This study examines the connections between Proust's *fin-de-siècle* 'nervousness' and his apprehensions regarding literary form. Michael Finn shows that Proust's anxieties both about bodily weakness and about novel-writing were fed by a set of intriguing psychological and medical texts, and were mirrored in the nerve-based afflictions of other writers including Flaubert, Baudelaire, Nerval and the Goncourt brothers. Finn argues that once Proust cast off his nervous concerns he was free to poke fun at the supposed purity of the novel form. Hysteria – as a figure and as a theme – becomes a key to the Proustian narrative, and a certain kind of wordless, bodily copying of gesture and event is revealed to be at the heart of a writing technique replete with pranks undermining many of the conventions of fiction.

Michael Finn is Professor of French at Ryerson Polytechnic University, Toronto. He has published on Proust in a wide variety of journals, has served in Bordeaux and Paris with the Canadian Department of Foreign Affairs, and for some years has written on food for *Toronto Life* magazine.

CAMBRIDGE STUDIES IN FRENCH 59

Proust, the Body and Literary Form

CAMBRIDGE STUDIES IN FRENCH

GENERAL EDITOR: Michael Sheringham (*Royal Holloway, London*)
EDITORIAL BOARD: R. Howard Bloch (*Columbia University*),
Malcolm Bowie (*All Souls College, Oxford*), Terence Cave (*St John's College, Oxford*), Ross Chambers (*University of Michigan*), Antoine Compagnon
(*Columbia University*), Peter France (*University of Edinburgh*),
Christie McDonald (*Harvard University*), Toril Moi (*Duke University*),
Naomi Schor (*Harvard University*)

Recent titles in this series include

JEFFREY MEHLMAN
Genealogies of the Text: Literature, Psychanalysis, and Politics in Modern France

LEWIS C. SEIFERT
Fairy Tales, Sexuality and Gender in France 1690–1715: Nostalgic Utopias

ELZA ADAMOWICZ
Surrealist Collage in Text and Image: Dissecting the Exquisite Corpse

NICHOLAS WHITE
The Family in Crisis in Late Nineteenth-Century French Fiction

PAUL GIFFORD AND BRIAN STIMPSON (EDS.)
Reading Paul Valéry: Universe in Mind

A complete list of books in the series is given at the end of the volume.

PROUST, THE BODY AND LITERARY FORM

MICHAEL R. FINN

CAMBRIDGE
UNIVERSITY PRESS

PUBLISHED BY THE PRESS SYNDICATE OF THE UNIVERSITY OF CAMBRIDGE
The Pitt Building, Trumpington Street, Cambridge CB2 1RP, United Kingdom

CAMBRIDGE UNIVERSITY PRESS
The Edinburgh Building, Cambridge CB2 2RU, United Kingdom   http://www.cup.cam.ac.uk
40 West 20th Street, New York, NY 10011–4211, USA   http://www.cup.org
10 Stamford Road, Oakleigh, Melbourne 3166, Australia

© Michael R. Finn 1999

First published 1999

Printed in the United Kingdom at the University Press, Cambridge

Typeset in 11/12.5pt Baskerville   [CE]

A catalogue record for this book is available from the British Library

Library of Congress cataloguing in publication data
Finn, Michael R.
Proust, the body, and literary form / Michael R. Finn
p.   cm.
Includes bibliographical references and index.
ISBN 0 521 64189 6
1. Proust, Marcel, 1871–1922 – Criticism and interpretation.
2. Neuroses in literature.   3. Hysteria in literature.
I. Title.
PQ2631.R63Z593   1999
843'.912–dc21   98-35829   CIP

ISBN 0 521 64189 6 hardback

In memory of my parents,
enthusiastic students of language both,
Clara Mary Elizabeth Raeburn
and Carroll Bernard Finn

Contents

Acknowledgements

The debts I acknowledge here have been accumulated over many years, and in many different circumstances. The first is both academic and human, and is to W. M. (Brick) Frohock, who tempted me to come to Harvard as a graduate student many years ago, and to his wife Nathalie, who helped to socialize a rag-tag, disparate group of us. My thanks go as well to Susan Read Baker and her sister Cathey for their friendship, advice and intellectual support over a period much longer than that of the writing of this manuscript. I have fond memories too of the encouragement received from my friend Joseph Hoare, scholar and Food Editor at *Toronto Life* magazine until his death in 1997.

Some hard-headed comments from Richard Terdiman regarding an early idea for this book helped to nudge it in a more fruitful direction. Barbara Bucknall made a number of useful observations about the manuscript. But my warmest thanks go to my colleague Kathleen Kellett-Betsos for her thorough inspection of this study, and for her unblinking, sensible advice on many aspects of the text. Ryerson colleagues John Cook, Errol Aspevig, Margaret MacMillan, Ingrid Bryan and Thomas Barcsay encouraged me, at various times and in various ways, to persevere. Maureen MacGrogan and Joseph Duggan helped to orientate me in the world of publishing. I owe a debt of gratitude to the reference librarians at that wonderful facility, the University of Toronto Library; and I thank particularly Perry Hall, who assisted me on a number of occasions. The research for parts of this study would not have been possible without access to the Bibliothèque Nationale in Paris and the assistance of its staff. I thank Bernard Brun of the Proust research group (ITEM) at the Ecole Normale Supérieure for putting the resources of his Proust collection at my disposal, and Anne Borrel, Secrétaire générale of the Société des Amis de Marcel Proust, for her help at various times.

Two travel and research grants from the Social Sciences and Humanities Research Council of Canada were an important impetus in getting this study airborne. I would like to thank the editors of *French Studies*, of *Revue d'Histoire Littéraire de la France* and of *French Forum* for permission to draw on articles already published in those journals for my chapter 1 (*FS*, 51, 3, July 1997; *RHL*, 2, March–April 1996) and chapter 3 (*FF*, 10, 2, May 1985). It has been a pleasure to work with my upbeat, straight-shooting editor Linda Bree at Cambridge University Press. I appreciated very much, as well, the opportunity to react to a set of even-handed and perceptive criticisms from the two readers who assessed the manuscript for Cambridge. Through many Canadian winters and a few Parisian summers, I talked out the points in this book with Elizabeth Park. I thank her for those exchanges, for the occasions on which she challenged me, and for her patience in putting up with my work habits.

Abbreviations

Double page references are provided (parenthetically, with volume and page number) for all quotations from *A la recherche du temps perdu*, except for those taken from Proust's manuscript sketches (esquisses). Here the translations are my own. The first reference is to the translation by C. K. Scott Moncrieff and Terence Kilmartin, revised by D. J. Enright, 6 vols. (London: Chatto and Windus, 1992), and the second to the most recent Pléiade edition, 4 vols. (Paris: Gallimard, 1987–9). I have, on occasion, modified the English translation when it did not illustrate adequately a point I was making in my own text. *Against Saint-Beuve and Other Essays* (below) does not contain all the material that figures in *Contre Sainte-Beuve*. Quite a few of the translations from the latter volume (those without the abbreviation *ASB*) are therefore my own.

ASB	*Against Sainte-Beuve and Other Essays*, trans. John Sturrock, Penguin
BIP	*Bulletin d'informations proustiennes*
BMP	*Bulletin Marcel Proust* (formerly *BSAMP, Bulletin de la Société des Amis de Marcel Proust*)
CSB	*Contre Sainte-Beuve*, Pléiade
Corr.	*Correspondance*, 21 vols., Philip Kolb (ed.), Plon
Esquisse	One of the sketches published in the appendices of *A la recherche du temps perdu*, Pléiade, 1987–9, 4 vols.
JS	*Jean Santeuil*, Pléiade

Introduction

Over time, I have come to believe that neurasthenia – that *fin-de-siècle* chronic fatigue syndrome – and, to a lesser extent, hysteria, are not simply surface features of the lives of certain characters in *A la recherche du temps perdu*, but figures that, in important ways, condition the Proustian notion of style, and organize and structure both the aesthetic debate in the novel and the life messages it conveys. It would be silly to want to reduce Proust's great work to an early twentieth-century case-study in the naturalist vein; but the novel should be read, at least on one level, as a *fin-de-siècle* moral tale in which art and aesthetics conquer medical determinism. It is, after all, the story of a 'nervous Narrator'[1] who struggles against negative hereditary factors in his family (personified in the semi-invalid aunt Léonie), and who suffers from a chronic lack of drive that makes him prefer salon time to productive time alone. If Proust's protagonist belongs to a long line of what Roy Porter has called articulate sufferers,[2] and if it is arguable that *A la recherche* is a narrative of disease, it is in part because there is a medico-psychological context to the novel, with familial, societal and literary components, that requires further exploration than it has received to date. We should not forget, for instance, that one of Proust's earliest titles for his work, 'Les Intermittences du cœur', had medical overtones as well as the emotional ones that are at first most evident. On at least two occasions, Proust indicated that this title alluded, in the world of the mind, to a disease of the body (*Corr.*, XI, 257; XII, 177). He might have noted discussions of nervous arrhythmia in a number of medical works, and perhaps especially in 1904–5 when he read the study of Dr Paul Dubois, *Les Psychonévroses et leur traitement moral*[3] as he considered treatment for his own neurasthenia.

What led me towards hysteria and neurasthenia was an initial focus on certain aspects of Proust's compulsive attitude towards

social language and non-fictional writing. There is a loathing of
conversation and social exchange in Proust which is both intriguing
and contradictory, given his lifelong practice of social writing genres
– his society columns, for instance, and his abundant correspondence. This anomaly is personified in Proust's reaction to Sainte-
Beuve. In his earliest adolescent writings, Proust likes to play the
Beuvian role of arbiter of literary taste. In December 1887, when he
was just sixteen years old, Proust wrote two columns for the
schoolboy review *Lundi*, entitled 'Causerie dramatique' and
'Causerie littéraire'. The style borrows from Sainte-Beuve and from
the drama critic of the *Journal des Débats*, Jules Lemaître, while the
titles recall the celebrated *Causeries du lundi*.[4] Not only is Proust
tremendously attracted by Sainte-Beuve's style, to the point of
appropriating it in pastiches that span twenty years, he also had
moments of self-doubt when he identified closely with Sainte-Beuve.
There are episodes in Proust's *Contre Sainte-Beuve* which clearly
suggest that Proust feared ending his career like the author of *Les
Lundis*, a failed creative writer who had abandoned art for
journalism.

What truly precipitated my interest, however, was Proust's label-
ling of Sainte-Beuve as a language hysteric (*ASB*, 37; *CSB*, 246), and
his characterization of social language as one that too closely mimics
bodily satisfactions and egocentric pleasure. If Proust longed to be
Sainte-Beuve, on the one hand, and repeatedly co-opted his language, but subsequently denied that language (because language
took Sainte-Beuve over and made his body speak in his mind's
place), then perhaps Proust was recognizing a psycholinguistic
process in himself and was actually defining himself as a language
hysteric. A second question seemed crucial: if hysteria was a
condition of social language, could it be absent from the language of
fiction?

At the same time, I began to be attracted both by what have been
called the new hysteria studies, especially those that relate to
narratives of hysteria in late nineteenth-century literature,[5] and by
the renewed focus, among specialists of Proust, on the relationship
between nervous ailments and writing. Some of the early French
sorties into this latter field were not well received. George Rivane's
book on the influence of asthma on Proust's writing was challenged
immediately,[6] while Charles Briand's tome *Le Secret de Marcel Proust*[7]
seemed to suggest that Proust's neuroses and complexes could be

explained by the 'fact' that he had had a sexual relationship with his mother. More recent studies in French, mostly in article form, redirect our attention to the medicalized discourse of *A la recherche*, the warring writing styles of the positivistic physician and hygienist Adrien Proust and his decadent son Marcel, and the interplay between nervous debility and the creative hygiene available through artistic creation.[8]

My study seemed to divide itself naturally into four areas. One was the extent to which Proust felt affinities with mentor writers – Flaubert, Nerval and Baudelaire in particular, but Senancour as well, even the Goncourts – who suffered from, and whose work depicted or reflected the effects of, nervous conditions similar to his own. *A la recherche* is a novel of a quest for literary form that is superimposed on a search for volition. It is aboulia, the absence of willpower which was the very basis of the condition called neurasthenia, that artistic creation finally cures in Proust's Narrator.

Proust's readings in the fields of psychology, medicine and philosophy become an important reference point in this first chapter. Anne Henry has argued for the significance of 1894 in his life, the year he took philosophy courses at the Sorbonne. She proposes that Schelling and Schopenhauer were the seminal influences on Proust's aesthetics.[9] I would not quarrel with the importance of the year, but I see Proust as much more preoccupied with what he perceives as a quasi-medical problem, a difficulty in focusing his energies, a deficit of willpower. The literary consequence, already clearly expressed as he struggled with the writing of *Jean Santeuil*, was an inability to organize a form for his fiction.[10] I have therefore explored the influences of two writers on him, the psychologist-philosopher Théodule Ribot, who wrote extensively about diseases of the will and about affective (or involuntary) memory, and Dr Adrien Proust.

An argument can certainly be made that Adrien Proust's writings play an intertextual role in *A la recherche*. In 1896–7, at a time when Proust's first attempt at a real novel was withering on the vine, his father published two texts that relate to his son's ailment, a preface to a study of asthma and a manual on neurasthenia,[11] both of which point to a single solution for nerve-based conditions: a return to an active, regular, fresh-air lifestyle that develops the backbone for a more positive approach to life. Since 1885, Dr Proust had held the Chair of Hygiene at the Faculty of Medicine in Paris, and in a number of publications – including the quite literary *Revue des Deux*

Mondes – he touted the universal benefits of hygiene. His son expressed a lifelong scorn for the doctor's literal-mindedness, and there are indications that *A la recherche* is structured to prove that art and literature, and not some more mundane contact with 'reality', represent the ultimate hygiene.

A second area of investigation was Proust's extraordinary anxiety about language. The obsessional fear of orality in Proust has many of the components of a hysterical phobia. The Proustian text endlessly presents spoken language as pure alienation. Proust the artist and the man are at home in silent contemplation, a form of intense communion, in a way they can never be when speaking. In the essay on reading which served as his preface to the Ruskin translation *Sésame et les lys*, Proust argues that speech diverts the individual from inner centredness, immobilizing him in a kind of trance where he is totally in the web of the Other. Social exchange sets up a dynamic that makes us copy language and external attitudes as though they were authentic phenomena, instead of simply words and attitudes copied in turn from others.

The surface texture of Proustian prose seems hysterical in the everyday sense: it has the aspect of an unstoppable flow, built of endless comparisons and reverberations, in which one senses an unconscious hunger not to stop. But there is a third sense in which Proustian language is hysterical. His protagonists – Jean Santeuil, the Narrator – act out a corporeal, gestural language that anticipates words. We often see the Narrator locked in wordless communion with objects and phenomena – the hawthorn, for example – that are kinetically simulated in order to be assimilated. The basic communication with our surroundings is thus via a mimetic language of the body which the writer's language, the language of art, must then reproduce in metaphor. Proust makes abundantly clear that this body language is the intuitive movement that prefigures writerly language; the objective of authentic writing must be to reproduce the initial mimesis of our impression.

Proust's encounter with Sainte-Beuve of 1908–9 was the occasion to confront the dilemma of orality versus writing. Proust's sense that the prelude to authentic style was the bodily copying of an impression had a dangerous pendant: his social habit of mimicking the voices and gestures of others. In Sainte-Beuve, Proust saw a slightly different level of oral mimicry being passed off as superior writing style. The text that labels Sainte-Beuve a language hysteric criticizes the constant witticisms in his prose as borrowings from the oral register.

Sainte-Beuve, and his hysterical desire to please through language, is very much present, just beneath the surface of the text, in the final aesthetic argument of *Le Temps retrouvé*, for his writing alerts the Narrator to two types of oral pitfalls in first-person writing. First, there is a constant naming activity that goes on in the individual as we ingest reality – the Proustian text calls it an oblique interior monologue – that classifies phenomenon and event. This voice masks the personal apprehension of reality in habitual language, that is, cliché. The mediocre writer never steps outside this voice. Second, a monologue in the first person also resembles another type of babble: talking to oneself. Interestingly enough, the Narrator frequently talks to himself. On a number of social occasions, for example, he catches himself re-creating the evening's dialogues as he tries to review and reposition experience to his own advantage. It is this Other-orientated, ego-based voice which he identifies as the Beuvian first person, and which he vows to exclude from his own writing.

This second chapter ends with an analysis of the relationship between oral voice, individuality and creativity in Proust's writer-character Bergotte. What is striking in the Proustian text's iterative and non-conclusive examination of this question, is the desire to conclude a pact between oral voice and tone, and accent and tone in literature. *A la recherche* appears to promote the notion that orality bears no relationship to the unique accent of a writer's fiction. At the same time, one senses in the text (in the attention devoted to understanding the rhythms and intonations of Bergotte's speech, for instance) a need to reconcile, or accommodate, this unique aspect of personality – oral accent – within the fuller individuality expressed in the writer's art.

In chapter 3, I investigate the need for another type of reconciliation: the acceptance that non-fictional forms have their role to play in shaping the Proustian 'text'. One of Proust's aesthetic anxieties is that literature remain pure. There is a correct hierarchy of writing styles, forms and genres that must be adhered to. Balzac is criticized because the style of his letters is hard to distinguish from that of his novels. Literary history has a trivial side because historians hold the naïve view that 'truth' is documentary and documentable: new finds of historical papers and manuscripts send them into orbit. Journal-

ism often represents a transfer of oral blabbing on to a newspaper
page, and the journalistic activity of Norpois, Brichot and Morel
during the war defines their limits. Erudition is a way of disengaging
the self from complex personal judgements about life and art. And
literary critics are subject to intellectual boredom, for an emerging
trend can quickly alter long-established, correct judgements: one day
Corneille's masterpiece *Le Cid* is up, the next *Le Menteur* is in vogue.
All these intellectual attitudes, with the writing stances that accompany them, are viewed as inferior to authentic creative writing.

The position of personal and social forms of writing poses a great
problem for Proust, whether he considers his own production or that
of others. What is the status of a writer's personal correspondence,
for instance? The hero of *Jean Santeuil* is troubled and attracted by
the exuberance of Balzac's and Flaubert's letters. Their conversation, the letters they write after a day of composition, must somehow
reveal an aspect of their creative being, even though Proust presents
them as 'inferior mechanisms' (*JS*, 486) of their thought. The
correspondence of a writer like Flaubert, even though he is totally
focused on an interior reality, may still communicate, in unarticu-
lated form, the raw materials of his inner self, or, from time to time,
even a perfectly sculpted literary phrase.

But given clear indications in the Proustian text that fiction and
personal letters are immiscible, sacred-and-profane entities, it would
be wrong to ignore two aspects of Proust's correspondence. Critics
have recently begun to point out considerable transfers of materials
from his letters to his novel,[12] and to wonder whether his letters
were not, in many instances, the initial locus of inscription for
certain ideas.[13] It is important to address this issue, for here is a clear
discrepancy in Proust's aesthetic position. His letters are a direct
extension of the social voice he insisted be absent from literature,
and therefore a comparison of that epistolary voice and the
narrating voice in *A la recherche* is essential.

Journalism was one of Proust's lifelong temptations. The perception, among members of the *Nouvelle Revue Française* group led by
André Gide, that Proust was essentially a social columnist for *Le
Figaro*, was a prime factor in their rejecting publication of his
manuscript. The *A la recherche* episode of the appearance of the
Narrator's article in *Le Figaro* was juxtaposed, in the early manuscripts, with the sleeping/waking sequence that now serves as the
definitive overture to *A la recherche*. The hero's reaction to that article

was subsequently set within a description of Sainte-Beuve's self-important reaction to his own articles (see *ASB*, 17–18; *CSB*, 226–8). The stage was set, early on in Proust's plans, for a demonstration of the inferiority of journalistic writing. This, in itself, is not of major interest, but what is, perhaps, is the patching of some of Proust's social columns, articles and essays into the text of the novel, as though socially orientated writing and fiction were not so mutually exclusive after all. Proust the *rentier*, whose family investments supported his lifestyle, was an inveterate reinvester[14] of his own material, whatever its origin.

With literary criticism and pastiche, we observe two other facets of Proust's non-fictional writing that were clearly more acceptable for the artist – and Proust's true *péchés mignons* – as long as they remained secondary activities. Proust's view of literary criticism as attention to unconscious, reiterated currents in a writer's style and personality is a key to his own aesthetic as a novelist. Proust's text also insists, as we shall see, that the physical mechanics of the *pasticheur* are exactly the same mimetic movements that authentic writing must adopt. All true writing, like good pastiche, begins in the preverbal stage of mimesis. To end this chapter, I examine the Goncourt pastiche in *A la recherche*. As the novel moves towards its aesthetic destination, that is, writing that is authentic because copied from personal impressions, it is natural and necessary that it pause over the phenomenon of the pastiche, pointing mutely to the semi-creative mechanism that underlies it, before finally laying it to rest.

Chapter 4 returns to the question of transforming language into form and examines how a series of Proustian anxieties is invested in the structure of the novel. The years immediately preceding the writing of *A la recherche* were years of doubt and true nervousness during which Proust feared he might be suffering from a malady that could prevent him from carrying out any major creative project. His concerns about levels and types of language and about the juxtaposition of pure literature and lesser writing forms are evident in the early stages of the writing of his novel, and they remain explicitly present in the final version of *A la recherche* which Proust left us. At the same time, however, that final version consciously transgresses certain formal rules of the genre, and a well-developed sense of *insouciance* and mischief regarding form begins to make itself felt.

The re-editing of *A la recherche* in the second Pléiade edition has given readers wider access to Proust's manuscript drafts,[15] and those manuscripts have brought critics back to absolutely basic issues of language and form. At one level, they have reopened the debate about the unfinished nature of *A la recherche*. In spite of a surface level of completion, an essential feature of the novel's form is that it remained open, both to new episodes and changed directions in old ones, until the end, that is, until the day in 1922 when Proust died. One position that has been put forcefully is that Proust's construction method was by fragments, and that perhaps the fragment has equal weight, in the evaluation of Proust's technique, with the author's efforts at sewing the narrative together.[16] An interesting aspect of these fragments is that they may recur, or be reused, across all of Proust's writing. At every level, the Proustian text structures itself through iteration, and iteration is copying. Albertine's love affair with the Narrator replicates aspects of Swann's relationship with Odette; sixteen iterative versions of the opening sleeping–waking sequence are written before the phrase 'Longtemps je me suis couché de bonne heure' is isolated; and one of the key artistic productions of *A la recherche*, the text on the Martinville spires jotted down by the adolescent Narrator, is actually a recontexted piece that Marcel Proust had published in *Le Figaro*.

Proust's habit of rewriting material should be viewed in the context of his self-quotation, his myriad borrowings from previous inscriptions of the same idea. The reiterated writing of important insights is the basic narrative act for Proust, and it seems not at all far-fetched to relate that copying process, in turn, to the quasi-hysterical mimesis that is the origin of Proust's style. The writer inwardly reproduces the physical attitude or movement or rhythm of an object or idea, until he recognizes how the form relates to the meaning, and until he can formulate one more copy, a metaphor which will replicate in words the inward copy he has produced.

Proust not only quotes himself in his novel, he copies what others have said as well, true to the image he presents us of his Narrator: a porous, impressionable individual who is invaded by the language of his every interlocutor. In *A la recherche*, much research is beginning to show the borrowings – even the plagiarism[17] – that are the fabric of the Proustian text. Quotations, borrowings and intertextualities in *A la recherche* have unusual significance for a writer who had an obsessional fear of the language of the Other. The process of domesticating the Other's language to make it absorbable and controllable is all-important.

The final section of chapter 4 reviews the nature of first-person narrative in *A la recherche* in the light of the linguistic obsessions mentioned above. Rather than following those who dwell on the differentiated 'I' in Proust and the distinctions between hero, Narrator and author, I believe emphasis needs to be placed on the way in which the first person very deliberately integrates all aspects of the Proustian personality, including Proust the translator, critic and journalist and, indeed, the director of the whole operation, Proust the organizer of his manuscripts. It is the unity of that voice, and its ubiquity, that guarantee the coherence of Proust's form. Expressed in that unique narrating tone and accent is the story of a writer, of a novel being written and of a search for voice. Encasement in that tone is a device that allows Proust to copy endlessly from himself, and into himself from outside, to align his personal, endless, hysterical flow of language with all sources of language, and to derive security and protection from the fragmentation of experience that is one of his novel's great subjects.

CHAPTER I

Proust between neurasthenia and hysteria

Studies of hysteria, as a socio-cultural phenomenon, as medical fact and myth, and as a subject for literature, represent a burgeoning field that is both important and, as Mark Micale has put it in a recent and readable overview, 'hopelessly fashionable'.[1] The medicalization of human experience – and particularly of female experience – in the literature of the second half of the nineteenth century has attracted a major subset of these new hysteria studies.

As we now know, although French interest in hysteria peaked during Jean-Martin Charcot's years at La Salpêtrière Hospital, and particularly in the 1880s and 1890s, there was voluminous research and writing on the topic years earlier. Ten to twenty years before Charcot's 1862 appointment to La Salpêtrière, almost a third of French psychiatric theses were already dealing with hysteria.[2] Literature was showing interest in hysteria in the 1860s even as it was becoming a more widely publicized societal phenomenon. Emily Apter has neatly labelled as 'pathography' the mix of biography, fiction and clinical case history we find in Zola's *Thérèse Raquin* (1867), in the Goncourts' *Madame Gervaisais* (1868), and in Huysmans' *Marthe* (1876).[3] The model of the genre was no doubt *Germinie Lacerteux* (1864), and its notoriety was guaranteed because the brothers chose to stress the time-honoured link between hysteria and nymphomania.[4] In fact, the Goncourts' first novel, *Charles Demailly* (1860), was also a pathography, and its subject is one of the earliest portrayals of a condition that came to be known as neurasthenia, a quasi-clinical state of hypersensitivity coupled with nervous exhaustion.[5]

Not only was the novel taking its documentation from medical cases during this period, it was to some extent occupying a limelight that medico-psychiatric research would have preferred for itself. In 1881 Jules Claretie published a very popular novel, *Les Amours d'un interne*,[6] that made some sensational speculations about contacts between doctors and their female patients at La Salpêtrière. Colleagues of Charcot such as Charles Richet, Alfred Binet and Henri Beaunis all wrote fiction that dramatized various aspects of hysteria.[7] There is evidence that Charcot was jealous of the success of some of the naturalist pathographies. To Edmond de Goncourt's chagrin, Charcot joined the hecklers at the première of the stage version of *Germinie Lacerteux*.[8] The play did not enjoy great success.

In 1857, two years before Briquet published his seminal *Traité clinique et thérapeutique de l'hystérie*, hysteria is sufficiently prominent in the literary reader's mind that Baudelaire uses the term to describe the poetic nature with which Flaubert has imbued Emma Bovary. After making that now famous connection, Baudelaire easily slips into a discussion of actual symptoms:

[hysteria shows up] in women in the sensation of an ascending and asphyxiating ball (I am speaking only of the main symptom), [and] manifests itself in nervous men in every kind of impotence and in the predisposition to every excess.[9]

The Goncourts, among others, championed the Romantic idea that artistic talent was in fact based on hypersensitivity. Some of their statements on the subject from the 1860s foreshadow quite directly the decadent mindset that became prevalent in the 1880s and 1890s: creativity was seen as nerve-based. According to the Goncourts, malady was almost a pre-condition for the novelist: 'Sickness sensitizes one's observational faculties like a photographic plate'.[10] Genius, they asserted, was in the nerves:

Man, by nature, does not love truth; and it is right that he not love it. Lies, myth, these are much more likeable. It will always be more agreeable to imagine genius in the form of a tongue of fire than in the image of a neurosis.[11]

By the mid-1890s, when Proust is writing his first novel, *Jean Santeuil*, the Goncourt view has become a literary stereotype. In Proust's young protagonist, hypochondria, insomnia and asthma are presented as incurable and 'the effect of genius' (*JS*, 732). Some twenty years later, the mature Proustian text is more ambiguous on this subject;[12] one senses that since the major work of the writer's life is at last close to completion, a certain peace has been made with the question of nerves. Still, the nervous defects of Charlus are seen as the probable basis of his artistic disposition, though he never develops his gifts. But it is left to the flashy, superficial Dr Boulbon to say that without a nervous disorder, there are no great artists or scientists. The ambivalence of this pronouncement is underlined by Boulbon's cavalier diagnosis that the Narrator's grandmother is suffering from nerves and that the albumin in her urine, from which she will shortly die, is therefore 'mental' (III, 347; II, 601).

It is of some importance, I believe, to examine Proust's 'nervousness' – both the biographical phenomenon and the presentation of nervous disorders in his fiction – against the backdrop of certain literary figures who were mentors for him. Some of the writers to whom he felt most closely attuned had suffered from nerve-related ailments just as he did. Proust turned both to their works and their lives, especially in the 1895–1908 period, for some confirmation that they had encountered creative hesitations similar to those that plagued him. For a time at least, Proust seems to have accepted the diagnosis, no doubt in part a self-imposed one, that his own chronic lack of willpower and tenacity was nerve-based, and that it was this nervous deficit that could explain his inability to conceive the form and structure of the great work he wanted to write. The problems with form, and the attitudes *vis-à-vis* form, of Flaubert, Baudelaire and Nerval, therefore came to interest him deeply.

At the same time, Proust had privileged access, through his doctor father Adrien, to the latest expert medical opinion on ailments of the nerves and to physician colleagues who were specialists in the field. It is not my purpose to retell the story of Proust's asthma, of his medical consultations, or of his self-prescribed drug regimen. Much more germane to an understanding of *A la recherche du temps perdu*, it seems to me, are the echoes of some of Proust's psychological and medical readings not only in the story the novel tells, but in the way its artistic message is shaped. For although Proust was diagnosed – and diagnosed by his own father, as we shall see – as a chronic sufferer from nerve-related problems, he was adamant that life problems were not solved by science, but rather by aesthetics.

To say that Proust suffered from anxiety of influence, to use Harold Bloom's phrase,[13] is to say that water is wet. His anxieties about literary inspiration and formal perfection hold a threefold interest. They can help us to define what he appears to have diagnosed in himself as a type of *fin-de-siècle* neurasthenia, a generalized lack of willpower based on weakness of the nerves. They also allow us to follow some of the suggested connections in the Proustian text between neurasthenia, hysteria and the creative process,

especially writing. And third, they open a perspective on the interplay between nervous dysfunction and certain aspects of the novel
form as it developed in Proust's hands.

Flaubert

Though Proust refers with sympathy to the neurotic natures of
Baudelaire and Nerval, his sentiments for Flaubert are never
expressed in terms of a kinship with his nervous makeup. Three
facets of Flaubert's artistry seem to have impressed Proust: certain
hard-won features of his actual writing technique, his striving for a
beauty of form, and his literary idealism. In the 1920 article 'A
propos du «style» de Flaubert', Proust lays out in some detail how
Flaubert's grammatical genius and sense of rhythm marked all of
French prose in the second half of the nineteenth century. Proust
sees greatness as well in Flaubert's insistence on beauty in structure:
'Where Flaubert links up with Balzac is when he says: «I need a
splendid end for Felicity»' (*ASB*, 68) ['Où Flaubert rejoint Balzac,
c'est quand il dit «Il me faut une fin splendide pour Félicité»'] (*CSB*,
276).[14] But the Flaubertian idea which Proust seems to cite most
approvingly and most often is one that connects to the essential
message of idealism that underpins *Le Temps retrouvé*. In his introduction to Louis Bouilhet's *Dernières chansons*, Flaubert wrote, 'life's
eventualities ... appear [to the writer] fully transposed as though
readied for the description of an illusion' (see *CSB*, 224, n. 1; 264–5).
Unlike Balzac but like Marcel Proust, Flaubert understood the value
of renunciation, the absurdity of life in society, and the fact that a
real-life event functions only as the sign of a deeper reality.

These are the main intellectual links between the two writers, and
the influences which Proust acknowledges. But each also suffered
from a nervous malady that, it can be argued, conditioned his
attitude towards speech, towards written language, and towards the
structuring of text into narrative. There is much to enlighten us in a
comparison of how the younger Gustave Flaubert and the younger
Marcel Proust, each from the starting point of an acknowledged
nervous malady, confront the activity of writing.

During his most hectic creative period, 1907–9, when he is at once
'rewriting' other writers (in a series of pastiches published in *Le*

Figaro), penning critical essays about them (in the *Cahiers* that will form *Contre Sainte-Beuve*), and seeing fictional threads develop out of the critical exercise, Proust is also consciously sifting through the resemblances between himself and other writers, including Flaubert. The *Carnet de 1908* contains a number of references to Flaubert, including the following passage on his letters to his niece, where we observe Proust's unusual habit of physically projecting himself into another writer's daily life and writing problems. There are passages in Proust's texts on Sainte-Beuve and Baudelaire where a similar transposition occurs:

Letters to Caroline. A splendid ending for *Un Cœur simple.* I read the Rouen newspaper, etc. I chat with servants whom I find no more stupid than people of a better class. I'm waiting for the book on the Middle Ages. How I envy you your work plans. I would happily stay in Concarneau for the whole winter.

[*Lettres à Caroline.* Fin splendide pour *Un Cœur simple.* Je lis le journal de Rouen etc. Je cause avec domestiques [que] je ne trouve pas plus bêtes que des gens bien. J'attends le livre sur le moyen âge. Comme je t'envie avec tes plans de travail. Je resterais bien à Concarneau tout l'hiver.] (*Le Carnet de 1908*, 75–6)

Many of these references have a dual resonance: they are Flaubert's comments on his own life, but the same events have happened in Proust's existence as well. Proust had enjoyed two prolific months in Begmeil and Concarneau as he began *Jean Santeuil* and may have been tempted to stay longer; he had awaited his own book on the Middle Ages, *L'Art religieux du XIIIe siècle en France* by Emile Mâle, loaned to him in 1898 by Robert de Billy as he documented himself for translations of Ruskin; in *A la recherche* the Narrator will repeatedly remark on the interest and usefulness of conversation with servants and working class people as compared to aristocrats; and Proust certainly envied Flaubert his work plans, for he himself never seemed to write from one.[15]

Flaubert's experience has become Proust's. And, if only unconsciously, Proust will also have absorbed other remarks in these same letters that connect anguish about creativity and nervous exhaustion:

I'm making no headway with Julien l'Hospitalier ... I have absolutely no idea what is going on in the world ... In order to write one page, I've crossed out twelve ... I'm so obsessed with work that I'm close to insanity.[16]

There are many externals that might make Flaubert and Proust medical soul-mates. Each was the son of an authoritative and some-times authoritarian doctor father. Proust was a frail, neurotic and later asthmatic child, while Flaubert had poor word skills that pointed to emotional difficulties and undermined his academic career. The patriarchal figure in both of these households was in a position to diagnose and to judge. It is interesting to reflect that it was Flaubert's father who prescribed treatment after his son's often discussed attack of January 1844. Proust's father, as I will argue later in this chapter, made a discussion of his son's nervous condition the subject of a book, *L'Hygiène du neurasthénique*, published in 1897. Both writers' creative lives are structured around a nervous crisis and the death of a parent, events which act as springboards for a retreat from the world and a sharpened focus on personal creativity.

In a letter of 13 May 1845, Flaubert speaks of his nervous attacks of a year before as the turning point between his early period and a later life fully devoted to art:

I have bid practical life an irrevocable goodbye. My nervous condition was the transition between these two states. All I shall want, for a long time, is six quiet hours in my room, a great fire in winter, and two candles each evening to give me light.[17]

After the death of his mother Jeanne, Proust spent about two months in the clinic of Dr Paul Sollier in Boulogne being treated for nervous exhaustion, leaving in January 1906. Sollier was the author of authoritative works on hysteria, but his clinic was also well known for its successful treatment of neurasthenics. In *Le Temps retrouvé*, a single sentence about the Narrator's unsuccessful sojourn in a clinic serves as a transition to the famous train stop in the countryside, when he appears to despair that he will ever recover his childhood gift for inspiration. Almost immediately, however, he again takes up his quest for a literary vocation. Symbolically, but unmistakably, confrontation and acceptance of malady are thematically paired with artistic development.

Both Flaubert and Proust worked through an 'acceptance' of their nervous disorders and saw that acceptance as a synonym of retreat from the world. In the preface of *Les Plaisirs et les jours*, the writer's malady transforms him into a Noah figure, confined to an ark which is at the same time a sickbed, and from which he has a clearer view of the world than from any point on land. Should the sickness be cured, there is a fall from true grace, the latter pointedly presented as communion with self: 'He had to begin living again, to turn away from himself. . .' ['Il fallut recommencer à vivre, à se détourner de soi . . .'] (*JS*, 7).

Flaubert took the same positive view of his 'maladie des nerfs'; accepting, and having others accept, his debility established the perfect conditions for creative self-absorption. In two letters from the year following his collapse in Pont-L'Evêque, he confirms his satisfaction:

My malady has had the advantage of allowing me to occupy myself as I please, which is an important point in life. I see nothing in the world more desirable for me than a nice, well-heated room, with the books I love and all the leisure time I want. As for my health, it is basically improved, but the cure is so long in coming, in these nervous afflictions, that it is almost imperceptible.[18]

As far as I'm concerned, I've been feeling quite well since I accepted that I will always be sick.[19]

Proust attributes his own impressionability to his malady. That he is porous, as it were, to the beauties of nature, is a positive part of his condition, for it represents his openness to inspiration. He sees the same poetic permeability in Senancour, and appears to wonder if the latter suffered from the same condition as himself:[20]

Senancour is myself. Moral reverie inspired by nature. He was sick, I believe. Indeed, one must be weak to be so enraptured with the simple phenomena of nature.

[Senancour c'est moi. Rêverie morale inspirée par la nature. C'était je crois un malade. Il faut être faible en effet pour s'enivrer ainsi avec les choses les plus simples de la nature.] (*CSB*, 568)

The feeling for nature, that is, the physical reaction to natural phenomena, is strikingly similar in Flaubert and Proust. The kind of ecstatic oneness with nature that readers identify as a Proustian privileged moment, whether an impression or a recollection, is based on an animal passivity that is described at some length in *Jean Santeuil*. The writer stipulates that this passivity is only relative, in that it affords the calm and mental space in which the imagination can function freely. But the state of waiting, of expectation that life stimulus will arrive from the outside, will have disadvantages that we will examine later in this chapter:

We envy the boa constrictor for whom digestion occupies a whole week and who can then sleep for several days in a row. We envy the lizard who sits for days on a warm rock soaking up the sunlight. We envy. . . seagulls who play in the midst of storms and let themselves be borne by the wind [... but] we derive enjoyment, at the same time, from our imagination ... It is only for the thinker and the sick person that the life of the instincts has all these exhilarations.

[Nous envions le boa pour qui digérer est l'occupation d'une semaine et qui peut alors dormir plusieurs jours de suite. Nous envions le lézard qui reste des journées sur une pierre chaude à se laisser pénétrer de soleil. Nous envions ... les mouettes qui jouent dans les orages et se laissent porter par le vent [... mais] nous jouissons en même temps par l'imagination ... Ce n'est que pour le penseur et le malade que la vie animale a tous ces enivrements.] (*JS*, 369)

The kind of passive absorption into objects and natural settings that we see in Proust and Flaubert becomes, in each, a key to their creativity in language. Sartre has argued persuasively that the capacity for animalistic 'stupidity' which Flaubert admires in himself ('What is best in me is ... the animal',[21] he writes to Louise Colet) is interchangeable with his capacity for appreciating sensation and feeling, and is synonymous with his capacity for literary inspiration. In Flaubert, that ability is the opposite of the ability to speak, to manipulate words, because, following Sartre's thesis, as a child Flaubert was ignored in favour of his older brother. The meaning of Flaubert's neurosis is that, in a sense, he was never designated in words. Because no verbal attention was paid to his existence, he began to define his existence as mutism and feelings left inarticulate.[22] A wonderful passage from *Les Mémoires d'un fou* shows how language breaks the cohesion of the self:

Infinity seemed more immense to me, if that is possible, than to God ... and then I had to descend from these sublime regions towards words ... How does one render in words this harmony that arises in the heart of a poet ... by what gradations does poetry lower itself without destroying itself?[23]

Here it is not cliché, Flaubert's lifelong *bête noire*, that the young writer fears in language, it is the fact that words interrupt the inner harmony of the self with the world. This is often the writer's experience, of course: readers of Joyce have spoken of the 'antinomy of impression and expression'[24] in his writings. The former is an intimate experience, the latter an activity of a more external order.

Moments of wordlessness in Flaubert's novels are tied in to his biographical epiphany moments. Emma Bovary's communion with nature recalls Flaubert's own silent 'ecstasies':

Silence was everywhere ... Then, in the distance, beyond the woods, on the other hills, she heard a vague, prolonged cry, a voice lingered, and she listened to it in silence as it fused like music with the last vibrations of her excited nerves.[25]

Of course, Flaubert and Proust come at their diffidence about language from apparently quite different directions. The younger Proust is someone conscious that there is an inner wellspring of words, an excess that corresponds to an excess of meaning. He cannot say 'enough'. Gently ironic portraits of the young Jean Santeuil speak of his exaggeration, the exaltation of his speech (*JS*, 259). A letter from Proust's seventeenth year provides a concrete picture of the irreversible flow that seems to have been Proust's experience of language:

Excuse my writing, my style, my spelling. I don't dare to re-read what I write! When I write at top speed. I realize that one shouldn't write at top speed. But I have so much to say. It just comes like waves.

[Pardon de mon écriture, de mon style, de mon orthographe. Je n'ose pas me relire! Quand j'écris au galop. Je sais bien qu'il ne faudrait pas écrire au galop. Mais j'ai tant à dire. Ça se presse comme des flots.] (*Corr.*, I, 106)

In contrast, even though he was a prolific writer during his adolescence, Flaubert sees himself as 'speechless'. He writes, 'I am a mute who wants to speak'.[26]

Voluble or silent by nature, these two men arrive at surprisingly similar conclusions about the alienating nature of language. Because I am essentially passive, sickly, the language of others, language from outside, invades me and defines me. I do not speak (for Proust this is especially acutely felt in social situations), I am spoken. The Narrator of *A la recherche* endlessly flags the danger of social dialogue: 'when we chat, it is no longer we who speak ... we are fashioning ourselves then in the likeness of other people and not a self that differs from them' (II, 563) ['quand nous causons, ce n'est plus nous qui parlons ... nous nous modelons alors à la ressemblance des étrangers et non d'un moi qui diffère d'eux'] (II, 261). There is a strongly developed physical fear in Proust, which we shall examine in the next chapter, of social language as a conduit through which one's identity flows out and is lost.

The object of social exchange is, in both men's perception, to find common ground. Conversation aims therefore necessarily at finding 'common language'. Because there is agreement and conceptions are shared, there must be stock phrases, cliché. Sartre articulates Flaubert's position as follows:

[the apparent meaning of language] has no other purpose than to unite people, to reassure them by enabling them to make a *gesture of agreement*, and on what could such impenetrable beings, with such diverse interests, agree, if not on *nothing*?[27]

Proust's diffidence about language focuses on speech, but also, at least in his pre-*Recherche* period, on correspondence. Letters are an extension of consensus-seeking, but in the physical absence of the interlocutor, we exaggerate the search for agreement. The letter is *the* locus of insincerity, and Proust sees a similar exaggeration in Flaubert's letters and his own:

[Flaubert's letters to George Sand or about Renan] are obviously not ... sincere and ... they make us tremble to think how people might judge our own literary ideas if, later, they were to find certain articles, or read certain letters if our correspondence were published.

[des lettres de Flaubert à George Sand ou sur Renan] ne sont évidemment pas ... sincères et ... nous font trembler en pensant à ce que croiront de nos idées littéraires ceux qui plus tard retrouveront certains articles, ou si notre correspondance était publiée, liraient certaines lettres. (*JS*, 488)

Literature, then, will provide the mechanism to express difference. How this will be done is not yet clear, since language will be the means at hand. But for Flaubert, at least, finding the exactly appropriate words to a situation is a dubious solution. Such precision will always remain the sign of 'agreement over nothing'. The individual who seeks an exact equation between expression and outer reality is the individual who has agreed to suppress his own identity. Naomi Schor reminds us that Emma Bovary is the character who cannot find the words, while Homais is always successful: '"What a terrible catastrophe!" exclaimed the apothecary, who could always find an expression to fit any situation imaginable'.[28]

It is important to recall that a similar ambivalence is embedded in Proust's aesthetics. He speaks often of the need to find the precise metaphor that will translate an impression; the comparison must appear 'inevitable'. 'Water only boils at 100 degrees', he chides Paul Morand (*ASB*, 284; *CSB*, 616). At the same time, metaphor is only a vehicle of comparison. A metaphor does not state or restate any thing, it simply alludes to it through an imitation. Beside Proust's requirement for precision, we should juxtapose his law regarding the element of mystery that is residual in any attempt to articulate a deeply rooted impression. A certain opacity of language is a measure and a gauge of the depth covered by the writer's investigative work.

Because of their mistrust of language, and because for both of them language is the sign of their potential for alienation, Proust and Flaubert lodge their ideal of style elsewhere than within language itself. Style has nothing to do with the surface features of text, it is, for Proust, 'a question of vision', as though he had in mind the famous phrase of Flaubert, 'style is, in and by itself, an absolute way of seeing things'.[29] Meditating on Stendhal, Proust sees style as a kind of unconscious, skeletal structure detectable beneath the conscious, intellectual structures of the novels. In Flaubert, says Proust, style is the fusion of the writer's intelligence with the objects he is describing – it is a movement in the prose: 'This rippling is the intellect transformed, which has been incorporated into matter' (*ASB*, 281) ['Cette ondulation-là, c'est de l'intelligence transformée, qui s'est incorporée à la matière'] (*CSB*, 612). Sartre's comment on Flaubertian style is valid for both writers: 'Style is the silence of discourse, the silence in discourse, the imaginary and secret object of the written word'.[30]

What one might add is that the Proustian/Flaubertian adoration of silence, and the movement of the intelligence that superimposes itself on matter and undulates with the oscillation of the molecules, in a wordless gesture of communication, is really the transfer to the level of literary technique of an epileptic/hysterical model of communication, with which both writers feel very much at home. Extending this model of artistic communication to the notion of literary structure seems reasonable for Proust and Flaubert both: their literature speaks not through language but through its internal rhythms and structures. Doris Lessing articulated this ideal of writing when she observed, 'My major aim was to shape a book which would make its own comment, a wordless statement: to talk through the way it was shaped'.[31]

Flaubert's gift for uniting his mind with matter is comparable to the talent for hysterical simulation which Proust points out in other writers, such as Racine:

And no doubt a hysteric of genius was struggling inside Racine, under the control of a superior intellect, and simulated for him in his tragedies ... the ebb and flow, and the manifold, yet for all that fully grasped lurchings of passion. (*ASB*, 283)

[Et sans doute une hystérique de génie se débattait-elle en Racine, sous le contrôle d'une intelligence supérieure, et simula-t-elle pour lui dans ses tragédies ... les flux et les reflux, le tangage multiple, et malgré cela totalement saisi, de la passion.] (*CSB*, 614)

Baudelaire had identified, in Flaubert, this same ability of the 'poète hystérique' to transform himself into his characters' emotions. No wonder Flaubert appreciated Baudelaire's use of the term hysteric, for during the writing of *Madame Bovary* he had found himself experiencing the same nervous fits he depicted in his heroine:

Earlier, at six o'clock, in the instant that I wrote 'attack of nerves', I was so carried away, I was bellowing so loudly and feeling so deeply what my little lady was feeling, that I was afraid I might have one myself.[32]

Proust's and Flaubert's ability to melt into matter (either could have written the phrase 'As a result, sometimes, of looking at a pebble, an animal, a painting, I have felt myself enter inside it'[33]) becomes their ability to create art. A propos of writing a love scene in *Madame Bovary*, its author admits, 'I was the horses, the leaves, the wind, the words that they were saying to each other and the red sun that caused eyelids drowned in love to close'.[34] In his notes on Senancour's *Rêveries sur la nature primitive de l'homme*, Proust identifies this transfer of animus to the plant and animal realm as what is most Proustian about Senancour. He marks the following passage 'très moi':

Delivered up, according to the natural order – that always mobile order – to what changes around us, we are what calm, shadow, the sound of an insect or the fragrance of a plant make of us: we share in that general life, and we flow along with these instantaneous forms. We find ourselves in what is active, in what grows, in the confident air of a chamois, in the bearing of a cedar, its branches hanging down to stretch themselves more easily, in every aspect of the world, which is full of oppositions because it is dependent on order, which changes constantly only to maintain itself forever.[35]

As *A la recherche* opens, this kind of surreal communion with the external world is presented as a potential narrative mode of the novel to be. A semi-dream state can produce the fusion of self and matter that is art: 'It seemed to me that I myself was the immediate subject of my book: a church, a quartet, the rivalry between François I and Charles V' (I, 1) ['Il me semblait que j'étais moi-même ce dont parlait l'ouvrage: une église, un quatuor, la rivalité de François 1er et de Charles Quint'] (I, 3).

Proust's and Flaubert's very similar attitudes towards language appear solidly anchored in their nervous dispositions. When they actively develop strategies of literary structure and form, their anxieties about language set them on similar artistic paths.

Baudelaire and Nerval

Two other writers whom Proust greatly admired were Baudelaire and Nerval. He formally credits both with major contributions to his own aesthetic of time and memory,[36] and, more tentatively, he points to overlaps in his and Baudelaire's experience of cruelty, sado-masochism and homosexuality. Here, however, I wish to focus more narrowly on the 'nervous' association Proust felt with the two earlier writers. In the 1907–9 period, Proust is struggling with the funda-mental question of which literary form to work in – philosophical essay, novel, criticism – while he fights a rearguard action with himself over how to sever certain still disturbing moral ties with his deceased parents.

In *Contre Sainte-Beuve*, Jeanne Proust plays the role of silent interlocutor in a dialogue where her son assesses Sainte-Beuve's contribution to nineteenth-century literary criticism. Nowhere is she more present than in the chapter on Sainte-Beuve and Baudelaire, where the text invokes the intimate 'tu' in almost every paragraph. Here, Proust's task is to explain to a maternal interlocutor Baude-laire's attraction to female homosexuality and the apparent cruelty of certain letters and poems. Part of his tactic is to underline that Baudelaire had a nervous nature and experienced acute suffering in his own life. Speaking of Baudelaire's poems on old women, he says 'one senses that he had felt the sufferings he makes sport of and presents so impassively down to his very nerve ends ... he is inside their bodies, he shudders with their nerves, shivers with their debilities' (*ASB*, 40–1) ['les souffrances qu'il raille, qu'il présente avec cette impassibilité, on sent qu'il les a ressenties jusqu'au fond de ses nerfs ... il est dans leur corps, il frémit avec leurs nerfs, il frissonne avec leurs faiblesses'] (*CSB*, 250).

The enforced presence of the mother during Proust's justification of cruelty towards the old in the poem 'Les Petites Vieilles' has a certain sadistic resonance. Now dead and unable to resist, she is made an observer of her son's faults and sins. In 1907, Proust had addressed head-on the question of liberation through parental death in his article on the real-life matricide perpetrated by an acquaint-ance, Henri van Blarenberghe.[37] This truly strange essay houses the most contradictory elements within itself, including a version of an often to be reused fragment on the morning routine of reading *Le Figaro* newspaper, the tone of which, given the horrific murder that is to be described, is knowingly cruel.

What is the connection between Baudelaire's poem, van Blaren-berghe's gesture and Proust's artistic search? All three are products of the nervous sensibility. At one end of the neurotic spectrum is the hypochondriac and, at the other, the madman:

Should a low pressure system be 'approaching the Balearic Islands', as the newspapers say, should earthquakes begin, even in Jamaica, at that very instant, in Paris, migraine sufferers, rheumatism victims, asthmatics, and no doubt the insane as well, experience their attacks. *This is a measure of the links that bind the nervous, from the farthest points of the globe, in a solidarity they often would prefer to be less intimate.* If the influence of the heavenly bodies, at least on some of them, were one day to be recognized (Framery, Pelletan, quoted by M. Brissaud), who better than a nervous person would suit the poet's line: 'And long silken threads link him to the stars.'

[Qu'une dépression 's'avance ver les Baléares', comme disent les journaux, que seulement la Jamaïque commence à trembler, au même instant à Paris les migraineux, les rhumatisants, les asthmatiques, les fous sans doute aussi, prennent leurs crises, *tant les nerveux sont unis aux points les plus éloignés de l'univers par les liens d'une solidarité qu'ils souhaiteraient souvent moins étroite.* Si l'influence des astres, sur certains au moins d'entre eux, doit être un jour reconnue (Framery, Pelletan, cités par M. Brissaud) à qui mieux appliquer qu'à tel nerveux, le vers du poète: 'Et de longs fils soyeux l'unissent aux étoiles'. (*CSB*, 154; the emphasis is mine.)

Proust appears to connect the matricide he is about to discuss with the exacerbated nervous systems of poetic natures like himself (the reference to Dr Eugène Brissaud is to the expert on asthma Proust himself consulted). The killing of a parent is an ultimate taboo, but it is one act on a continuum of actions caused by the nervous hysteria that can affect certain over-sensitive minds. As we have seen, Proust labelled Racine a hysteric because of his abilities as a simulator and an interpreter of the other gender. He sees in Baudelaire another aspect of the hysterical spectrum, the inability to resist blasphemy. In a letter of early 1905 he writes:

People have said he was a decadent? There is nothing more false. Baudelaire is not even a Romantic. He writes like Racine. In fact, he is a Christian poet and that is why, like Bossuet and Massillon, he speaks endlessly of sin. Let's say that, like all Christians who are also hysterics (I don't mean that Christians are hysterics, you understand, I mean 'those Christians who by chance are also hysterics'), he experienced the sadism of blasphemy.

[A-t-on dit que c'était un décadent? Rien n'est plus faux. Baudelaire n'est même pas un romantique. Il écrit comme Racine. Du reste c'est un poète chrétien et c'est pour cela que comme Bossuet, comme Massillon il parle sans cesse du péché. Mettons que, comme tous les chrétiens qui sont en même temps hystériques (je ne veux pas dire que les chrétiens sont des hystériques, vous me comprenez bien, je veux dire 'ceux des chrétiens qui par hasard sont aussi hystériques') il a connu le sadisme du blasphème.] (*Corr.*, V, 127)

Proust did not, of course, invent Baudelaire's nervous nature. The image of the decadent poet inwardly consumed by a defective nervous system is one that the author of *Les Fleurs du mal* accepted and cultivated. The caption under an 1852 Félix Nadar caricature of Baudelaire reads, 'young nervous poet, bilious, irritable and irritating'.[38] One of Baudelaire's most famous statements about himself, 'When just a child, I felt two contradictory sentiments in my heart, the horror of life and the ecstasy of life', is completed by the less-quoted line, 'This is certainly the characteristic of a lazy, nervous person'.[39] And in his description of Emma Bovary/Flaubert as a hysteric, Baudelaire appears to be defining himself when he imagines hysteria in men: 'it manifests itself in nervous men in every kind of impotence and in the disposition to every excess'.[40]

Proust is troubled by certain aspects of repetition in Baudelaire's poetry and appears to relate these formal problems to the poet's nerve defects. Juxtaposed to Proust's most celebrated pre-*Recherche* statement of frustration in the search for literary form is a cryptic remark about Gérard de Nerval that will lead us to Baudelaire as well:

Laziness or doubt or helplessness [impotence] taking refuge in uncertainty over artistic form. Should it be a novel, a philosophical study, am I a novelist? (What consoles me is Gérard de Nerval. See page XXX of this notebook.)

[La paresse ou le doute ou l'impuissance se réfugiant dans l'incertitude sur la forme d'art. Faut-il en faire un roman, une étude philosophique, suis-je romancier? (Ce qui me console, Gérard de Nerval. Voir page XXX de ce cahier.) (*Le Carnet de 1908*, 61)

Though Baudelaire and Nerval are probably two of Proust's favourite writers in French, during the years he is casting about for an artistic form, he identifies what, to his mind, are structural weaknesses in their work, and sees these as a confirmation that even the greatest writers shared his own self-doubts about form. It is the origins and nature of these hesitations over structure, as Proust views them, that are intriguing. In Proust's most negative assessment of Nerval, where he almost goes so far as to say that the author of *Les Filles du feu* was a second-rank writer, he focuses on the fact that neither Nerval nor Baudelaire *ever arrived at a definitive idea of form*. Their hesitation shows up in repetitions: lines from Nerval's poetry recurring in the short story 'Sylvie', poetry on the same subject and employing similar language in *Les Fleurs du mal* and *Petits poèmes en prose*.[41] For Proust, these are not paltry faults. In a diagnosis of the problem in Nerval, he explicitly relates these formal difficulties to his own and to disease, a medical deficiency in willpower:

In such geniuses the inner vision is very sure, very strong. But, be it *a malady of the will* or the lack of a determinate instinct, or a predominance of intellect indicating different paths rather than going down just one, they try in verse and then, so as not to waste the original idea, in prose, etc. (*ASB*, 26)

[Chez de tels génies la vision intérieure est bien certaine, bien forte. Mais *maladie de la volonté* ou manque d'instinct déterminé, prédominance de l'intelligence qui indique plutôt les voies différentes qu'elle ne passe en une, on essaye en vers, puis pour ne pas perdre la première idée on fait en prose, etc.] (*CSB*, 234–5; the emphasis is mine.)

One senses the judgement of a practising writer in these lines, someone who felt himself on shaky formal ground as he wrote in every imaginable genre: short story, poem, autobiographical novel, essay, social column, etc. Baudelaire is no better than Nerval. He is depicted as lacking the ability to establish an overall plan for his work, which he approaches with 'certainty in the detailed execution, uncertainty in his overall scheme' (*ASB*, 52) ['avec des certitudes d'exécution dans le détail, et de l'incertitude dans le plan'] (*CSB*, 259). These two writers reinforce Proust's pre-*Recherche* view that his own weakness is working in repetitive fragments, and that that weakness cannot simply be overcome with intellectual effort, for it is based in nervous weakness and permanent neuroses.

There is self-reference and a tone of real anguish in the above quotation about Nerval's absent willpower. During the *Contre Sainte-Beuve* period, contradictory observations swirl around the roles of intelligence and intuition/instinct in the creative process. To repeat oneself is lamentable, but is there an aspect of repetition that is intuitive, and therefore revelatory of genuine individuality? 'It is true', says Proust, 'that certain repetitions in Baudelaire seem to be a taste and can hardly be looked on as filling out the line' (*ASB*, 53) ['Il est vrai que certaines répétitions chez Baudelaire semblent un goût et ne peuvent guère être prises pour une cheville' (*CSB*, 260). He praises Nerval for his gift of transforming his personal illusions into reality in 'Sylvie', then criticizes him for being too intellectual about it: 'Perhaps there is still a little too much intellect in his story...' (*ASB*, 31) ['Peut-être y a-t-il encore un peu trop d'intelligence dans sa nouvelle ...'] (*CSB*, 240). At the same time, of course, Proust is prefacing his *Contre Sainte-Beuve* with the remark 'Daily, I attach less value to the intellect'. But in classifying Nerval as potentially a second-class writer, Proust seems to say as well that his weakness is a lack of reasoned reflection on what literary form one's thoughts should take. Nerval is *too* intuitive, he has no really determined genius, because he 'creates the form of his art at the same time as his thought'. Thus, intuitive inspirations cannot function alone; distance and perspective on one's revelations must be a part of the creative process too. And of course, they will be in the final version of *A la recherche*, when the intelligence will be allowed a role in ordering the intuitive material that is provided to it. In this earlier period, as I will argue at length shortly, Proust is still very much under the influence of some early readings in the medical and psychological literature that make him want to strictly limit the role of the intelligence.

The Goncourt brothers

It is generally accepted that Proust's interest in the Goncourt brothers centred on their *Journal* and its celebrated 'style artiste'. In part, as critics have suggested, the Goncourt pastiche in *Le Temps retrouvé* is an attempt to contest that style and the aesthetic that underlies it. At the same time, the 'style artiste' appears precariously close to Proust's own; within it, consciously or unconsciously, he seems to navigate with ease. Proust's final comment on the brothers' contribution to literature – it appeared in *Le Gaulois* in May 1922 – continues the same schizophrenia. He calls the *Journal* 'a delightful and entertaining book' ['un livre délicieux et divertissant'] (*ASB*, 311; *CSB*, 642), suggests he has an essentially positive view of its style, but condemns the content as sub-literary, and the brothers' naturalist works as outmoded. This ambivalence recalls the push and pull of his feelings about another journalist-critic, Sainte-Beuve, whose prose he parodied with equal delight. 'Now I more than anyone', said Proust, 'have indulged in veritable orgies with the deliciously bad music that is the spoken, ornate language used by Sainte-Beuve' (*ASB*, 270) ['Je me suis permis plus qu'aucun de véritables débauches avec la délicieuse mauvaise musique qu'est le langage parlé, perlé, de Sainte-Beuve'] (*CSB*, 596).

Certainly, Proust's reading of the Goncourts' *Journal* seems to have been extensive, and research has shown the stylistic and thematic relationships between the various Goncourt pastiches[42] and actual texts from the diary.[43] But the Goncourts defined themselves primarily as the novelists of nervous disorders. Might Proust have been interested in the exploration of neurasthenia, hysteria and degenerate sexuality that dominates certain Goncourt novels? There is in fact some evidence to this effect. Proust had met Edmond de Goncourt socially, and he had a certain familiarity with the brothers' fiction and theatre. Perhaps he had read the famous letter from Edmond de Goncourt to Zola, commenting on the death of Jules. Edmond insisted that the latter's demise was nerve-related, and that his end was a logical one for a frail, delicate personality whose nervous constitution had been strained from the beginning.[44] Edmond wrote,

One should realize that our entire *œuvre*, and there lies, perhaps, its originality, rests on nervous malady, that we drew these images of malady from ourselves, and that by dint of studying ourselves, minutely describing ourselves, dissecting ourselves, we developed a super-acute sensitivity that was wounded by the infinitely small things in life. I say 'we' for, when we wrote *Charles Demailly*, I was sicker than he was.[45]

Paul Bourget, to whom Proust was introduced through Laure Hayman in 1888, may have been one of the conduits leading Proust to this letter and to the novel it describes, *Charles Demailly*. Both letter and novel are mentioned in the chapter devoted to the Goncourt brothers in Bourget's *Nouveaux Essais de psychologie contemporaine*. This text would have made suggestive reading for a young writer concerned by his own weakness of purpose. Bourget asserts that willpower deficit is not only at the heart of the Goncourt brothers' literature, but a central element in the naturalist school's subject matter, in Zola, Daudet, Huysmans and Maupassant:

This weakening of the will, which is the usual subject the Goncourts study, is truly the malady of the century. This was the term used fifty years ago; later it was the great neurosis; today we speak of pessimism and nihilism.[46]

Bourget then reviews the plot of *Charles Demailly*. Originally published in 1860 under the title *Les Hommes de lettres*, *Charles Demailly* reads in a number of episodes like an intertext for *A la recherche*. The protagonist, surrounded by journalists who threaten his autonomy and success, is a case-study in neurasthenia before the name. A doctor diagnoses Demailly as suffering from the 'maladie du siècle', and the description he provides could have been lifted from the writings of the official apostle of neurasthenia, the American George Beard, whose first discussions of the condition would appear only ten years later. According to the diagnostician in *Charles Demailly*, the condition is attributable to the innumerable pressures of modern society, unlimited competition, career stress, the multiplication of people's activities and output, and the insalubrity of modern city life:

I consider it ... to be an organic disease characteristic of the nineteenth-century race, at least in its generality and excess. I believe it to be the malady of all those who inhabit large cities ... Modern life is changing from the fresh air of a farming life to concentrated life, to life sitting down, to a life of coal gas, a life of lamp gas, a life nourished by falsified, sophisticated, deceptive food, a life in which all the normal conditions of our physical being are reversed ...[47]

Fictional threads and psychological patterns seem to overlap between *A la recherche* and the Goncourt novel. Demailly shares his Christian name Charles with Proust's gifted but unproductive trio Charles Swann, Charlus and Charlie Morel, and although Demailly is a published novelist, the tragedy of his life – not unlike that of Swann's – is that his artistic development is stifled prematurely after a miscalculated marriage to an attractive but coarse young actress. Demailly's mixed racial origins and nervous nature also look forward to those of Marcel Proust and Swann: 'a delicate, sickly nature, from a family where the sickly delicacy of two races had crossed and of which he was the last child and the full expansion' (*Charles Demailly*, 72). He is both highly impressionable and lacking in energy: 'even furniture seemed friendly or inimical to him ... He lacked that kind of active energy, the energy that makes us jump out of bed' (*ibid.*, 73).

It is interesting that Demailly marries an actress; Odette had been an actress as well before she married her first husband, M. de Crécy (*Recherche*, II, 985, n. 2). More suggestive is that one of the characters in *Charles Demailly*, an attractive *cocotte* often seen at the theatre who continually flirts with Charles, is named 'la Crécy'. Her first appearance is in glorious, white, English lace, like Odette, the eventual *dame en rose*, who appears in white at Combray. Like Odette as well, she has a highly developed taste for Saxe porcelain: 'Food was served on a white Dresden service, with a barley flower pattern. The Crécy woman had old Spanish tastes in porcelain: white Dresden, white Sèvres, or Chinese white' (*Charles Demailly*, 194).[48]

The deeper connection in the life patterns of Charles Demailly and Charles Swann is the use they make of their intellectual and artistic capacities. Though Demailly has an important manuscript underway (with the evocative, Proustian title, *Souvenirs de ma vie morte*), he abandons the reality of art for the illusion of emotional attachment. The text chastises him in the same way the Narrator will chide Swann and other unproductive 'célibataires de l'art'. Demailly knows better than to take the marital plunge. He reflects: 'Love is basically the poetry of a man who writes no poetry, the idea of a man who has no ideas, and the novel of the man who does not write' (*Charles Demailly*, 198). Demailly has a further trait that is critical to the art-versus-life debate in which Swann and the Narrator are plunged. The attraction of an intellectualized social life is strong for him. He needs the *words* of others, as though artistic inspiration were dependent on social interaction: 'I believe an exciting, irritating regimen is required for one's intellectual hygiene; in a word, a certain intoxication of the mind in good intellectual company ...' (*Charles Demailly*, 160–1).

The placing of all these common threads in the context of a novel structured specifically around the figure of a neurasthenic, a sensitive would-be artist with a pathological lack of willpower, foreshadows the shared vocational dilemma of Charles Swann and the Narrator. We cannot be sure that Proust had read *Charles Demailly*, though the title does surface in one of the drafts for the Goncourt pastiche published in *Pastiches et mélanges*.[49] It is evident, however, that Proust was aware of a stage version of the novel, directed by Koning, that premièred in Paris in December 1892,[50] because a section in the pastiche just mentioned is based directly on the entry in the Goncourt *Journal* of 22 December 1892, which bemoans the play's poor reception. The Goncourt entry reads, in part,

Without a doubt, this is an accumulation of unlucky circumstances: bad press, politics, the jinx of the theatre world, and perhaps a personal jinx where December is concerned, the month in which my brother and I were charged in criminal court, in which *Henriette Maréchal* opened, in which, in recent years, I have had pneumonia that has left me with bronchitis.[51]

In the second section of Proust's pastiche, also dated 22 December, we read,

And for an hour I complain in whispers to Rodenbach about the jinx that has always hung over the heads of my brother and myself ... Rodenbach immediately confesses his conviction that this month of December has always been unlucky for my brother and me, that it led to our being charged in criminal court, to the failure, instigated by the press, of *Henriette Maréchal*, to the pimple I had on my tongue the day before the only speech I have ever had to deliver, a pimple that led people to say that I had been afraid to speak on the grave of Vallès when it was I who asked to do so.

[Et c'est de ma part toute une révolte chuchotée pendant une heure à Rodenbach sur cette guigne qui nous a toujours poursuivis, mon frère et moi ... Alors Rodenbach de me confesser le fond de sa pensée, qui serait que ce mois de décembre nous a toujours été malchanceux, à mon frère et à moi, ayant amené nos poursuites en correctionnelle, l'échec voulu par la presse d'*Henriette Maréchal*, le bouton que j'ai eu sur la langue à la veille du seul discours que j'aie jamais eu à prononcer, bouton ayant fait dire que je n'avais pas osé parler sur la tombe de Vallès, quand c'est moi qui avais demandé de le faire.] (*CSB*, 26)

Although Proust's text closely reflects the Goncourt original, the pastiche demonstrates his gift for concentrating the stylistic tics of the *Journal*,[52] a gift which is more completely developed in the Goncourt pastiche placed in *Le Temps retrouvé*. Richard Sayce has argued that the brilliance of Proust's later pastiche is to have taken advantage of a network of stylistic and thematic associations between the Goncourt *Journal* and his own novel, some of these actually resident in the Goncourt diary (for example, visual and tactile impressions of food and drink), many others seeded in the pastiche by Proust himself. The result is an eclipse of the *Journal*, absorbed into a stylistically superior and less naïvely configured vehicle for representing reality, *A la recherche du temps perdu*.[53]

There is further evidence that the Goncourts' preoccupation with nervous ailments left a lasting impression on Proust's own writing. The chief fictional work of the brothers which stood out in his memory was *Germinie Lacerteux*. As a teenager, Marcel went to see the stage version of *Germinie* at the Odéon theatre with his friends Jacques Bizet and Jacques Baignières, and Mr and Mrs Strauss (*Corr.*, I, 161–2).[54] In the memory of the sensitive and neurotic young Proust, the emotions of that evening remained strong; it was Réjane's performance in the lead role that made a particular impact. In one letter he writes,

The art of Madame Réjane has filled my mental life. The sorrows of Germinie Lacerteux were some of the greatest of my life; I still suffer, thinking of them, and I am moved for hours by the memory of that heartrending voice.

[L'art de Madame Réjane a rempli ma vie intérieure. Les chagrins de Germinie Lacerteux ont été dans les plus grands de ma vie, j'en souffre encore et souvent je suis remué pour des heures par le souvenir de la voix déchirante.][55]

In his 1922 tribute to the Goncourt brothers, Proust expands somewhat on these lines, recalling that his eyes were so red from sobbing that members of the audience approached him after the performance wondering, as he said, whether he had been beaten (*ASB*, 311; *CSB*, 643).

The sobbing and the 'beating' Marcel took, the 'cruelty' and 'sublimely horrifying' scenes he witnessed (*Corr.*, XIX, 312), if we are to accept his language at face value, suggest that some part of Germinie's suffering must have coincided with Proust's own. Her story, let us remember, centres around the need to keep powerful, 'deviant' sexuality secret. It is also a tale of visceral jealousy and borderline sadism, with hints of male/female gender trading. The heart of the story is the relationship between Germinie and the Jupillon family, formed of a devoted but treacherous mother figure and her malicious son. At the same time, it is the portrait of a hysteric, based of course on the life of the Goncourts' servant Rose Malingre, but also on documentation the brothers assembled from medical studies of the condition. Edmond de Goncourt's preface to the 1886 re-edition of *Germinie* lays much emphasis on the sordidness of Rose's double life, and the brother's amazement at what they see as her hystero-nymphomania.

It was in 1892–3, only a short time after seeing *Germinie* as a play, that Proust wrote four stories which appear to owe much to his exposure to its hysteric protagonist: 'Violante ou la mondanité', 'La Confession d'une jeune fille', 'Avant la nuit' and 'La Fin de la jalousie'. The latter two in particular connect uncontrollable sexual urges to nervous disorders, just as Germinie's 'uterine furore' is a central fact of her hysteric nature. The young women in Proust's stories suffer from intense guilt that tends to coalescence – with overtones of masochism and sadism – around maternal figures. The guilt Germinie feels *vis-à-vis* her own surrogate mother, Mme de Varandeuil, has a very similar flavour.

The nervous excitement champagne causes in the heterosexual heroine of 'La Confession d'une jeune fille' demands instant sexual release and immediate submission: 'My nerves needed release ... I simply let it happen to me' ['j'avais ... besoin ... de dépenser mes nerfs ... je ne fis plus que me laisser faire'] (*JS*, 94–5). Germinie has no willpower where sex is concerned. Her desire is pictured as 'that emotion of one's whole being, that almost animal sensation of the approach of a master'.[56] For her part, the heroine of 'Violante' has an attack of nerves after reluctantly resisting Honoré's advances. In 'Avant la nuit', Françoise attributes her lesbianism to a deterioration of the nervous system (*JS*, 169). And in 'La Fin de la jalousie', the carnal suspiciousness of Honoré, who has a nervous disposition and suffers from nervous asthma, recalls Germinie's bitter jealousy over the liaisons of her lover Bibi.

It is the maternal figure that truly haunts Proust's protagonists and the Goncourts' heroine in certain key scenes where shame is externalized as an image of guilt reflected in a mirror. Germinie sees Mme de Varandeuil as a mother confessor to whom she cannot confess her secret drinking and hidden pregnancies:

And in the midst of this horrible pretence, a pious, almost religious feeling came over her, like the feeling of a daughter lying openly to her mother so as not to break her heart (*Germinie Lacerteux*, 144).

A few pages later, when Germinie contemplates robbing her mistress, she catches a glimpse of herself in the mirror:

She lifted her eyes: the mirror reflected her face. Before this countenance of hers, she grew afraid; she started backwards in horror and shame at the sight of her crime: it was the head of a thief that she had on her shoulders (*Germinie Lacerteux*, 150).

The integration of these two moments in 'La Confession d'une jeune fille' – a flash of insight followed by a mirrored reflection of sin – creates the primal scene of Proustian guilt. The suffering inflicted on the mother figure lifts her to the level of a religious saint. At the same time, guilt can exacerbate one's enjoyment:

Then, as the feeling of pleasure held me ever more tightly, I felt, in the depths of my heart, the stirrings of an infinite sadness and desolation; it seemed to me that I was making my mother's soul weep, the soul of my guardian angel, the soul of God.

[Alors tandis que le plaisir me tenait de plus en plus, je sentais s'éveiller, au fond de mon cœur, une tristesse et une désolation infinies; il me semblait que je faisais pleurer l'âme de ma mère, l'âme de mon ange gardien, l'âme de Dieu.] (*JS*, 95)

The intense combination of pleasure and shame gives way to an intuition that there is a connection between suffering, causing suffering, and personal pleasure:

I had never been able to read stories of the torture that villains inflict on animals, on their own wife, on their children, without shuddering from horror; it now seemed to me, in a confused way, that in any voluptuous, culpable act, there is just as much ferocity in the body that is enjoying itself and, within ourselves, just as many good intentions and just as many pure angels are martyrized and weep.

[Je n'avais jamais pu lire sans des frémissements d'horreur le récit des tortures que des scélérats font subir à des animaux, à leur propre femme, à leurs enfants; il m'apparaissait confusément maintenant que, dans tout acte voluptueux et coupable, il y a autant de férocité de la part du corps qui jouit, et qu'en nous autant de bonnes intentions, autant d'anges purs sont martyrisés et pleurent.] (*JS*, 95)

Immediately following these thoughts the young woman sees her own sensual, guilty reflection in the mirror, along with that of her male friend. At the same instant she glimpses her mother observing the embrace from the balcony, and their eye contact is interrupted by an act in which inflicted pain and remorse meet: the mother falls backwards and catches her head between the balcony rungs.

It appears eminently arguable that *Germinie Lacerteux* serves as an intertext not only for these stories but in *A la recherche* as well, projecting forward into the Narrator's courtyard a drama of shop-keepers, sexuality and hysteric behaviours. First of all, the close homonymy of the names Jupillon/Jupien is striking when one considers the interactions of the triangular groupings *mother Jupillon/son/Germinie*, and *father Jupien/niece-daughter/Morel*. The physical in-stallation of Jupien and his niece in the courtyard of the Narrator's apartment building affords him the same observation post that he would have enjoyed as a reader of *Germinie Lacerteux*. In the Goncourt novel, we look down on a courtyard where mother Jupillon runs a *crémerie* as she brings up her son Bibi. Bibi's professional aspirations are similar to those of the waistcoat maker Jupien and his dressmaker niece: he is a glove cutter and eventually persuades Germinie to set him up in a glove shop.

Some of Germinie's humiliations appear to move forward into *A la recherche*. The episode in which Morel berates Jupien's niece, calling her a whore, recalls a host of scenes in the Goncourt novel where Germinie is publicly humiliated by the young Jupillon. (In the stage version, the 'scène de l'engueulade' was apparently one of the powerful moments in the drama.[57]) The episode is prepared by a repeated focus on Morel's neurasthenia (V, 179–80; III, 668–9), and the actual exchange with the niece is introduced – and, in part, excused – by the remark that Morel suffers from 'a malicious nervousness' which explains his hurtful outbursts. The Narrator overhears Morel in Jupien's shop with the niece, whom he is shortly expected to marry. The girl stands silent and trembling under a rain of insults: 'Didn't I tell you to get out of here, *grand pied de grue, grand pied de grue*. Go and fetch your uncle till I tell him what you are, you whore' (V, 180) ['Je vous ai dit de sortir, grand-pied-de-grue, grand-pied-de-grue, allez chercher votre oncle pour que je lui dise ce que vous êtes, putain'] (III, 670).

It is noteworthy that the Proustian text internalizes and transposes to the masculine the nerve-based ailment that had explained Germinie's promiscuity. When, later, the Narrator happens upon Morel who is weeping over the cruelty of his behaviour, there are repeated references to the recurrence of his neurasthenia. It is to this condition that the text, always with hesitations and qualifications, attributes the violinist's emotional and moral instability.

There are other narrative threads shared by *A la recherche* and *Germinie*. The story of Germinie's torments as an adolescent, her rape, and especially her brutal treatment at the hands of her own sisters when she becomes pregnant (41–2), may lay the groundwork for some of the sadistic sub-themes of *A la recherche* that relate to pregnancy and the family. One of Proust's texts is enticing here, referring to the fact that Jupien's niece was 'in trouble' when quite young (V, 47; III, 558), as though in her mature years, like Germinie, she might be paying the price of an early pregnancy. Kitchen maids in Proust are treated with great brutality: the cook Ernestine tortures her assistant in *Jean Santeuil*, while in *A la recherche* a pregnant kitchen maid receives brutal treatment from Françoise before her delivery, and is the object of even more cruelty after her post-partem complications. Of course, Mme de Varandeuil herself is the model for such relationships: Germinie's elderly mistress was treated with squalid brutality by her own father and most of her family, and reduced, like Germinie, to the role of domestic, but in her own house.

Perhaps what is most suggestive of all in the Goncourt novel, for a reader of Proust, is the current of androgyny that winds through the narrative, touching most main characters. Like the 'hommasse' Charity of Giotto, Germinie has crude, mannish features. The intensity of her sexual desire is presented as abnormal for a woman: she sleeps with anyone, seeking 'pain in pleasure' (*Germinie Lacerteux*, 192). The Goncourts describe Rose Malingre's career as 'a secret life of ... uterine furores which made her lovers say: «One of us, she or I, won't leave this place alive!»' (*ibid.*, 250). But Germinie/Rose is not the only androgyne. Mme de Varandeuil is an image of maternal protectiveness and goodness housed within a mannish exterior. Her willpower is described as male, her stoicism and her features as masculine, even her goodness is 'virile' (*ibid.*, 35, 46). Her counterpart Jupien is womanly in his goodheartedness, while his maternal/paternal instincts are tested in the extreme when he must play both mother and father to his niece/daughter, whom he first places under the protection of and then defends against the bisexual Morel.

Surely, however, the most intriguing possible echo of *Germinie Lacerteux* in *A la recherche* is in a portrait of the young Jupillon, an individual whose malicious behaviour looks forward directly to Morel. Here is how Jupillon, the non-stop seducer of servant girls, is presented in one passage:

his appearance was uncertain, and made more ambiguous by his smooth-cheeked face which was marked only by two little brushes of a moustache, and his sexless features in which passion and anger had injected all the nastiness of a nasty little female face. (*Germinie Lacerteux*, 82)

Sharing all the ignorance and maliciousness of Morel but none of his artistic gifts, this 'voyou' does not appear to practise the double-edged sexuality that stands out in his traits. Proust may well have appropriated the kernel of bisexuality hinted at here to help flesh out the character of Charlie Morel, the androgyne who completes the trio of the heterosexual Charles Swann and the homosexual baron Charlus. Each of these would-be artists shares in one or another of the symptoms that *fin-de-siècle* medicine diagnosed in the hystero-neurasthenic male. Surprisingly, we may owe some of Proust's fascination with the literary exploration of certain sexual and 'nervous' behaviours to the outmoded fiction of the *frères* Goncourt.

Nerve-based ailments are thus resonant markers in the private lives and literature of a range of writers from whom Proust drew diverse types of inspiration. The question remained, before *A la recherche* was begun: in what way would his own nervous condition inhibit or favour his own writing? Proust's correspondence, especially of the 1895–1905 period, reveals endless references to nerve-based disorders. In addition to the constant allusions to his own problems, the letters ascribe nervous conditions to, among others, Lucien Daudet, Alphonse Daudet and his wife, Antoine Bibesco, Anna de Noailles, princesse Brancovan, Fernand Gregh, and Proust's uncle Georges Weil. Proust's preoccupation with his neurotic lack of focus and drive was not his alone, but a broad feature of the 1890s. Maurice Barrès, his own personal life marked by a malady of the nerves which saw him taking rest cures in Switzerland as early as age ten, wrote a first novel, *Sous l'œil des barbares* (1888), whose protagonist's ideal is life as a kind of self-nurturing convalescence from excessive sensitivity. The neurasthenic overtones of his fiction caught the spirit of the age and were obvious to his contemporaries. Edmond de Goncourt spitefully remarked that Daudet viewed Barrès as an exhausted individual whose fiction reflected that exhaustion.[58] When André Gide's *Cahiers d'André Walter* appeared in 1891, Marcel Schwob interpreted the work as a symbolic representation of the nervous exhaustion that seemed to have affected a whole generation of *fin-de-siècle* youth:

You have captured with great perception that terrible malady of the will faced by young men of the second half of the century – a malady that results from a weak will that is slow to develop, and which is neglected in our education for many reasons ... Alas, I have seen, and close up, other André Walters. Their sad stories held me in their grip as I read your book.[59]

These fictional willpower deficits are remarkably similar to that identified by Proust both in himself and in his hero, Jean Santeuil.

A la recherche du temps perdu contains several texts which discuss the two most popular nerve maladies of Proust's day, neurasthenia and hysteria. Two of these passages can provide an initial illustration of the ways in which the two conditions impinge on character and creativity in the novel. The first is a discussion of the water-lily, the second a portrait of the character Charles Morel.

One of the Narrator's observations is that when the water-lily is caught in a river current, its captive to-and-fro movements mimic the manic behaviour of a human neurotic:

I would still find [the water-lily] there, on one walk after another, always in the same helpless state, suggesting certain victims of neurasthenia, among whom my grandfather would have included my aunt Léonie, who present year after year the unchanging spectacle of their odd and unaccountable habits, which they constantly imagine themselves to be on the point of shaking off but which they always retain to the end; caught in the treadmill of their own maladies and eccentricities, their futile endeavours to escape serve only to actuate its mechanism, to keep in motion the clockwork of their strange, ineluctable and baneful dietetics. (I, 202)

[Je ... retrouvais [le nénuphar] de promenade en promenade, toujours dans la même situation, faisant penser à certains neurasthéniques au nombre desquels mon grand-père comptait ma tante Léonie, qui nous offrent sans changement au cours des années le spectacle des habitudes bizarres qu'ils se croient chaque fois à la veille de secouer et qu'ils gardent toujours; pris dans l'engrenage de leurs malaises et de leurs manies, les efforts dans lesquels ils se débattent inutilement pour en sortir ne font qu'assurer le fonctionnement et faire jouer le déclic de leur diététique étrange, inéluctable et funeste.] (I, 167)

All the explicit and implicit identifications in the passage are of interest: the coupling of the mechanical flower movements with the manic behaviour of Aunt Léonie just as, later in the story, the behaviour of the Narrator will be paired with that of his aunt. A glance at some of the Pléiade sketches for this passage shows, unexpectedly, that there are sexual references suppressed within it. The published version relates both to a sketch on adolescent masturbation and to the odd reproductive life of another waterplant, the vallisneria.[60] Are we to see in the Narrator's patterns of entrapment in habit and the nerve-based inertia he shares with his aunt, Morel, Germinie and Charles Demailly, the explanation of his fitful, but unproductive devotion to a literary vocation? Is there also a connection between artistic potential, nervous disorders and degenerate sexuality, or between nervous malady and literary impotence? Without ever answering these questions, the Proustian text, just beneath its surface, constantly alludes to them.

Pushed a step further, neurasthenia can turn to hysteria.[61] In the latter part of *A la recherche*, the violinist Morel undergoes a transformation. He is trying his hand at writing, more particularly journalism and satirical pamphlets with his former lover Charlus as his target. The would-be man of letters is presented as a human counterpoint to the water-lily, trapped by an uncontrollable urge to copy. In Morel's imitation of the novelist Bergotte, the author sees a hysterical nature at work:

Morel imitated Bergotte marvellously. It was even unnecessary, after a while, to ask him for an impersonation. Like those hysterics whom one doesn't have to hypnotise to make them become such or such a person, he entered spontaneously and immediately into the character. (VI, 12)

[Morel imitait Bergotte à ravir. Il n'y eut même plus besoin au bout de quelque temps de lui demander d'en faire une imitation. Comme ces hystériques qu'on n'est plus obligé d'endormir pour qu'ils deviennent telle ou telle personne, de lui-même il entrait dans le personnage.] (IV, 278)

The hysteria of imitation was, as we shall see, a nervous problem which Proust had to overcome in his own life. Here it arrests a would-be writer in his tracks. The ability to imitate is a gift, but when it takes place directly at the nerve ends, as it were, the product is simply a copy without individual personality. The degenerate Morel can perform art (he is a violinist after all), but he cannot, in a sense, get beyond performing the Other.

Did some of Proust's medical readings on conditions such as neurasthenia and hysteria have an effect on the way he developed the story of the search for an artistic vocation that is *A la recherche du temps perdu*? It is time to examine Proust's own diagnosis.

THE NOVEL OF THE NEURASTHENIC

It was the American George Beard who, in the early 1880s, first 'discovered' neurasthenia in his study *A Practical Treatise on Nervous Exhaustion (Neurasthenia)*.[62] A year later Beard produced a related volume designed more for the lay person, *American Nervousness, its Causes and Consequences, a Supplement to Nervous Exhaustion (Neurasthenia)*.[63] Beard's more specialized study, *Sexual Neurasthenia (Nervous Exhaustion, its Hygiene, Causes, Symptoms and Treatment)*, was the only one translated into French, and not until 1895,[64] but Charcot had already brought Beard's ideas into the medical mainstream in his lectures of the late 1880s.[65] In 1891 Charcot would write the preface to Fernand Villain's primer *La Neurasthénie*.[66] Treatment for neurasthenia varied little between the 1850s and 1905, when Proust committed himself to Dr Sollier's clinic and received what sounds very much like the Silas Weir Mitchell rest-cure treatment (minus the electricity) for his nervous exhaustion.[67]

In its day, neurasthenia enjoyed the status of an intellectual epidemic in France. As hysteria became a kind of catch-all diagnosis for various female ailments, so neurasthenia was a condition that appeared to capture the nervous complaints of many men, and particularly of upper-class men with delicate constitutions.[68] In spite of the fact that Briquet's famous 1859 treatise on hysteria opens with a discussion of seven male hysterics, and in spite of the fact that Charcot had published over sixty case histories of male hysteria in the 1880s and 1890s, there was a tendency in the medical community to reserve the diagnosis for adolescent boys and effeminate men.[69] The time was not quite ripe to hystericize the male's emotional makeup or to confront the ambiguous aspects of male sexuality. Neurasthenia as a term and as a distinct condition had a social role to play.

Hysteria and neurasthenia were highly popularized notions. In 1895 Max Nordau published a study of degeneracy which quickly became a national bestseller,[70] and in it he claimed that the French as a nation were predisposed to nerve-weakness and neurasthenia. The problem was especially evident in literature and art:

The physician especially if he has devoted himself to the special study of mental and nervous maladies, recognizes at a glance, in the ... tendencies of contemporary art and poetry ... the confluence of two well-known conditions of disease, with which he is quite familiar, viz. degeneration (degeneracy) and hysteria, of which the minor stages are designated as neurasthenia.[71]

In *A la recherche du temps perdu*, as we will see, the distinction between hysteria and neurasthenia is similarly unclear, and their link with degeneracy just as marked. Debate on the national weakness of the nerves spilled over into *La Revue des Deux Mondes* (where Proust's father had written as early as 1893), and Alfred Fouillée proposed for the nation the fresh air and exercise cure that doctors like Adrien Proust would suggest for his son.[72]

Certainly between 1890 and 1905, neurasthenia was widely treated, in Europe and the United States, as a serious medical condition.[73] And along with hysteria, it began to become a subject for literature. In *Les Morticoles*, an 1894 French bestseller, Léon Daudet published an unsubtle send-up of Charcot, in the person of Dr Foutange from the Hôpital Typhus. (The story goes that Daudet had refused the hand of Charcot's daughter and had, as a result, been failed in his final medical examination.) The novel contains a dramatic scene featuring a group of medical orderlies packing a financially ruined neurasthenic off to an institution. The condition is real enough to be treated, but bothersome to physicians because they cannot cure it.[74] A year earlier, Dr Pierre Janet, a rising star of hysteria studies, had received better treatment than Charcot, portrayed as the sensitive Dr Daumier in Marcel Prévost's novel, *L'Automne d'une femme*.[75]

In 1904 neurasthenia was still being described as France's 'fashionable disease'. The writer was Dr Paul Dubois,[76] one of the most prominent clinicians treating the condition. Proust referred his friend Fernand Gregh to Dubois and intended to seek treatment from him himself (*Corr.*, IV, 279, n. 3). In the same year, Proust mentions reading a front-page article in *Le Figaro* entitled 'Neurasthénie' where the writer Henry Roujon reflects on the moral necessity of suffering from the condition (*Corr.*, IV, 288). Of course, neurasthenia was well known in the artistic community. In the company of Mme Greffuhle, Proust first saw Nijinsky dance in Paris in June 1910 (*Corr.*, X, 113); it was in that year that the great dancer himself was diagnosed as neurasthenic. Years later, Marcel Pagnol (born in 1895) was probably poking fun at some of the societal idiosyncrasies of his youth when he included the following exchange in the opening scene of *Marius* (1929):

CESAR You're pale, you're sad: you're like a teetotaller.
MARIUS Perhaps I'm a neurasthenic.
CESAR You?
MARIUS Why not?
CESAR Where would you have caught it?
MARIUS You just get it.[77]

In the United States, neurasthenia became a less popular diagnosis after 1900, especially after Freud's lectures at Clark University in 1909, in favour of other neuroses for which symptoms could be more precisely identified.[78] In a more general sense, neurasthenia has suffered the same fate as hysteria: it has been 'dismembered' (in the phrase of Joseph Babinski) to permit a reconstruction of new and different clinical categories.[79]

Neurasthenia made a dual impact on the Proust household. In 1897, Dr Adrien Proust published, with his colleague Gilbert Ballet, *L'Hygiène du neurasthénique*,[80] a practical guide to identification and treatment of the condition. Some ten years later, Marcel Proust began the writing of *A la recherche du temps perdu*, a novel whose neurotic Narrator struggles throughout his life against the character-istic neurasthenic absence of willpower, a deficit which inhibits his writing for many years.

The writings of the Proust family provide fertile ground for the study of the relationships between medicine and literature. The 'style' of malady in Proust, the sleep patterns of the author of *A la recherche*, the ideology of hygiene promoted by Dr Adrien Proust and the reaction of his son Marcel, these are but three of literally scores of medically related questions that continue to be of interest to the Proust research community.[81] Proust was extremely well informed about neurasthenia and other nervous disorders. The vocabulary of nervous ailments is constantly in evidence in his fiction, character-izing men and women from the heroine of 'Violante ou la mon-danité' and Jean Santeuil to Swann, Charlus, Madame Verdurin and the Narrator. I wish to re-examine here the notion that, in the early stages of its conception, *A la recherche du temps perdu* may well have been seen, by its author, as the biography of a neurasthenic, the story of an individual who suffers from a disease of the will, but succeeds in understanding his ailment, and overcomes it by dis-covering special sources of energy.

In *Contre Sainte-Beuve*, Proust appears to be considering the possible interest of making the protagonist of his novel a neurasthenic. Speaking about certain novels of Balzac, he states, 'Whoever writes the life of the family of a neurasthenic may paint a picture of the same kind' (*ASB*, 61, n.) ['Celui qui écrira la vie de la famille d'un neurasthénique pourra faire une peinture du même genre'] (*CSB*, 269, n.). But at this very time Proust is also suffering from chronic doubts about the form his story should take: 'Should it be a novel, a philosophical study, am I a novelist?' he asks in *Le Carnet de 1908*. There is good reason to ask whether the rediscovery of self that dominates *A la recherche*, of a self that is not totally cured but is at least conscious of the mechanisms of its condition, is not presented according to schematics borrowed from the medical diagnoses of diseases of the will and of the nerves of Proust's time. In other words, the question we may now ask is to what extent the aesthetic argument and the construction of Proust's novel integrate various diagnoses of diseases of the will in order to challenge certain medical ideas of his time.

WRITING AND VOLITION

Proust's very first writings, both critical and creative, reproduce endlessly the image of individuals with artistic gifts who do not have the willpower to execute their projects. An 1892 article on Louis Ganderax begins with the picture of a person 'whose strength is not the equal of the obligations at hand, who says «Tomorrow I will possess, in some magical way, the willpower that I lack»' ['dont les forces n'égalent pas le devoir qu'il faudrait remplir, [qui] se dit: «Demain, j'aurai comme par quelque enchantement cette volonté qui me manque»'] (*CSB*, 343). Proust admires the enormous vitality and self-assurance of comte Armand-Pierre de Cholet (his lieutenant during his military service), who published *Voyage en Turquie d'Asie* in 1892. He lauds the man's tenacity and capacity to complete projects, 'the energetic life of a will that knows no limits and no weaknesses, which pursues the difficult enterprises and carries them off' ['[la] vie énergique d'une volonté sans limites et sans défaillances qui poursuit les entreprises les plus difficiles et les mène à bonne fin'] (*CSB*, 351).

The inertia that affects certain creative individuals has overtones of moral degeneration in Proust's writing, as though he always bore in mind the medical diagnoses of his time which assimilated the literary impotence of the decadent writers to degeneracy and even sexual impotence. One thinks, for example, of the heroine of 'Violante ou la mondanité', who, out of apathy, refuses to cultivate what is best in herself, seeks out the social life instead of a more productive solitude, and by that preference alone plunges into vice. But the young Marcel Proust also reacts to the simplistic aspects of medical diagnoses. In a mocking comment on an article in *L'Echo de Paris* (1892), he attacks the naïve medical recipes of hygienists of the period: 'in spite of its prestigious title, this article is no more than a piece of advice on hygiene and, dare I say, a prescription of cold baths to cure impotence' ['malgré son titre prestigieux, [...cet article] se réduit à un conseil d'hygiène et, si j'ose le dire, à une prescription de bains froids contre l'impuissance'] (*CSB*, 352). We see the same type of juxtaposition in 1893 in a phrase that is already a sketch for the famous opposition between instinct and intellect that will dominate *Contre Sainte-Beuve*: 'Art is an instinct, and reflective individuals suffer, in a sense, from impotence' ['L'art est un instinct, et les réfléchis sont un peu des impuissants'] (*CSB*, 358).

In an early article on Robert de Montesquiou, Proust adopts the count's mocking tone to castigate a class of nerve-sufferers of whom Proust himself is a member:

If you know one of these young men, you know them all. They're all the same. First, they all suffer from a 'malady of the will'. They are without willpower, and thus they cannot act and don't wish to think. Most of them glory in it, others pretend to regret it, as though it were an infinitely distinguished weakness. Some sense the depth of the problem, the toll it takes on the mind and on our actions, but they can't change, because to do so they would require willpower. If it weren't the most pitiful misfortune, it would be the most disgusting of trivialities.

[Vous les connaissez tous, ces jeunes gens, si vous en connaissez un. Ils sont tous pareils. D'abord ils ont tous une 'maladie de la volonté'.[82] Ils ne peuvent pas vouloir, d'où ils ne savent agir et ne veulent pas penser. La plupart s'en glorifient, d'autres affectent de s'en plaindre, comme d'une faiblesse infiniment distinguée. Quelques-uns sentent la profondeur du mal, ses ravages dans l'esprit et dans l'action, mais ne peuvent changer, justement parce que pour cela il faudrait vouloir. Si ce n'était pas la plus pitoyable des misères, ce serait la plus écœurante des banalités.] (*CSB*, 407)

What this text seems to confirm is that in 1894 Proust was already familiar with *Les Maladies de la volonté* by Théodule Ribot. Proust will not forget the lessons learned in this work, for he refers to it in two important texts, the introduction to *Sésame et les lys* and *Contre Sainte-Beuve*, in contexts where he is discussing creative beings who suffer from aboulia that prevents them from conceiving their work as a whole.

It is the crucial problem of willpower that haunts the hero of *Jean Santeuil*, Proust's abandoned novel begun in autumn 1895. In the episode of the bedtime kiss that reappears in *A la recherche*, Mme Santeuil and a medical friend, Dr Surlande, are discussing Jean. His mother adopts the peremptory tone of her husband as she indicates the life path the parents have chosen for their son:

He is only seven, Doctor ... But we have some very firm ideas about his future. Not that we would wish to thwart our son's own wishes in any way, as long as his preferences run to a true career, such as the magistrature, Foreign Affairs or the bar.

[Il n'a que sept ans, docteur ... Mais nous avons pourtant sur son avenir des idées très arrêtées. Non que nous voulions contrecarrer en rien les désirs de notre fils qui sera toujours libre ici, du moment que ses préférences n'iront qu'à une carrière véritable, comme la magistrature, les Affaires étrangères ou le barreau.] (*JS*, 202–3)

Dr Surlande immediately identifies and limits Jean's possibilities, while Mme Santeuil appears to raise questions about his sexuality: 'He is what we call a nervous child, said the doctor, smiling as though he had pronounced a witticism. His facies indicates that clearly enough' ['C'est [ce] que nous appelons un nerveux, dit le docteur, en souriant comme après un bon mot. Son faciès l'indique d'ailleurs assez'] (*JS*, 202). 'My husband and I want to bring him up in a manly way' ['Nous voulons, mon mari et moi, l'élever virilement'], continues the mother. It is on this evening, after Jean's nervous tantrum, that his mother frees him forever from his guilt. His reprehensible behaviour is not a product of his 'responsible willpower', she suggests, but of 'an involuntary nervous state' (*JS*, 210).

The initial fever of writing *Jean Santeuil* did not last long. Already in September 1896, compositional problems are apparent: the writer cannot arrive at an overall plan for the novel (*Corr.*, II, 124). The letters of 1896–1900 record Proust's progressive detachment from *Jean Santeuil*. Towards the end of 1899, there is the discovery of Ruskin, which seems literally to supplant the fictional project in his mind.[83] But the success of the articles about and translations of Ruskin was no compensation for a lack of more personal writing, as far as Proust was concerned. Writing about others was a secondary activity, a semi-creativity that he found frustrating. Visiting Léon Yeatman on his birthday in 1901, Proust exclaims, 'I'm thirty years old today, and I've accomplished nothing'.

His correspondence from the 1900–05 period reflects his increasing sense of frustration, an absence of inspiration, and the realization that he lacks the conceptual powers to imagine the structure of the major work he has within him. In 1904, he tells Marie Nordlinger that he will refuse to translate *St Mark's Rest*, and in the same year he writes to Barrès, 'I have two more Ruskins to do and after that I will try to translate my own poor soul, if it hasn't died in the interim' ['J'ai encore deux Ruskin à faire et après j'essaierai de traduire ma pauvre âme à moi, si elle n'est pas morte dans l'intervalle'] (*Corr.*, IV, 93).

Proust's apprehensions about artistic aboulia grew more intense and crystallized around his second Ruskin translation, *Sésame et les lys*. This project is, in fact, almost a physical image of Proust's semi-creativity during the period, with its poetic beginning (a miniature version of the Narrator's childhood in Combray) that rapidly transforms itself into an essay on reading. It is, without doubt, a creative piece, bubbling over with ideas about the difference between various belle-lettrist approaches to writing and true creativity, but it is an essay that poses its own basic contradiction. Reading is at the threshold of spiritual life, it is not in itself a spiritual exercise, Proust tells us. His *Sésame et les lys*, his 'reading' of Ruskin, comes up against the same obstacle, for the fine introduction frames a translation, a pure reproduction of the Other's language.

Within the larger essay on Ruskin there is a smaller one which analyses reading as a means of therapy for those suffering from lack of willpower. The text targets certain almost pathological cases of spiritual depression for which reading provides a curative discipline; books are said to play a role analogous to that of psychotherapists for certain cases of neurasthenia (*ASB*, 211; *CSB*, 178). The real subject of these experimentations with reading is the artist who lacks willpower. In a note in which Proust refers to what he calls Ribot's 'fine book', *Les Maladies de la volonté*, he alludes to the aboulia that struck Fontanes and undermined Coleridge's career. The long, quasi-clinical introduction to these considerations on willpower and art begins with the portrait of an individual almost paralysed by his neuroses, half-way between Beard's neurasthenic and Charcot's hysteric:

We know that in certain affections of the nervous system, without any of the organs themselves being affected, the patient is mired in a sort of impossibility of willing, as if in a deep rut, from which he cannot escape unaided and where ultimately he would waste away, if a strong and helping hand were not held out to him. His brain, his legs, his lungs, his stomach are sound. He is not truly incapacitated from working, from walking, from exposing himself to the cold, from eating. But he is incapable of willing these various actions, which he would be perfectly capable of performing. And an organic degeneration, which would end by becoming the equivalent of the diseases he does not have, would be the irremediable consequence of this inertia of the will, if the impulsion he is unable to find in himself were not to come to him from outside, from a doctor who will will for him, until such time as his various organic wills have been re-educated. Now there exist certain minds that might be compared to patients such as these, who are prevented by a sort of laziness or frivolity from descending spontaneously into the deeper parts of the self where the true life of the spirit begins ... they live on the surface in a perpetual forgetfulness of themselves, in a sort of passivity which makes them the plaything of every pleasure and reduces them to the stature of those roundabout who excite them. (*ASB*, 212)

[On sait que, dans certaines affections du système nerveux, le malade, sans qu'aucun de ses organes soit lui-même atteint, est enlisé dans une sorte d'impossibilité de vouloir, comme dans une ornière profonde d'où il ne peut pas se tirer seul, et où il finirait par dépérir, si une main puissante et secourable ne lui était pas tendue. Son cerveau, ses jambes, ses poumons, son estomac, sont intacts. Il n'a aucune incapacité réelle de travailler, de marcher, de s'exposer au froid, de manger. Mais ces différents actes, qu'il serait très capable d'accomplir, il est incapable de les vouloir. Et une déchéance organique qui finirait par devenir l'équivalent des maladies qu'il n'a pas serait la conséquence irrémédiable de l'inertie de sa volonté, si l'impulsion qu'il ne peut trouver en lui-même ne lui venait de dehors, d'un médecin qui voudra pour lui, jusqu'au jour où seront peu à peu rééduqués ses divers vouloirs organiques. Or, il existe certains esprits qu'on pourrait comparer à ces malades et qu'une sorte de paresse ou de frivolité empêche de descendre spontanément dans les régions profondes de soi-même où commence la véritable vie de l'esprit ... ils vivent à la surface dans un perpétuel oubli d'eux-mêmes,[84] dans une sorte de passivité qui les rend le jouet de tous les plaisirs, les diminue à la taille de ceux qui les entourent et les agitent.] (*CSB*, 178–9)

For these irresolute souls, one of whom seems to be Proust himself at this juncture, reading represents a powerful incitation to personal activity.

INVOLITION'S WAY

As we have seen, the first direct mention of Ribot's work by Proust dates from 1894. The year is an important one for Proust from a number of points of view. In the autumn, he enrolled for the *licence* in philosophy. Anne Henry has argued that the philosophy courses he took that year had a profound influence on his thought. She singles out, in particular, a course in aesthetics taught by Gabriel Séailles[85] that was broadly influenced by Schelling's philosophy of art, and she sees that aesthetic position transposed directly into *Jean Santeuil*, begun in 1895. Schopenhauer probably exercised an even more direct influence on Proust. The French translation of *The World as Will and Idea* appeared in 1888,[86] the year Proust did his *baccalauréat* philosophy year at the Lycée Condorcet. Henry's discussion of the similarity of Schopenhauer's and Proust's ideas on music, and of the probable absorption, by Proust, of the German notion of *Einfühlung*, the state of intuitive fusion with external objects which Schopenhauer advanced as a necessary preliminary for artistic creation, is convincing.[87]

At the same time, it has been pointed out that the raw material for *A la recherche du temps perdu* existed in abundance, in embryonic form, in the last three decades of the nineteenth century.[88] In his book on Schopenhauer, for instance, Théodule Ribot observes that one tendency which characterized nineteenth-century metaphysics as a whole was to explain the world by the notion of will (or intuition), and to downplay the importance of the rational intelligence.[89]

The anxiety about personal willpower deficit evident in all of Proust's writing up until about 1906 – the stories in *Les Plaisirs et les jours, Jean Santeuil*, his letters – did not diminish after his encounter with Schopenhauer. On the contrary, in the two years following the death of his father and subsequently, both before and after the death of his mother in September 1905, Proust continued to seek psychological and medical answers to his condition. He speaks, beginning in September 1904, of the possibility of being treated for his neurasthenia by Dr Paul Dubois of Bern, then wonders in December if he should consult Dr Jules-Joseph Déjerine of La Salpêtrière. After his mother's death he seems determined to take treatment, but is undecided between Dubois and Déjerine until he eventually accepts the advice of his asthma specialist, Dr Brissaud, and is admitted to Dr Paul Sollier's sanatorium in Boulogne-sur-Seine in December 1905. Proust's reading related to questions of willpower, neurasthenia and asthma appears to have been considerable in this period. The notes and preface to *Sésame et les lys* and Proust's correspondence suggest familiarity with Dubois' famous lecture of 1901 *De l'influence de l'esprit sur le corps*, and his major work, published in 1904, *Les Psychonévroses et leur traitement moral*. Proust had also consulted works by Dr Wilhelm Brügelmann on asthma as well as Brissaud's *L'Hygiène de l'asthmatique*, and a study by two students of Déjerine, Drs Camus and Pagniez, entitled *Isolement et psychothérapie* (1904), which contains an excellent summary of Déjerine's methods.[90] It seems to me, therefore, that more emphasis needs to be placed on the medico-psychological rather than the philosophical framework surrounding Proust's insecurity about willpower.

The psychological and medical aspects of willpower and memory were of course already receiving close scrutiny in the early 1890s. In an important study which Proust's father quotes in his works, *L'Etat mental des hystériques*, Pierre Janet devotes a chapter to aboulia in hysterics.[91] Janet cites a Freud-Breuer essay approvingly, agreeing that the hysteric suffers above all from reminiscences.[92] But it is not the conscious memory which functions in the hysteric. Like the Proustian Narrator, Janet's hysteric depends on surges from unconscious states to reconstitute full-fledged memories:

remembrance seems to disappear every time [the hysteric's] personality is concerned, every time [he/she] is compelled to say 'I remember'. The remembrance, on the contrary, seems present in various other circumstances – in dreams, hypnotic sleep, thoughtless acts, writing, and speech obtained while the patient's mind is diverted by another conscious operation.[93]

One of Janet's most discussed patients, from his earlier study *Automatisme psychologique*, has the same first name as tante Léonie from Combray; Léonie also makes her appearance in *The Mental State of Hystericals*, notably in the chapter on 'idées fixes'.

October of 1894 also marked the appearance of Théodule Ribot's first article on involuntary memory – or 'mémoire affective', as he called it – in the *Revue Philosophique* which he had founded in 1876.[94] It would be surprising that Proust, so keen on questions of philosophy since he had been turned on to the subject by his philosophy teacher Darlu, did not know of Ribot by the late 1880s, given the latter's notoriety. At just 180 pages, Ribot's digest of Schopenhauer's philosophy would have been a useful and practical reference text for lycée students, and some of his other publications, *Les Maladies de la mémoire* and *L'Hérédité psychologique*, for example, bore titles that were bound to interest Proust.[95] Like his study of diseases of the will, Ribot's research on involuntary memory promotes the superiority of involuntary processes over intellectual ones. Feeling precedes knowing, and consciousness is, in the first instance, visceral.[96] There is a quasi-militant fervour in Ribot's desire to put the intellect in its place, a sentiment that we find echoed fairly exactly in Proust's writing:

The object is to show the distinctive nature of sensibility, its basis, its matter, its content: to establish that the affective life and the intellectual life are heterogeneous, not reducible one to the other.[97]

In his discussion of involuntary memory, Ribot invokes the experiences of Chateaubriand, Nerval and Sully Prudhomme, and makes reference to memories embedded in childhood, in music, and in the experience of another's death.[98] What strikes a reader of Proust, more than these external parallels with *A la recherche*, is Ribot's frequent assertion that an involuntary memory is far more powerful than the initial impression to which it refers, and that such memories actually resuscitate previous experience which overlaps and shunts aside our current state of perception:

True or concrete affective memory consists in the reproduction in the present of an earlier affective state with all its characteristics. This is necessary, at least theoretically, so that it can be complete. The closer it approaches totality, the closer it approaches exactness. In this case, memory does not consist solely in the representation of conditions and circumstances, that is, in intellectual states; but in the recollection of the affective state itself, as such, that is, as it was experienced.[99]

But let us return to the one study of Ribot to which Proust makes direct and pointed reference. The title *Les Maladies de la volonté* should not lead us astray. The book is by no means simply a pathology of morbid states of the will. On the contrary, the author examines the notion of the will itself and discovers that there is a type of willpower that one might call 'involuntary'. In parallel to voluntary attention, which demands an effort of concentration, there exist states of spontaneous attention, for example, that of a child absorbed by an object it is gazing at, or that of an animal contemplating its prey. In connecting voluntary attention to an effort of the intellect, Ribot seems to give priority to more spontaneous feelings, and he makes an essential distinction that will form the basis of Proust's argument that intuition must precede intellectual efforts, a distinction which contains the seed of the Proustian cleavage between deep self and social self.

Spontaneous attention may be observed, among others, in the poet possessed by an internal vision. Quoting Ferrier, Ribot evokes certain habits and an attitude that are those of the Proustian Narrator absorbed in a profound impression:

In the most intense attention, any movement that would diminish internal diffusion is also stopped. Thus, when we think deeply, automatic actions are themselves arrested, and one notes that a man who falls into deep meditation while walking stops and remains at rest.[100]

In *Contre Sainte-Beuve* (*ASB*, 6; *CSB*, 214), Proust remarks on the way images absorb him; the Narrator of *A la recherche* is similarly transfixed: 'How many times at Combray... I returned with such an image, before which I had come to a stop for a moment and which I felt to be but a lid that covered something else' ['Que de fois à Combray ... je revins avec une telle image, devant laquelle j'étais tombé en arrêt un instant, que je sentais n'être qu'un couvercle'] (IV,

823). Conscious intellectual efforts are insufficient to bring us to the state of heightened sensitivity described by Ribot:

I would define this state of intense, spontaneous attention, with Sergi, as a difference of perception producing a greater psychic energy in certain nervous centres with a sort of temporary catalepsy of the other centres.[101]

The beauty of Ribot's argument, for a reader like Proust, is the way it reverses a value system that enshrines conscious willpower alongside 'intelligence'. These two operate at a surface level, creating the feelings with which they work instead of allowing attention to focus on the spontaneous ideas that rise from the deeper layers of the mind. Ribot equates conscious willpower and intelligence with artificiality and inauthenticity. Moreover, and this may surprise us when we think of the fragility of the products of involuntary memory in Proust, Ribot depicts voluntary attention as precarious and unstable, precisely because it depends on a sustained effort of intellectual concentration:

voluntary attention is an artificial state in which, with the aid of factitious feelings, we maintain with some difficulty certain conscious states that tend only to vanish (for example, when out of politeness we follow a very boring conversation). In one case [= spontaneous attention] what determines this specialization of the consciousness is our whole individuality; in the second [= voluntary attention], it is an extremely weak and limited portion of our individuality.[102]

Even the small details in this passage strike a reader of Proust. The example of boring conversations listened to in stoic politeness looks directly forward to the Proustian dynamic that opposes social language to interior silence. But in a more general sense these lines seem closely linked to the anti-intellectual arguments in *Contre Sainte-Beuve* and to several passages in *Le Temps retrouvé* that deal with the aesthetics of intuition and chance.

Already in *Jean Santeuil* Proust argues that consciously willed investigations cannot pierce the surface of phenomena or events:

in the instant that I lived these scenes of my life, it was my will that registered them for purposes of pleasure or fear, of vanity or maliciousness. And their intimate essence escaped me. I could have gazed at them with great intensity and they would have escaped me all the same.

[au moment où je ... vivais [les scènes de ma vie], c'est ma volonté qui les connaissait dans un but de plaisir ou de crainte, de vanité ou de méchanceté. Et leur essence intime m'échappait. J'y eusse fixé les yeux avec force qu'elle m'eût échappé de même.] (*JS*, 490)

In *A la recherche*, in terms borrowed even more closely from Ribot, Proust connects everything that is voluntary to the artificial:

The thought that there is a vast difference between the real impression which we have had of a thing and the *artificial* impression of it which we form for ourselves when we attempt *by an act of will* to imagine it did not long detain me. (VI, 220)

[Sur l'extrême différence qu'il y a entre l'impression vraie que nous avons eue d'une chose et l'impression *factice* que nous nous en donnons quand *volontairement* nous essayons de nous la représenter, je ne m'arrêtais pas.] (IV, 448; the emphasis is mine.)

Because they are both the product of an artificial attitude, Proust assimilates intelligence and willpower. What these two produce is mediocre and superficial. The *avant-textes* of the episode of 'l'esthétique dans le buffet' turn endlessly on this observation, which is provoked by Elstir's compliment: whatever his other problems, the Narrator can always enjoy the pleasures of the intellect and of the spirit. But appreciating an intellectual joy is a command performance: 'Whatever I tried to recall of what I had seen, the image that my will drew from my memory seemed to me as boring as reality itself' ['Quoi que je voulusse évoquer de ce que j'avais vu, l'image que ma volonté tirait de ma mémoire me semblait aussi ennuyeuse que la réalité même'] (IV, 802). The mediocrity of the Narrator's life is not so much related to its substance, but to the images requisitioned by his conscious will, which are like 'facsimiles of the intelligence' (IV, 807). It is the image born of chance, 'without the intervention of our will, or of our reason' (IV, 817), 'before there has been any intervention of our will or our intelligence' (IV, 824), that is the only authentic image. The repeated juxtaposition of the words 'volonté' and 'intelligence' melds them into synonyms:

I understood what an abyss there was between a past regained by chance and the inexact and cold facsimiles which, under the guise of the term 'past', my conscious memory... presented to my intelligence at the bidding of my will.

[je compris quel abîme il y avait entre un passé retrouvé par hasard et les inexacts et froids fac-similés que sous ce nom de passé ma mémoire consciente ... présentait à mon intelligence sur la réquisition de ma volonté.] (IV, 813)

Ribot's dissection of the ailments of the will provides Proust with a major trump card: the real disease is to be too responsive to the conscious willpower of the intelligence, which can only suggest reasonable acts (following a boring conversation out of politeness, for instance). To be healthy is to heed spontaneous, intense impressions, for in them our whole individuality is engaged, our true deep self.

Like the preface of *Sésame et les lys* in which Proust refers to it, Ribot's study of willpower also deals with reading as a remedy against the absence of willpower. Ribot is preoccupied by the moral inertia of the literate and neurotic, the fine minds that have the potential to be creative. Unlike Proust who, in *Sésame et les lys*, pictures the act of reading as an energizing, therapeutic activity for the undecided creative person (Proust's example focuses on the individual who allows himself to be absorbed by the charm of a text), Ribot describes an individual without willpower whom reading defeats. The effort of intellectual concentration required is too great:

Conscious of this weakening of energy, the patient attempts to gain it back; he takes up a book, resolved not to give in to his feelings of intellectual incapacity, psychic languor, cerebral weakness ... In these attempts to understand the meaning of what is before his eyes, he reads and resolutely rereads certain striking passages, with the apparent energy of victory, but without being able to understand a set of very simple ideas or to pursue successfully an elementary line of reasoning. (*Les Maladies*, 100)

This repeated effort to read certain 'striking passages', the intense intellectual attention of this patient, recall in a powerful way the intellectual contraction of the Narrator struggling with the obscure sensations that the madeleine evokes. Of course, the Narrator succeeds in this early effort of memory and will, but much time will pass before he interiorizes the lessons learned. The metaphor of reading appears to continue its journey from Ribot to *Le Temps retrouvé*, the finale of the novel where the reading of oneself becomes the essential activity of the artist and where, finally, the intellect is assigned the essential but limited role that it has to play in art.

There are more pathological cases, according to Ribot, where one observes the progressive degeneration of the will. The judgement and good sense of individuals in this state are perfectly intact:

The patients can exercise their will internally, mentally, according to the requirements of their reason. They can feel the desire to act; but they are powerless to act appropriately. In the depths of their understanding, there is an impossibility. (*Les Maladies*, 38)

There are parallels between this being – intelligent, quite capable of humour, still receptive to the sensations he feels, but impotent – and both the Narrator and Charles Swann. The child protagonist of Combray is equipped with a prodigious sensibility and is excited by the idea of writing. He is open to the profound rhythms of nature, the inspirational force of the sun and the wind. His problem (a retrospective one) is to integrate these pulsations into a unified view of the world and, in addition, as the short composition on the Martinville spires demonstrates, to translate his impressions into words. Swann is almost as sensitive as the child in certain moments of deep perception, for example, when he listens to music. But both suffer from a kind of artistic inertia, for too often they abandon their efforts to get to the bottom of their impressions and to build out of them a new construction which would be their creative response.

Certain aspects of Swann's character seem composed from Théodule Ribot's formulae for diseases of the willpower. One is struck, for instance, by the emphasis on Swann's intelligence. Intelligence, Proust says elsewhere, is an organizing force that manipulates data provided to it; it cannot create anything. According to Ribot, 'intelligence is savings and will is expenditure' (*Les Maladies*, 29). Swann makes his savings on two levels, so to speak. He refuses to become involved at an emotional, personal level in exchanges of ideas, nor does he ever offer a deeply felt comment on even the most important questions: 'He appeared unwilling even to risk having an opinion, and to be at his ease only when he could furnish, with meticulous accuracy, some precise detail' (I, 116) ['Il avait l'air de ne pas oser avoir une opinion et de n'être tranquille que quand il pouvait donner méticuleusement des renseignements précis'] (I, 97).

His sensibility, his taste, his talents hold much promise, but he always opts for the facile solution while carefully protecting his reputation as a discriminating person. His predilection for things intellectual hides the fact that he has given up on any determination to explore his own individuality. According to Ribot once again, 'a malady of the will produces, as far as is possible, an individual reduced to pure intelligence' (*Les Maladies*, 50). The statement, in the introduction to *Contre Sainte-Beuve*, that its author attaches less importance to intelligence with each passing day, reads very much like an echo of Ribot from a reader taking comfort in the hope that the only way to overcome a disease of the willpower is to fully assume the disease and to accept that, in everything, the involuntary should have first priority.

The relationship Ribot constructs between intelligence and inac-

tion thus governs Swann, even if the latter retains a certain superiority over other characters in *A la recherche*. But Swann's evolution as
a person resembles that of the vast majority of the society who
people the novel. Proust will reiterate that these individuals live
through imitation, imitation being the way of politeness and
common sense which leads us not to upset applecarts, and thus not
to be upset ourselves. On this particular point Ribot appears to have
provided Proust with rules of conduct for his characters:

If one calculates, in each human life, what is to be attributed to
automatism, *habit, the passions* and, above all, *imitation*, one sees that the
number of purely willed acts, in the strict sense of the word, is quite small.
For most men, *imitation* is sufficient; they are satisfied with what *was* the will
of others and, since they think using everyone else's ideas, they act
according to the will of everyone else. (*Les Maladies*, 173; the emphasis is
mine.)

The role Proust assigns to art, in lines that appear to draw on the
above passage very closely, is to restart life on a different footing,
eliminating from it the unconscious copying of the behaviour and
ideas of others: 'Our vanity, *our passions, our spirit of imitation, our habits*
have long been at work, and it is the task of art to undo this work of
theirs' (VI, 255) ['Ce travail qu'avaient fait notre amour-propre, *notre
passion, notre esprit d'imitation*, notre intelligence abstraite, *nos habitudes*,
c'est ce travail que l'art défera'] (IV, 475; the emphasis is mine).

Even though the Narrator experiences moments of inspiration
and deep insight, his goal of becoming a writer long remains just
beyond the horizon. He will experience life as dispersion and
disintegration. What it lacks is a centre. The search for a fixed,
stable core of personality constitutes, in one sense, the entire drama
of *A la recherche*. Ribot had also identified this problem of absence at
the nucleus in certain indecisive individuals who experience life only
as scatteredness, and who seem to have lost the sensation of living:

My existence is incomplete; I have retained the functions and actions of
ordinary life; but in each of these something is missing, that is, *the sensation
that characterizes them and the joy that follows them*. . . Each one of my senses,
each part of myself is separated from me, so to speak, and can no longer
provide me with any sensation. (*Les Maladies*, 50–1; the emphasis is mine.)

This image of a person dispersed into tiny atoms and having lost the
key to reintegrating them into a self is not so far from our vision of
the Narrator. As a young person he suffers from a similar feeling of
being separated from the physical objects of the outside world: he

speaks of the 'thin spiritual border' which prevents any contact. The terms 'sensation' and joy' from Ribot's text are weighty ones in our context: these are the two key aspects of the Proustian theory of the re-creation of life by art. It is a kind of joy resembling certainty that becomes the sign of reality emerging from the habitual: 'But it was precisely the fortuitous and inevitable fashion in which this and the other *sensations* had been encountered that proved the trueness of the past which they brought back to life ..., since we feel, with these sensations, the effort that they make to climb back towards the light, feel in ourselves the *joy* of rediscovering the real' (VI, 233) ['la façon fortuite, inévitable, dont la *sensation* avait été rencontrée, contrôlait la vérité du passé qu'elle ressuscitait ... puisque nous sentons son effort pour remonter vers la lumière, que nous sentons la *joie* du réel retrouvé'] (IV, 457–8; the emphasis is mine).

The Narrator's only hope resides in certain brief moments packed with vivid sensations and inexplicable joy. How can this momentary happiness be converted into lasting happiness, perpetual bliss? It is here that intellectual willpower, the will of the intellect, has its role to play. The realization that, in most individuals, willpower is a periodical thing, seems to have been confirmed by Ribot, who defined three types of willpower: firm, weak and intermittent. Assessing the incidence of these three forms from the point of view of their effectiveness, Ribot sees a hierarchy at the summit of which resides the genius, the individual whose actions seem to be a direct extension of his will:

The most perfect co-ordination is that of those with the greatest will, the great active ones, whatever their order of activity: Caesar, Michelangelo or Saint Vincent de Paul. That co-ordination may be summarized in a few words: unity, stability, strength. The exterior unity of their life is in the unity of their purpose, always pursued, which creates as circumstances evolve new co-ordinations and adaptations. But this exterior unity is, itself, but the expression of an internal unity, that of their character. It is because they remain the same that their purpose remains the same. In their heart is a powerful, inextinguishable passion that co-opts ideas for its own purposes. That passion is themselves, it is the psychic expression of their constitution as nature made it. (*Les Maladies*, 169–70)

Proust clearly does not consider himself one of the 'co-ordinated' geniuses, but the passage appears to have struck him. In a letter to Reynaldo Hahn where he examines the problem of willpower and productivity, this idea of the coherency of genius surfaces again:

for the elite, for thinkers, saints, etc., it is ... clear that they believe one can
do whatever one wishes, or rather that one is worth what one wishes, or
rather what one can do. (That is, our willpower, our power over ourselves
gives the measure of our worth.)

[pour les personnes d'élite, les penseurs, les saints, etc., il est ... clair qu'ils
croient qu'on peut ce qu'on veut, ou plutôt qu'on vaut ce qu'on veut, ou
plutôt ce qu'on peut. (C'est-à-dire que notre volonté, notre pouvoir sur
nous donne la mesure de notre valeur.)] (*Corr.*, II, 112)

Théodule Ribot's 'fine book' presents itself as an unexpected
inheritance to Proust. Its argument, studded with the intuitions of a
paternal figure, provides the features for a nervous hero, suffering
from incapacities of the will, suspicious of intelligence, subject to
intermittent poetic visions, who learns to reject pure intelligence and
intellectual willpower in favour of the spontaneous, the intuitive and
the involuntary. If the intense focus on memory is something
particularly Proustian, the insistence that involuntary memory is the
more magical genus may be read as directly related to the promi-
nence which Ribot gives to the involuntary in his study. Among all
the 'Proustian' ideas in Ribot's text, however, it may be that of
intermittence that conditions most profoundly the deep structure of
the novel and of life experience in the novel: 'A rung beneath this
perfect co-ordination [of the genius], there are *those lives that are
traversed by intermittence*, whose centre of gravity, which is ordinarily
stable, oscillates from time to time' (*Les Maladies*, 170; the emphasis is
mine). It is in that oscillation that all of meaningful life resides for
the Proustian hero, and the notion of intermittence is transformed
into a positive force, a prefiguration of the artistic meaning of the
involuntary memory, itself intermittent. The universality of the
aesthetic credo of *A la recherche* turns on the idea that any individual
with artistic gifts can employ momentary flashes of insight and
inspiration to create a durable work. Intermittence marks the life of
every man, but it can be transformed into an artistic mindset that is
not unlike the 'perpetual adoration' of the monk.

NEURASTHENIA: DIAGNOSIS AND RESPONSE

If Théodule Ribot's ideas appear as a kind of spiritual heritage into
which Marcel Proust dipped to complete the psychological traits of
his Narrator, it should not be forgotten that Dr Adrien Proust also

wrote a detailed analysis of the state of absent willpower which preoccupies his son in the preface to *Sésame et les lys*.

During the period 1896 to 1903, when Marcel's creative production falters, his father's publication list grows as he returns enthusiastically to his speciality, therapeutic hygiene. Dr Proust becomes general editor, for the publishing house Masson, of a series of treatment manuals for all sorts of common conditions. In 1896 he writes an important preface for the work of a colleague, Dr Eugène Brissaud, *L'Hygiène des asthmatiques*. In 1897, in conjunction with Dr Gilbert Ballet, he produces *L'Hygiène du neurasthénique*. Ballet and Dr Proust had already worked together, attempting to apply certain experimental uses of magnets that Charcot had employed with hysterics to other patients with other complaints. They had presented a paper on the topic – later published by Masson[103] – to a medical conference in Amsterdam. In the second edition of *L'Hygiène du neurasthénique* (1900), the editors mention three titles in the new series, *L'Hygiène du goutteux*, *L'Hygiène de l'obèse* and *L'Hygiène du diabétique*. In 1901, Adrien Proust completes the introduction to the third edition (in 1245 pages) of his very popular *Traité d'hygiène* (*Corr.*, II, 34).

Dr Proust's extremely pessimistic verdict on neurasthenia and asthma is that, once the patient has entered adolescence, he is no longer curable unless he has been taught good principles of hygiene. By their simple juxtaposition in time, *L'Hygiène du neurasthénique* and the preface to the volume on asthma stand as negative diagnoses of Marcel Proust's literary production. In 1896 Marcel had published *Les Plaisirs et les jours*, a non-homogeneous collection of short writing – stories, poems and poems in prose, pastiches – and in 1896–7 he was already in the process of abandoning *Jean Santeuil*. Any neurasthenic artist, according to the analysis of Dr Proust, would have 'production' difficulties, for his problem would by definition be an inability to persist and to follow through:

Neurasthenics try out occupations and subjects of study that seem to them likely to excite their interest and to revive their activity; but the attraction of novelty is ephemeral for them. They tire quickly, become disenchanted with their undertaking and soon abandon it to move on to other subjects (77–8).

L'Hygiène du neurasthénique requires careful reading for, while analysing a very modish condition, 'la maladie du siècle' as Dr Proust calls it, he is venturing on to land well tilled by his son, an area where Marcel is as expert as the physician. The basis of the treatment Dr Proust will propose for neurasthenia – and Marcel saw this as well as anyone – was to be drawn from his recipes for proper physical hygiene.

Eugène Brissaud's 1896 study on asthma, which Marcel Proust read with care, is very much in the mould of Adrien Proust's thought. An asthmatic's treatment must involve fresh air and exercise; a day is not complete without a moment reserved for a shower, work in the gym, cycling or fencing. In his introduction to the volume, Dr Proust goes so far as to assert that sensible hygienic principles should prohibit marriages between those afflicted with nervous disorders. He appears to forget that the neurasthenia from which his son suffered would likely have been inherited from his own side of the family, from his sister Elisabeth Amiot to be precise. Already in Brissaud's study Dr Proust maintains that hygiene is the panacea for many neuroses and psychoses, especially neurasthenia, since the condition is the result of an overworked brain. But Adrien Proust also saw hygiene as a response to the ailments of society as a whole:

hygiene ... includes the study of all those conditions that ensure the prosperity of the individual and the species, which improve them morally and physically, in a word, which favour and drive their development. [The programme of the hygienist] must be at one with the aspirations of humanity and all its tendencies towards continued and indefinite improvement, improvement which may be expressed in a single word: progress.[104]

The style of Dr Proust, with its Homaisian potential, must have rankled Marcel, but there are other reasons for reading *L'Hygiène du neurasthénique*. Not only does this study discuss real problems faced by Marcel Proust, it dips into the same pool of images and family experiences as *A la recherche*. At times, in fact, it takes on the tone of an *avant-texte* of that novel.

Let us imagine that at a relatively early point in its evolution, Proust conceived *A la recherche du temps perdu* as the fictional autobiography of a neurasthenic. Obviously, the nervous protagonist would not end his days in total apathy, never having produced anything or having been able to rise from his moral degeneracy. He would rather suffer from a nostalgia for creative activity until a final moment of epiphany, when all hesitations would disappear. Let us examine the various contributions that Marcel's father might have made to this composition, basing ourselves on the portrait of the neurasthenic supplied in *L'Hygiène du neurasthénique*.

One Proustian theme that is familiar to us from Proust's early stories onwards (one sees it in 'Violante et la mondanité', for example) is the culpabilization of social life, sometimes to the point where it is indistinguishable from more obviously troubled or degenerate pleasures. Some would ascribe the guilt to a kind of transfer: a young person with creative abilities wastes his genius and energies in the social round. It happens that she or he is also homosexual. The delinquency is dual, and the two-part guilt meshes into a single feeling.

Proust's correspondence shows clearly that Adrien Proust condemned his son's attraction to society life, but it is surprising to witness the degree to which, in *L'Hygiène du neurasthénique*, Dr Proust medicalizes the relationship between the taste for the social round and neuroticism:

If one reflects on the conditions of the social life as it is practised here ..., on the excitations of every sort that it occasions, on the physical fatigue that it causes, which results almost inevitably from the habit of meals that last too long and are too copious, eaten in rooms that are often overheated, if one thinks of the late nights, the insufficient sleep, at least sleep enjoyed at regular times, it is not surprising that the social life is frequently the cause of the development of nervous asthenia. (31).

It is rare to contemplate works of science where a father appears publicly to dissect the weaknesses of his offspring. Dr Proust follows this passage with another in which he connects directly an excess of socializing and degeneracy:

There is nothing so enervating, nothing that is more likely to unbalance the nervous system and to weaken it than a single-minded preoccupation with the search for pleasure and the satisfaction of the lowest, least noble desires ... Neurasthenia is often the legitimate though unfortunate price one pays for idleness, laziness and vanity. (32).

Adrien Proust refers to the works of Beard, but cautiously. He makes a distinction between American 'nervous exhaustion' and the continental neurosis that stems from exhaustion. Above all, he joins others in expressing his wariness about the label of neurasthenia, because the term often hides erroneous or incomplete diagnoses. (It must be said that original sin in this area is attributable to Beard himself; he spoke of the increasing popularity [*sic*] of baldness as one of the minor but very instructive expressions of nervous sensibility.[105])

In turn-of-the-century medical circles, there was acceptance of the connection between symptoms of sexual weakness (nocturnal emissions, ejaculatio praecox, masturbation) and the exhaustion-based neurosis described by Dr Proust.[106] Without perhaps wishing to be too categorical in his wording, Adrien Proust sees neurasthenia as the affliction of the effeminate male: 'These neurasthenics are almost always men: they are the «emaciated type» whose nervous system is excessively fragile and yields to the least shock' (11).

What is the origin of this fragility? For Adrien, heredity is either the main cause, or it creates a predisposition for all nervous ailments, although the condition only very rarely passes from one generation to the next in the same form. Hypochondria, migraines, irritability may affect the grandparent but transform themselves into gout or nervous weakness in the grandchild.[107] In the case of neurasthenia, however, heredity is presented as a factor in only about forty per cent of cases. Dr Proust's analysis seems a bit shaky here. Medically speaking, heredity does exist as a cause for neurasthenia. But he appears to feel that the life of neurotics would be too simple if they were not responsible for their condition, and he thus invokes concomitant causes, an irregular lifestyle, excessive time spent in the social round, capricious parents and even, as 'le père Norpois' will reiterate in *A la recherche*, the disastrous effects of a bad education:

One can easily see that incorrect methods of education which cause or hasten the development, in children, of bad tendencies and character faults can exercise a disastrous influence on their physical and moral energy.[108]

If Adrien Proust's book seems to provide, on several levels and from several points of view, a stock of images and ideas which Marcel Proust will employ to animate his novel, it is because Dr Proust's focus is on an in-house nervousness, a family affair. Speaking of the influence of family members on the behaviour of the neurotic, Adrien Proust appears to transfer into his medical text twenty-five years of disagreement with his wife on the manner in which their son should be raised:

Nothing is more likely to stir up or maintain, in these patients, depression and hypochondriacal preoccupations than the assiduous ministrations, the endless questions about their state of health and the recommendations which people in their family circle rain upon them. (80)

Proust's correspondence demonstrates that when Marcel and his mother were separated (for example, when his parents took their annual cure at Evian or Vichy), their correspondence was rife with questions and answers about his state of health.

It is impossible to judge whether Elisabeth Amiot, the sister of Adrien Proust, was as nervous in life as Aunt Léonie was in fiction, but we do know from his writings that the image of this type of female hypochondriac struck Adrien as it did Marcel:

We have seen that certain female neurasthenics, without being paralysed in any way, felt themselves completely incapable of walking and standing up and ended up confined to their bed, relegated for years at a stretch to an immobility which is deplorable. (*L'Hygiène*, 79)

When he lives with Albertine, the Narrator will understand more clearly in what ways he resembles his whole family, including his father and his aunt. The latter are both interested in the weather, the father in a more scientific and external way (the act of consulting the barometer follows him in *A la recherche* like a leitmotiv), the aunt in a more internalized fashion, for often she 'observes' the weather from her bed. Sufferers from neurasthenia are extremely sensitive to cold, heat and atmospheric change. 'It has been said correctly of some of them', notes Dr Proust in his study, 'that they were genuine living barometers' ['de véritables baromètres vivants'] (56). It is intriguing to see Proust revisiting this comparison to characterize his Narrator in this same context of family resemblances:

And as if it were not enough that I should bear an exaggerated resemblance to my father, to the extent of not being satisfied like him with consulting the barometer, but becoming a living barometer myself, as if it were not enough that I should allow myself to be ordered by my aunt Léonie to stay at home and watch the weather, from my bedroom window or even from my bed (V, 82)

[C'était assez que je ressemblasse avec exagération à mon père jusqu'à ne pas me contenter de consulter comme lui le baromètre, mais à devenir moi-même un baromètre vivant, c'était assez que je me laissasse commander par ma tante Léonie pour rester à observer le temps, mais de ma chambre ou même de mon lit?] (III, 586)

Adrien Proust examines the surface of things and employs the barometric comparison to enliven his medical text with a touch of irony. But the tiny barometric personage that inhabits the Narrator is affiliated, via his pure joy, to the self that recognizes the essence of experiences, the self that is capable, in spite of his nervous ailments, of reliving important sensations in order to transform them into creative energy.

The process of internalizing paternal ideas has its stages: reading/ absorption, a parodic rewriting, repudiation by inverting value systems, and a final assertion that becomes an apotheosis. The older he gets and the more his literary inactivity weighs upon him, the more Marcel Proust retires from society life. It is clear, however, that he is not ready to accept the values that his father would substitute for the social ones. Admonitions like the ones we have seen from Dr Proust reappear in ironic surroundings in *A la recherche*, often in language marked by heavy parody.[109]

Dr Proust's diagnosis of the neurasthenic identifies additional factors that are central to the aesthetic preoccupations of his son Marcel. Some of these dovetail closely with certain ideas of Théo- dule Ribot. *L'Hygiène du neurasthénique* returns constantly to the feeble determination of neurasthenics, the 'ineffectiveness ['impuissance'] of their intellectual faculties' (48), which they are not prepared to admit. Their inertia makes any complex intellectual task, any serious effort at co-ordination of thought, impossible, and leaves the patient full of hesitation and self-doubt (74–80). One description of the problems that affect the memory of neurasthenics and, as a con- sequence, the stable core of their personality, recalls Ribot and prefigures the Narrator's inability to recall the real content of his life through his conscious, voluntary memory:

The evoking of memories is defective because [neurasthenics] are incapable of sustaining the effort of attention required by *the search for lost memories* ['*la recherche du souvenir perdu*']; because most of the events that took place after the onset of their malady are only weakly perceived by them and are therefore not strongly linked to their conscious personality. (76; the emphasis is mine.)

This impossible search for a lost memory could be seen as a paternal challenge. The young Narrator is at first duped, adopting the reasonable but superficial point of view that our conscious person- ality is involved in the search. At the same time, this medical text proposes a programme for mnemonic education, the education of the Narrator who has been alerted to the importance of the unconscious and who will, henceforth, direct his efforts towards the reconquering of the essence of his experience.

I see anchored here, in this medical text, parts of the foundation for a narrating character who is not only congenitally naïve, but who suffers from the conscious impression of a lack of cohesion at the centre of his existence, just like certain patients described by Ribot. The inability to sustain intellectual effort, according to Adrien Proust's study, means that the neurasthenic cannot resist the incursion of external ideas and influences:

They are often obsessed by some fixed idea, some hypochondriacal preoccupation and live, so to speak, in a state of perpetual *distraction* ... This is one cause for their perceiving the events which they witness in a vague and uncertain manner. They are thus incapable of relocating them in their memory even when they are still recent. (76–7)

The result of this weakening of the personality, according to Dr Proust, is a relaxing of the links that ensure the synthesis of the self. What is left is a personality open to surrounding influences, naïve, infinitely suggestible (166), and, as we have seen, living out daily experience with only a tenuous recollection of events.

Suggestibility is one of the Narrator's most basic characteristics. The word strikes us, because it is imposed with great force from the opening page of *Du Côté de chez Swann* where one contemplates the Narrator marvellously at ease in a state of half-sleep in which he cannot distinguish between past and present, between the various rooms in which he has slept, between dream and reality. It is around this episode of the 'dormeur éveillé' that the first line of *A la recherche* crystallized and the work finally took off.

It is absorbing to see Dr Proust employ this same image, in a concrete, medicalized way, when he discusses certain treatments available to neurasthenics – treatments that are in fact drawn from the field of hysteria. But the image of the neurasthenic which Dr Proust presents us is, for once, that of a patient enjoying all aspects of his willpower, who seems to control the direction of his experiences even when apparently hypnotized:

The 'state of sleep' generally imposed on neurasthenics, which corresponds to the first stages of hypnosis according to the classification of M. Bernheim, is quite different from true induced hypnosis. Patients do not lose their self-awareness: they take part in the 'session' in spite of having their eyes closed and feeling happy to be absent and to be sleeping. They are sleepers who are awake ['dormeurs éveillés']. Hence, when they obey the verbal suggestions of their doctor after waking, they do not act by virtue of a real unconscious and involuntary suggestion. The mental phenomenon that takes place has but the appearance of suggestion, and is quite different. The instruction they have received has been received in full consciousness; it has not escaped monitoring by their personality. (192)

Willpower is the one thing which Dr Proust refused to admit his son possessed. It is true that he inculcated in him a desire, almost an obsession for it. *A la recherche* is a kind of epic search for artificial willpower, that is, of the conscious variety. But in the state of hypersuggestibility that is hypnosis, and which Dr Proust calls the state of the 'dormeur éveillé', the doctor appears to concede to his patient a special kind of willpower, for the latter is quite conscious of every experience that happens to him. Superimposing two states of consciousness, one present, one remembered or sensorially related, will become the technique for releasing the unchanging essence of the Narrator's personality.

It is hard to resist the question: How much does the dream-state overture of *A la recherche*, so poorly understood at first, so static, so mysterious and opaque, owe to Dr Proust? How much does the narrative, that long, curvilinear quest for willpower, which ends in an enshrining of the involuntary, owe to the desire of the nerve-wounded son Marcel to play with the figure of the neurasthenic in all the senses proposed by his father's medical manual in order to make of it a literary creation a hundred times more subtle and many-faceted than the humiliating portrait painted by Dr Adrien Proust?

Marcel's interest in the potential connections between artistic creativity and ailments like neurasthenia and hysteria was intense. His manipulation of his father's medical ideology, his recontexting of Ribot's ideas on spontaneous willpower, his attraction to some of the Goncourts' attempts to translate nervous conditions into literature, all these show Proust struggling to devise an original, creative alternative to some of the medical diagnoses that provided pat answers to these questions. In a sense, however, this struggle was the easy part of Proust's task, for irony and laughter were his great strong points. The central problem he had to face was also nerve-related, but much more complex. Like Flaubert, he would have to work painstakingly at the construction of a literary form using as building blocks the object of his most basic anxiety, words. Proust's concern about the viability of language itself is the subject of our next chapter.

CHAPTER 2

An anxiety of language

However one might nowadays diagnose the nervous disorder from which Proust suffered, the social mark of his condition was an openness to external stimuli, a kind of porosity that might be called neurasthenic. This attitude of unprotectedness was positive, on the one hand, since it attuned him to the world of sensation, the source of inspiration for the artist. But Proust's awareness of his openness is the source of an acute concern about linguistic dependency and authenticity of language that flavours all his major reflections on literary aesthetics. For this potential writer, the spoken word, which floats in the air between interlocutors, authorless, unassignable, represents language at its most ambivalent and most threatening.

One of Proust's most insightful early readers pictured him as an individual who responded totally to anything that made an impression on him: 'Proust's soul is a function when seen in relation to the changing variables of reality, of life. It does not represent and does not protect an independent spirituality', said Ramon Fernandez in the 1940s.[1] French students of characterology have followed in this vein, classifying Proust variously as emotive-non-active-primary, or perhaps secondary, terminology which denotes an emotional, susceptible personality especially permeable to external stimuli.[2]

The Narrator of *A la recherche* criticizes his open disposition, but recognizes that it facilitates the crucial first step in writing, which is to get into the skin of one's subject:

Unfortunately, I should have to struggle against that habit of putting oneself in another person's place which, if it favours the conception of a work of art, is an obstacle to its execution. (VI, 371)

[Malheureusement, j'aurais à lutter contre cette habitude de se mettre à la place des autres qui, si elle favorise la conception d'une œuvre, en retarde l'exécution.] (IV, 564)

Proust's unprotected psychological stance *vis-à-vis* other people in social situations affects his stance as a writer, for language is a continuum: how can I differentiate between social formulae which relationships oblige me to employ, and a set of essentially similar words which I choose to write down for a more complex purpose? Words and ideas that come to me through exchange with another person are part of the specially moulded phrases I set down as distinctive, personal, sacred, as art. What is me in this mixture? Proust's comments about the alienation inherent in social exchange show his anxieties coalescing around language and self-expression.

It is not surprising, in light of this, that the problem which *A la recherche* poses is that of its own form, and beyond that, of literary form in general. The substratum of form is language, and what underpins Proust's dissatisfaction with form is his diffidence about words. His difficulty in identifying a literary form for himself was an effect of his basic mistrust of the very medium he chose to convey his art. Proust had no faith in the spoken word, and the written word could easily prove dangerous because of its interchangeability with the spoken.

SPEAKING THE OTHER

More than is the case with 'normal' people, the physical presence of others seems to have had a particularly jangling effect on the Proustian psyche. Gobineau's *boutade*, 'la présence gêne', seemed to Montesquiou an appropriate line to slip into a letter to the elusive Proust (*Corr.*, XVI, 28). Proust was perfectly conscious of a kind of nervous absenteeism that came over him when in the presence of someone he admired. Prefacing a portrait of Léon Radziwill, he writes, 'Though I admire him infinitely, because of an unpleasant nervous phenomenon, as soon as he is in my presence, I am absent from myself, I can say nothing, I become stupid' ['Moi qui l'admire infiniment, par un phénomène nerveux très pénible, dès qu'il est là, je suis absent de moi-même, je ne puis rien dire, je deviens stupide'] (*CSB*, 477). The speaker sees the problem as an 'absence', an alienation from the self that results in a kind of stupor and an inability to articulate feelings. But in fact, as countless witnesses of Proust's communication have volunteered, there was no inability to articulate, but rather an inability to articulate anything other than what the interlocutor wanted to hear. If I am absent from myself, it is because I am drawn to the Other; if 'I' can say nothing, it is because the Other speaks through me, in my place, replacing my words with his.

Few of Proust's adult acquaintances dared to bring his linguistic alienation to his attention (his school chums were not so reticent), but a letter from Maurice Barrès reads like the finger snap of a hypnotist trying to bring his subject out of a trance. After contemplating Proust's gushing comparison of their contemporary Maurice Maeterlinck to Racine, Barrès writes: 'Proust! Proust! Marcel! There are ways of admiring genius that are more dishonest than the brutal coarseness of barbarians' (*Corr.*, IV, 89).

Proust's Narrator is perfectly conscious of this outward displacement of the self. The basic dynamic of *A la recherche* is established as a pendulum swing between a permeable social disposition and a closed, self-attentive mental stance:

Alone, at times, I felt surging from the depths of my being one or other of those impressions which gave me a delicious sense of well-being. But as soon as I was with someone else, as soon as I was talking to a friend, my mind as it were faced about, it was towards this interlocutor and not towards myself that it directed its thoughts. (II, 364)

[Seul, quelquefois, je sentais affluer du fond de moi quelqu'une de ces impressions qui me donnaient un bien-être délicieux. Mais dès que j'étais avec quelqu'un, dès que je parlais à un ami, mon esprit faisait volte-face, c'était vers cet interlocuteur et non vers moi-même qu'il dirigeait ses pensées.] (II, 95)

The physicality of oral communication interrupts Proust's thought processes. The soundedness of speech, the materialization of abstract thought in the tongue, the movements of the lips, throat and jaws, impede connections with the intellect and the sensibility. Speech has a physical taint. 'When I speak, I don't think', wrote Proust to Lucien Daudet (*Corr.*, XVI, 29). All the more logical then, that spoken information presented by others cannot be absorbed intellectually. Proust does not like to listen to readings of literature:

the only advice I can give, if I give any at all, is written or verbal advice, but based on something I have *read* while alone. Over dinner, I would never know what people have read to me.

[les seuls [conseils] que je puisse donner, si tant est que je le puisse, sont des conseils, écrits ou verbaux, mais d'après une chose *lue* quand je suis seul. Dans un dîner, je n'aurais jamais su ce qu'on me lisait.] (*Corr.*, XVI, 106)

Describing this deficiency to another correspondent, Proust suggests that the Other's presence causes his own absence, and to depict the kind of susceptibility from which he suffers, he employs the eerie image of a crab-like creature that must scuttle back into a deep, protected hiding-place to rearrange itself:

I only read well if I read myself, and when I am alone. What is read to me arrives only through the interposed person of the reader. Because I am attentive to that reader and wish to communicate my impression to him, I don't have the freedom to allow it to create itself in the depths of my being; I inhabit my own surface, and it is only when I am alone that I descend once more into the hole from which I can see more clearly.

[je ne lis bien que si je lis moi-même, et quand je suis seul. Ce qu'on me lit ne m'arrive qu'à travers la personne interposée du lecteur. Attentif à ce lecteur, à lui faire connaître mon impression, je n'ai pas le loisir, la possibilité, de la laisser se créer dans les profondeurs de mon être; j'habite ma propre surface, et ne redescends qu'une fois seul, dans le trou où je vois un peu clair.] (*Corr.*, XIV, 53)

The jangling effect is produced by sound itself. Reading while alone poses no problem; in the absence of sound, the mind can apprehend the notions directed to it by another intellect. Deep reflection is impossible during conversation because communication does not penetrate to the mind when the exchange takes place 'through the intermediary of sounds'.[3]

There are few activities that elicit more contempt in Proust's fiction than conversation. Social language – and the view that social yardsticks can be used to assess the meaning of reality or of art – are devalued money. Loathing for talk is expressed in many ways, and set in numerous contexts. Proust refers constantly to the impurity of conversation, to the fact that personal vanity and pride make it self-referential. In an early work like *Jean Santeuil*, the hostility may be subsumed in a maxim, apparently de-emotionalized, almost as though inherited from La Rochefoucauld:

If theatre is the saving grace for talkers whose friend is mute or whose mistress is a bore, conversation, even when it is exquisite, is the pleasure of men who have no imagination.

[Si le théâtre est la ressource des causeurs dont l'ami est muet ou la maîtresse insipide, la conversation, même exquise, est le plaisir des hommes sans imagination.] (*JS*, 53)

There is great cynicism about the value of talk on 'serious' subjects. Any activity, however outwardly trivial, that engages the Narrator's imagination is superior to 'conversations of a humanitarian or patriotic or internationalist or metaphysical kind' (VI, 237; IV,

461). Flaubert's conversations with his niece or watchmaker are safe because they lack pretension. But more important, Proust's writing constantly alludes to a loss of psychic tension in conversation, as though the reservoir of our personality had been punctured. Like Antonin Artaud, Proust seems to have experienced speech as robbery of the body's breath.[4] The drop in psychic pressure registers in passages like the following:

the apparent animation of my conversation [disguised] from others *a profound intellectual torpor.* (VI, 34)

[l'activité apparente de ma conversation dont l'animation masquait pour les autres *un total engourdissement spirituel.*] (IV, 296)

the intellectual power which ... conversation *dispels* instantly. (*ASB*, 208)

[la puissance intellectuelle ... que la conversation *dissipe* immédiatement.] (*CSB*, 174; the emphasis is mine.)

Talk is thus almost a form of psychic bleeding for Proust. If the life of the creative person can be reduced to two physical poses, conversation is the one in which muscles sag because they are pouring out their tone. Silence, reading, contemplation, allow the sinews to feed off their inner strength; this is a self-connected stance, where no energy is lost to the outside. In the preface to *Sésame et les lys*, Proust distinguishes these two states quite explicitly. Our mode of communicating with human beings implies what he calls 'a weakening of the active forces of the soul',[5] while reading constitutes a recharging of those forces:

reading being the reverse of conversation [consists ...] for each one of us in receiving the communication of another's thought while still being on our own, that is, continuing to enjoy the intellectual power which we have in solitude and which conversation dispels instantly, and continuing to be open to inspiration, with our minds still at work hard and fruitfully on themselves. (*ASB*, 208)

[la lecture, au rebours de la conversation, consist[e] pour chacun de nous à recevoir communication d'une autre pensée, mais tout en restant seul, c'est-à-dire en continuant à jouir de la puissance intellectuelle qu'on a dans la solitude et que la conversation dissipe immédiatement, en continuant à pouvoir être inspiré, à rester en plein travail fécond de l'esprit sur lui-même.] (*CSB*, 174)

If the Proustian text demonstrates considerable anxiety about the invasiveness of speech, part of the reason is that the invader sometimes will not leave: Proust's Narrator is saddled with the habit of talking to himself. Throughout *A la recherche*, conversing with oneself is presented as a flawed narrative mode that threatens to substitute itself for writing. The inner voice, a hysterically active one, constantly tries to cover over silence and short-circuit the process of reflection. Arriving home after spending time with the Swanns and their daughter Gilberte, the adolescent Narrator catches himself in unforeseen word games. Instinctively, he organizes a drama out of the words left behind in the salon, playing all the roles, taking special care to leave openings in the dialogue so that his own persona will shine:

[once] back at home, my isolation was apparent only, my mind was powerless to swim against the current of words on which I had allowed myself mechanically to be borne for hours on end. Sitting alone, I continued to fashion remarks such as might have pleased or amused the Swanns, and to make this pastime more entertaining I myself took the parts of those absent players, putting to myself fictitious questions so chosen that my brilliant epigrams served simply as apt repartee. (II, 177–8)

[une fois … rentré à la maison, … ma pensée ne pouvait plus remonter le courant du flux de paroles par lequel je m'étais laissé machinalement entraîner pendant des heures. Seul je continuais à fabriquer les propos qui eussent été capables de plaire aux Swann et pour donner plus d'intérêt au jeu, je tenais la place de ces partenaires absents, je me posais à moi-même des questions fictives choisies de telle façon que mes traits brillants ne leur servissent que d'heureuse repartie.] (I, 569)

The Narrator talks to himself not just in his impressionable youth, but in all his age incarnations. Irritated by a banal remark of the Duchesse de Guermantes, he realizes that often, in what he normally views as conversation, he is not expressing his own ideas at all:

Those were the words I said to myself, but they were the opposite of what I thought; they were purely conversational words such as we say to ourselves at those moments when, too excited to remain quietly alone with ourselves, we feel the need, for want of another listener, to talk to ourselves, without meaning what we say, as we talk to a stranger. (III, 261)

[Tels étaient les mots que je me disais; ils étaient le contraire de ma pensée; c'étaient de purs mots de conversation, comme nous nous en disons dans ces moments où trop agités pour rester seuls avec nous-mêmes nous éprouvons le besoin, à défaut d'autre interlocuteur, de causer avec nous, sans sincérité, comme avec un étranger.] (II, 526–7)

Orality, spokenness, is a trap. Speech feels as though it is directed at others, but it resembles more a conductor that connects speaker and interlocutor. Into that connecting flow the conversationalist can pour all the reserves of his being and identity in a futile attempt to reverberate with the Other, to reproduce linguistically what that person will appreciate, and what will essentially be that person. Out of our own consciousness we create a double, and converse with him as though he were separate from us, a stranger. Alienation is literally personified.

Characteristically, the relationship between creative language and orality surfaces again in the aesthetic discussions of *Le Temps retrouvé*. The narrator/novelist is still troubled by memories of talking out loud, as though he were still having to resist the encroachment of oral voice upon written tone even as his future literary opus is about to take shape. The work to come must be a product of silence, not of talk:

Above all I should have to be on guard against those phrases which are chosen rather by the lips than by the mind, those humorous phrases such as we utter in conversation and continue at the end of a long conversation with other people to address, factitiously, to ourselves. (VI, 256)

[Plus que tout j'écarterais ces paroles que les lèvres plutôt que l'esprit choisissent, ces paroles pleines d'humour, comme on en dit dans la conversation, et qu'après une longue conversation avec les autres on continue à s'adresser facticement à soi-même.] (IV, 476)

The meanings of speech, the author seems to be suggesting, are the opposite of what we 'mean' when we write. But if written language, compared to speech, has no innate prestige (since it can be tainted by containing loose ends of pure orality), why does the written monologue that is *A la recherche du temps perdu* benefit from the immense prestige it seems to have in its own creator's eyes? The question of orality in the novel begs an answer, in part because of the obvious tensions it arouses. In one of his innumerable letters of self-defence after *A la recherche* began to be published, Proust angrily dismisses any comparison between himself and a poet known for his exploration of repetition, Charles Péguy. Péguy is accused of the worst sin, oral chattering: 'If I had blabbed (all alone, but one can blab to oneself) *Swann*, I would never have published it' ['Si j'avais bavardé (tout seul, mais on peut bavarder pour soi) *Swann*, je ne l'eusse jamais publié'] (*Corr.*, XVI, 65).

The novelist's fear of never being able to write appears to surface here once again, wedded directly to another admission of talking to oneself. The profusion of texts on this same subject invites us to explore the connections between orality and writing in Proust's text, so adamant is Proust's denial that the spoken monologue might be a key to the understanding of his writing style. Later in this chapter we will examine how the debate on oral/written style crystallizes around the person of Sainte-Beuve, critic and journalist, hesitant poet and novelist. In the final chapter, we will return to the question of oral and written tone, in order to assess how tone may act as a unifying, structuring force in Proust's prose.

If the invasion of the written by the oral is disquieting enough to warrant mention in Proust's discussions of the writer's aesthetic, then his personal speech habits also deserve at least a passing glance. Those habits, as recorded by friends and acquaintances and some-times referred to ironically by Proust himself, have a large com-pulsive element: there is an irresistible urge to mimic others, a verbal dilation that tended to entrap objects of attention or desire in a morass of words, and an intriguing sense of laterality, rather than forward progress, in the story-telling style.

It might be argued, of course, that all the testimonials I am about to cite originate in observers who were struck by the intricacies of Proust's prose style. Their recollection of his speaking voice might be influenced by the more durable impression a book leaves. Still, the feeling that Proust's writing voice equalled his oral voice was firmly rooted among many people who knew him well, and the references to the relationship deserve attention, particularly in the context of the constant Proustian fear that oral voice can supplant authentic writing style.

There are instinctive techniques for defending oneself against language that is experienced as too invasive. We can create space for self-assertion by manipulating the powerfully characterized language of others, winding it up like a toy, and turning the mechanism back towards its originator. One observer of Proust's impulse to mime is the writer Albert Flament, whose first entry under Proust in his memoirs recounts the aftermath of a dinner that included Edmond de Goncourt and Robert de Montesquiou, themselves both famous for their verbosity.

Flament describes how, at 1 a.m. in the vestibule outside the dining room, Proust did a virtuoso imitation of Montesquiou's speech, punctuated by the man's piercing cries, for the benefit of Flament and two young women, a performance which he extended to most of the other guests at the party as he drove Flament home in a cab.[6] The latter mentions a similar occasion on which Proust talked about having his portrait done by the painter Jacques

Blanche. As Proust evokes the long conversations that took place during the sittings, his voice slips naturally into another register, the 'whining sinuosities' of Blanche's voice.

Several other observers have recorded their impressions of Proust's gift for oral and gestural mimicry. Fernand Gregh, a school chum, witnessed Proust's reaction to two important literary figures, while Elisabeth de Clermont-Tonnerre remembers his 'impressions' from society receptions:

There were prodigious sessions of continually invented and inventive humour, which exploited their subject to the full. For several minutes Proust would 'do' Anatole France or Robert de Montesquiou with true genius; this was to be found later in the remarks of Françoise and M. de Norpois, remarks which are nothing if not marvellous impersonations.[7]

Proust imitated Montesquiou's voice and manners to such a point that he had adopted his laugh and the way he had of hiding his mouth so that you wouldn't see his black teeth ... Then he would stamp his foot like Montesquiou, which was very ugly, for he was short.[8]

Then would come the *monkey-business*. Proust imitated Montesquiou's laugh and admired that of Madame Greffuhle ... He impersonated Madame Lemaire showing her guests out: 'Madame de Maupeou, you sang like an angel tonight! That Brandès woman is astounding, she still looks twenty years old!' Etc.[9]

Proust's subsequent attempts to pass off his Montesquiou parodies as complimentary and even deferential lack conviction, though they employ some of the musical metaphors which recur in Proust's more formal discussions of the function of literary pastiche; the oral voice is comparable to the literary one, both require the continual practice of a singer in training:

As for your hypothesis concerning my 'imitations', which were never anything but scales, or better, singing exercises, having no pretension to render a melody, nothing of the original genius, they were simply exercises and games of admiration, *ludi solennos festivolia*, naïve canticles practised and enjoyed out of adolescent admiration.

[Quant à l'hypothèse que vous hasardiez au sujet de mes 'imitations', qui ne furent jamais que des gammes, ou mieux des vocalises, n'ayant aucune prétention de rendre aucune mélodie, rien du génie original, mieux, elles étaient de simples exercices et jeux de l'admiration, *ludi solennos festivolia*, de naïfs cantiques où s'exerçait et se complaisait une admiration juvénile.][10]

Oral parody is one of Proust's instinctive reactions, part of a mimetic attunement to the tones and 'songs' that ring in voice registers, but partly too a hysterical re-enactment which, through linguistic and gestural re-creation of the Other, poses the question of personal identity.

Most of the characters who are labelled as hysterical in Proust are pictured as would-be creative artists or writers, individuals in whom the creative instinct has been blocked. Hysterics tend to be language hysterics. There is a professor named Ralph Savaie in *Jean Santeuil* who teaches at the Ecole des sciences politiques; he is given to flights of verbal fantasy that amaze his colleagues:

People considered him a genius who is delightful, a hysteric who is interesting, one came home delighted, not knowing if one was returning from the Sorbonne or from La Salpêtrière.

[On le regardait comme un homme de génie qui ravit, comme un hystérique qui intéresse, on rentrait chez soi ravi, ne sachant pas si on revenait de la Sorbonne ou de la Salpêtrière.] (*JS*, 275)

Bloch has a hysterical desire to lie; the Narrator himself is called a hysterical flatterer by Norpois. In Charlus, hysteria is a kind of spasm, a public pulsing of the female spirit that inhabits the male homosexual:

And it must be admitted that, among certain of these newcomers, the woman is not only inwardly united to the man but hideously visible, convulsed as they are by a hysterical spasm, by a shrill laugh which sets their knees and hands trembling, looking no more like the common run of men than those apes with melancholy ringed eyes and prehensile feet who dress up in dinner-jackets and black ties. (IV, 23)

[Et il faut avouer que chez certains de ces nouveaux venus, la femme n'est pas seulement intérieurement unie à l'homme, mais hideusement visible, agités qu'ils sont dans un spasme d'hystérique, par un rire aigu qui convulse leurs genoux et leurs mains, ne ressemblant pas plus au commun des hommes que ces singes à l'œil mélancolique et cerné, aux pieds prenants, qui revêtent le smoking et portent une cravate noire.] (III, 21)

A man of great intellectual and emotional gifts, Charlus is an oral virtuoso, an artist of the spoken word whose imaginative potential has been sidetracked into a salon. He associates with creative people but has never had the courage or perspicacity to turn his creative gifts on his own inner life. The sign of his disorder is linguistic: he endlessly spouts poetic, imaginative language that in his mind somehow transforms the objects that surround him, as though through speech we could apply to reality a coat of artistic prestige. The Narrator sees a kind of intellectualized materialism at work here, a refusal to look inward to the true bases of artistic transformation.

The hysteria–language connection seen in Morel's oral pastiches of Bergotte seems to point to another model of narrative, the mimetic 'recital', which we might juxtapose with our initial model of talking to oneself. There is self-reference and retrospective self-questioning in the portraits of both Morel and Charlus: each is a Marcel-like performance hysteric trapped in the oral and social stage from which one must escape before one can access the personal, creative voice. As a young man, the Narrator resembles Morel, for he too is a fervent admirer of Bergotte's prose, and is marvellously attuned to the musicality of the writer's language, even to the way his speech intonations represent certain stylistic stresses in his prose.

Proust's habit of verbal embellishment – overloading objects of observation with epithet or metaphor – is a further connection between the oral and the literary register. One school friend, Pierre Lavallée, has the following memory of Proust reading his French compositions in class:

I remember Marcel's dissertations, rich in impressions and images and already quite 'Proustian' with their sentences loaded down with parenthetical clauses ... I can still see and hear Marcel reading his assignments out loud, and the excellent, charming M. Gaucher commenting, praising, criticizing, then suddenly laughing uncontrollably at the audacities of style which, to be truthful, delighted him. (*Corr.*, 1, 107, n. 7)

Fernand Gregh had one of the most vivid recollections of Proust's oral effusiveness. He and other students created the verb 'proustify' to describe their friend's speech:

Proust sometimes exaggerated that grace in simpering but always witty ways, as he sometimes exaggerated his amiability in flattery that was always intelligent; and we had even created, among ourselves, the verb 'proustify' to describe an attitude of kindness that was a bit too self-aware, with a tangling of sentiments that the average person would have called interminable and delicious 'fussing'.[11]

Such excess, with the resulting ambivalence it creates in the observer (for in the habit of being cloying, there is the kernel of a desire to entrap), will dominate in Proust's correspondence during his whole lifetime. Some early examples have been preserved. A letter to Antoinette Faure, daughter of the future French president, written in July 1887 just as Proust turned sixteen, shows a fondness for adjective triads and precious epithets that suggests familiarity with the prose of Anatole France[12] and the Goncourt diaries:

Although Boulanger is very common, a vulgar bass drum player if you will, his great enthusiasm, which is so unexpected, so *novelistic* in our banal, never-changing lives, stirs in one's heart all that is primitive, untamed and bellicose. You can see I'm no great philosopher and that I find only adjectives when I'm searching for reasons.

[Quoique [Boulanger] soit très commun et un vulgaire batteur de grosse caisse, ce grand enthousiasme si imprévu, si *roman* dans la vie banale et toujours la même, remue dans le cœur tout ce qu'il y a de primitif, d'indompté, de belliqueux. Vous voyez que je ne suis pas grand philosophe et je ne trouve guère que des adjectifs quand je cherche des raisons.] (*Corr.*, I, 97)

Some of Proust's letters to Daniel Halévy are equally verbose, but more florid, scented with sexuality and the Symbolist graces of the period:

You have administered a proper little punishment, but your rods are so bloom-covered that I can't hold it against you, and the brilliance and perfume of the flowers have intoxicated me so sweetly as to soften the cruelty of the thorns. You have beaten me with strokes of the lyre. And your lyre is enchanting.

[Tu m'administres une petite correction en règle mais tes verges sont si fleuries que je ne saurais t'en vouloir, et l'éclat et le parfum de ces fleurs m'ont assez doucement grisé pour m'adoucir la cruauté des épines. Tu m'as battu à coups de lyre. Et ta lyre est enchanteresse.][13]

The writer of *Jean Santeuil* is painfully aware of his protagonist's image as an emotional *poseur*, as is Jean's philosophy professor Beulier who criticizes Jean's essay style because he heightens the tone simply to utter banalities. The writing stance of the Proustian-type correspondent is defined with some irony in *Jean Santeuil*: 'Jean had written such a beautiful letter, so sincere, so eloquent, that tears came to his eyes as he wrote it' ['Jean avait écrit une si belle lettre, si sincère, si éloquente que les larmes lui venaient aux yeux en l'écrivant'] (*JS*, 258).

Proust's prolixity is not simply loquaciousness. There is a tactic at work. The object of attraction must be surrounded and immobilized by a flow of words. The object is also, literally, 'exhausted' by the endless pulse of phrases, just as the number of possible perspectives on it are 'exhausted' by the various linguistic options presented. Proust's mature literary style has exactly the same property, an apparent prolixity that translates the writer's effort to stabilize phenomena by verbally exploring, from every perspective, their every attraction.

Elisabeth de Clermont-Tonnerre may have caught this Proustian need to surround and adhere most picturesquely in her comparison of his speaking voice to a pair of baby's hands – sticky, clammy, invasive:

It was somewhat of a puerile voice, caressing, pleasant, full of a thousand gracious inflexions, giving the impression of those sweet little paws, smeared with jam, with which very young children touch your face and clothing; the experience is tender and sticky, one is at once flattered and a bit annoyed.[14]

The endlessness of Proust's oral style poses at least one other important question, that of its direction. As the story line of *A la recherche* lacks linearity, and appears continually to circle backward on itself, so too his speech seems to have been marked by a series of asides and tangential reflections, as though his mental process was one of continual comparison and qualification, caused partly by a deep sense of irony, and partly by hesitancy over the adequacy and completeness of a statement from the instant that statement was uttered.

The writer-diplomat Paul Morand, one of Proust's sometimes exasperated friends, describes the first time he experienced the Proustian oral monologue in what sounds very much like a pastiche of the actual Proustian manner. Marcel travels in deliberate circles to get to the point, constantly testing the distance to his interlocutor with sidewards reflections as though to ensure agreement and parallel progress at exactly the same snail's pace:

Proust began to speak right away with gentle authority and a discursive skill in which I immediately recognized his writing and the style of the entire man:

Henri Bardac telegraphed me from London to let me know that you were arriving in Paris and that you were staying at his place. You'll find, and you're right – please, go back to bed, you'll catch your death – (I was in my pyjamas, and still in the entrance hall) you will doubtless judge it unseemly to be awakened at this hour, but I hardly ever go out, I get up late – and indeed it's wrong of me to get up because the next day I pay for it with terrible suffering and an excess of ridiculous, endless treatments, which are none the less a necessity, for a chronic condition is like an old lady who loves people to show regard for her (you would be right to complain yourself – although you're a young man and not an old woman –

that I'm showing little regard for you knocking on your door at midnight);
if I took the liberty of doing so, it's because I had a great desire to know
someone (I mean yourself) who expressed about me – it was reported to me
– (I don't know you well enough yet for anyone to report anything other
than observations that are pleasant, even delightful to hear), who expressed
about me, or more precisely about my book – I wouldn't have the nerve to
say 'the most discerning' judgements (in the du Bos style) – but certainly
the most delicate . . .

The sentence had only begun.[15]

Jean Cocteau as well was struck by the laterality of Proust's
speech. The two knew each other for the last ten years of Proust's
life,[16] and a few months after Proust died Cocteau wrote down his
recollections of Proust the storyteller. Normal forward progression of
the story line was replaced by tangential reflections, but these
Cocteau saw as somehow germane to the discussion at hand. He
contended that the rhythm of Proust's prose was totally evocative of
his speaking voice. There was an undertone of suppressed laughter,
and attached to it an acute desire to recount a story. Even as the
story began, however, its forward impetus was absorbed by a series
of introductory pauses, wayside stops, apparent asides (which were
really innate to the story mode) that held back the main flow
momentarily.[17]

In its simplest terms, Proust's nervous problem is to *convert* his
somewhat hysterical sociability, experienced as a compulsive oral
gush, into a calmer, more controlled narrative stream: to transfer the
compulsion to mimic and to embellish into a narrative mode that
allows and flatters his natural impulse to regard events from every
angle before moving on. The difficulty with Proust's oral compulsiveness is the loss of control. The images of the younger Proust as
an endless embellisher of language, a manic flatterer, demonstrate
that loss. The social impulse to praise, to create verbally an image
that will reflect positively on the person admired, seems related to
the more creative but still obsessive habit of pastiching the language
of speakers and writers. The Narrator's impression of his chatty
habits captures the medical symptoms of hysteria: mechanical
imitation, momentary possession by another, with the clear perception that the performance is somehow nerve-related. When the
Narrator converses, another person inhabits his body and he
becomes what he calls a 'simple medium' (IV, 239; III, 203), uttering
machine-like phrases that serve an emotional but not an intellectual

purpose, 'words uttered mechanically to imitate others or to give satisfaction to our nerves' ['des mots dits mécaniquement pour imiter les autres ou pour donner satisfaction à nos nerfs'] (IV, 829). This is the type of false creator we encounter in Morel, or, by extension, in a whole category of unoriginal writers who imitate out of habit, and who cannot divest themselves of that habit. Unaware, uncritical copying is the problem in much literary production, 'all those banalities of form which are acquired through imitation' (VI, 257) ['toutes les banalités de forme acquises par imitation'] (IV, 477).

The hysteric copies by internalizing, by reperforming, and this particular style of simulation Proust recognizes as a powerful creative force. As we have seen, in Racine's talent for inwardly miming and then exteriorizing passion Proust saw the essential hysterical nature of the creative artist.[18] The problem of the hysteric coincides with that of the writer searching for his own way among the various anxieties of influence. He is at once drawn to the linguistical profusion and energy of others, but he is obsessed by the desire for original expression, without which, as a source of discourse above all, *he does not exist*. As Lacan has pointed out, the hysteric is in search of a master.[19] But the search is an impossible one: 'The request that is implied in all speech introduces a dissonance between what is at the origin of the message and what responds to its call: that is never that. This, basically, in its universal value, is the complaint of the hysteric.'[20] This idea turns around slightly a Hegelian argument about language that is at the very heart of the frantic Proustian search for non-clichéd discourse:

They *mean* 'this' bit of paper on which I am writing – or rather have written – 'this'; but what they mean is not what they say. If they actually wanted to *say* 'this' bit of paper which they mean, if they wanted to *say* it, then this is impossible, because the sensuous This that is meant *cannot be reached* by language, which belongs to consciousness, i.e. to that which is inherently universal.[21]

According to Hegel, Proust loses on two counts: there can never be real expression of sensory material through words, and words, in any case, are universal, not personal. If language is universal, that is, if the language we use to establish our meaning in social situations is essentially derivative of others, how can the artist select the same medium, language, and fashion an independent, free-standing structure that speaks about his life? If all language is derivative, how can language be used as a building material in such a structure? It is impossible to create a 'safe' literary form.

This dilemma provides the essential contradiction that undermines Proust's early novel *Jean Santeuil*. In this period Proust is caught in an aesthetic bind. He promotes the notion of a poetic novel, a 'récit pur', as Maurice Blanchot called it,[22] structured as a juxtaposition of moments of insight, but at the same time part of his subject is the aristocratic society of his time, the Dreyfus Affair, other political events, etc. The prefatory lines of *Jean Santeuil* picture composition as a simple positioning of recipients to catch condensed moments of inspiration. There seems little room for the socio-historical aspect of the story:

Can I call this book a novel? It is less, perhaps, and much more, the very essence of my life, captured without impurities, in those hours when the vein opens and it flows. This book was never written, it was harvested.

[Puis-je appeler ce livre un roman? C'est moins peut-être et bien plus, l'essence même de ma vie, recueillie sans y rien mêler, dans ces heures de déchirure où elle découle. Ce livre n'a jamais été fait, il a été récolté.] (*JS*, 181)

The protagonist and his young friend Henri de Réveillon are especially interested in how the writer's social self is filtered into his art. Their objective is to understand 'the secret links, the necessary metamorphoses that exist between a writer and his work, between reality and art' ['les rapports secrets, les métamorphoses nécessaires qui existent entre la vie d'un écrivain et son œuvre, entre la réalité et l'art'] (*JS*, 190). This phrase immediately evokes the image of the novelist whose personal life appears most visible in his literature, at least in Proust's estimation. Balzac is both a monster and mentor-figure for Proust and the attraction/repulsion operates on at least three levels.

First, as we have seen, Proust had already diagnosed himself during this period as suffering from a pathological lack of willpower. Balzac attracts him because of his physical energy, his sudden enthusiasms and his colossal will to produce. The writer-figure C., who appears at the beginning of *Jean Santeuil*, seems to be the product of a kind of nostalgia for Balzac. He is an artist, but also an athlete who dives from the boat when seas are heavy and swims for hours. One has the impression Proust would literally like to enter Balzac's skin because Balzac appears to have integrated in his own life, in a way that troubles Proust but attracts him, two antinomical elements: poetic inspiration and a voracious ability to live and to enjoy life. For a writer like Proust who sees the social and the creative self dissociated by definition, Balzac's life appears sound because of its healthy sensuality.

Proust's admiration turns to horror when he is obliged to observe that, at the same time as Balzac integrates the poet and sensualist in his own life, his personal and fictional writing styles are also integrated. In this *Jean Santeuil* period, Proust is carefully reading Balzac and Flaubert's letters to uncover the links between these writers' talents as conversationalist or correspondent and their literary production. As a mighty conversationalist and correspondent himself, Proust is very concerned about the answer. The writer's anxiety is articulated in a very awkward passage following a reflection about the disturbing similarity of Balzac's novels and correspondence:

until he is dead, an author remains a thing that can be modified, and it is essential that his thought absorb his entire being, bit by bit, so that everything he says will be the language of thought, but not in such a way that others can draw his thought to themselves, with the result that he would simply be thinking their words and would be destroyed.

[un auteur jusqu'à ce qu'il soit mort reste une chose qu'on peut modifier, et il faut que la pensée qui est en lui absorbe peu à peu tout son être, si bien que tout ce qu'il dira sera le langage même de la pensée, mais non pas que les autres puissent tirer à eux jusqu'à sa pensée, si bien qu'il penserait simplement leurs paroles et serait anéanti.] (*JS*, 487)

Alarm bells ring in this passage. In a discussion of artistic thought and individuality, Proust inadvertently uses the verb 'to say', that is, he has his author begin to speak. But the spoken word is anonymous, anti-individual. The image of being drawn out, like a crab somehow vacuumed from its hiding place and absorbed into the void through a transparent tube of words connected to the Other, illustrates the most fundamental level of fear in the Proustian individual, a fear of being drained of individuality by language. The intellectual articulation of that fear is Proust's contention that the work of a true artist must be directed, or perhaps is directed naturally, to the absorption of his material life by his art. But to be art, literature must be expressed in a distinctive, individual language; otherwise, art becomes cliché. The writer enjoys existence only through language, and if his prose is built of the indifferent social language of his letters or of his interlocutors, he simply loses the status of existence, he is 'obliterated' ('anéanti').

How then does the artist arrive at the tenuous balance that allows the intellect to extract truth from mimesis? The final answer, an ambiguous one, comes in *Le Temps retrouvé* and will occupy us later. But a preliminary response is provided by *Contre Sainte-Beuve*, or, more precisely, the figure of Charles Augustin Sainte-Beuve,[23] as it is developed in that work and subsequently set in the much broader context of *A la recherche*.

THE LANGUAGE HYSTERIA OF SAINTE-BEUVE

There is ample evidence to interpret *Contre Sainte-Beuve* as the oxymoron of Proust's whole literary endeavour. The decision about the form it would take itself involved hesitations between a quasi-oral and a more literary approach. One option considered was a classical essay in the style of Taine, but what seems to have won out (though the structure of the work remains exploded, since its parts were never stitched together), was an essay-cum-aesthetical-argument preceded by a chat between the writer and his mother. The subject of this extensive conversation was, in effect, the nothing-ness of talk. Sainte-Beuve, after all, called his Monday-morning columns in *Le Constitutionnel* 'Les Causeries du lundi' (the Monday-morning talks), and the mother–son dialogue could therefore be neatly structured around the morning routine of the delivery of *Le Figaro* newspaper to Marcel and the discovery, in it, of an article authored by Marcel himself. Oral voices would respond to Sainte-Beuve's oral style, but then the argument would shift to a more formal plane.

The encounter with Sainte-Beuve was a moment of superposition, of identifying oneself in another writer. We have seen Proust's impulse to fuse with the figures of admired writers like Flaubert, Baudelaire, Nerval, even Balzac. His realization, around 1907–8, that his quasi-journalistic career to date and his mixed literary production made him a replica of Sainte-Beuve, produced what is clearly both his most combative work and a work in which denial is ubiquitous.

The external parallels between the two men's lives may have significance at one level. It is intriguing to reflect that both had unhappy careers as library employees. Gabriel Hanotaux, a one-time French foreign minister, had helped Marcel obtain a non-paying position at the Bibiothèque Mazarine. He had also warmly promoted, in discussions with the young Proust, the career of documentalist/writer, very probably using as examples Sainte-Beuve and Leconte de Lisle.[24] Sainte-Beuve's abandonment of literature for journalism after some early partial successes is a rough equivalent of Proust's shift into criticism, translation and journalism after the non-event that was *Les Plaisirs et les jours* and the failure of *Jean Santeuil*.

But I would contend that the most wounding recognition, when Proust contemplates Sainte-Beuve, is the sensation that at the heart of the Beuvian personality is a loss of control which expresses itself in uncontrolled language. The most viscerally bitter of Proust's observations about Sainte-Beuve are reserved for his moments of slippage into the hysteria of cliché:

I cannot believe that in writing [of Baudelaire] the words 'nice young fellow', 'gains on acquaintance', and 'thoroughly classical in his manners', Sainte-Beuve was not giving way to that sort of hysteria of language which led him now and again to derive an irresistible pleasure from speaking like a bourgeois who does not know how to write, from saying about Madame Bovary: 'The beginning is delicately done.' (*ASB*, 37)

[Je ne peux pas croire qu'en écrivant les mots *gentil garçon, gagne à être connu, classique dans les formes* [à propos de Baudelaire], Sainte-Beuve n'ait pas cédé à cette espèce d'hystérie de langage qui, par moments, lui faisait trouver un irrésistible plaisir à parler comme un bourgeois qui ne sait pas écrire, à dire de Madame Bovary: 'Le début est finement touché'.] (*CSB*, 246)

There is a palpable fear in certain of Proust's texts that he actually *is* the kind of oral performer that Sainte-Beuve was, and the author of *Les Lundis* thus provides him with the occasion for substantial development of the relationship between orality, a social stance in writing, and cliché. It was with exasperation that Proust came upon a passage in *Chateaubriand et son groupe littéraire* where Sainte-Beuve defined his literary ideal as a kind of tasteful, courtly gab-fest with friends:

To write pleasant things from time to time, to read both pleasant and serious ones, but above all, not to write too much, to cultivate one's friends, ... to give more to one's personal life than to the public, to reserve the finest, most tender part, the essence of oneself for the inside, to enjoy the final seasons of youth in moderation, in a sweet commerce of intelligence and sentiment, this was for me the dream of the literary *galant homme* ...[25]

Agreeable social exchange, pleasant writing: Proust sees in this juxtaposition the admission that Sainte-Beuve did not distinguish between true creativity in language and writing what one spoke, or as one spoke. It is really around this perceived seepage of orality into potential literary discourse that Proust's denunciation turns bitter:

What one gives to sociability, that is to conversation (however refined it may be, and the most refined is the worst of all, because it falsifies our spiritual life by associating itself to it: Flaubert's conversations with his niece or with the clockmaker are without risk) or to those productions intended for one's intimates, that is to say reduced so as to appeal to a few and which are barely more than written conversation, is the work of [an...] external self, not of the deep self. (*ASB*, 15)

[Ce qu'on donne à l'intimité, c'est-à-dire à la conversation (si raffinée soit-elle, et la plus raffinée est la pire de toutes car elle fausse la vie spirituelle en se l'associant: les conversations de Flaubert avec sa nièce et l'horloger sont sans danger) et à ces productions destinées à l'intimité, c'est-à-dire rapetissées au goût de quelques personnes et qui ne sont guère que de la conversation écrite, c'est l'œuvre d'un soi ... extérieur, non pas du moi profond.] (*CSB*, 224)

Writing that directly bears its audience in mind is calibrated, just like speech, argues Proust, to synchronize with that audience's tastes. The linguistic content of such writing is cliché, because it is an imitation of the perceived desires of its audience served up to them in a language shared with them.

In two of the rare moments when Proust does speak with affection of Sainte-Beuve, one can see that his emotion springs from the feeling that they share the dilemmas of the would-be creative writer. Proust notes how the great critic expended every poetic image and thought in his arsenal to produce his weekly column. 'He' becomes 'we':

For ten years everything that he might have kept back for friends, for himself, for a work long meditated which he would no doubt never have written, had to take on form and come ceaselessly forth from him. Those reserves where we keep precious thoughts, the one around which a novel was to have crystallized, that other which he would work up into a poem, a third whose beauty he had one day sensed, would rise up from the depths of his mind as he was reading the book he had to write about and bravely, so that his offering might be all the finer, he would sacrifice his most cherished Isaac, his supreme Iphigenia. 'I am calling on all my resources', he would say. 'I am spending my last powder.' (*ASB*, 16–17)

[Pendant dix ans, tout ce qu'il eût réservé pour des amis, pour lui-même, pour une œuvre longuement méditée qu'il n'eût sans doute jamais écrite, dut prendre une forme, sortir sans cesse de lui. Ces réserves où nous tenons de précieuses pensées, celle-ci autour de laquelle devait se cristalliser un roman, celle-là qu'il développerait dans une poésie, telle autre dont il avait, un jour, senti la beauté, se levaient du fond de sa pensée, tandis qu'il lisait le livre dont il devait parler et bravement, pour faire l'offrande plus belle, il sacrifiait son plus cher Isaac, sa suprême Iphigénie. 'Je fais flèche de tout bois, disait-il, je tire mes dernières cartouches.'] (*CSB*, 225–6)

Later, when Proust speaks with equal measures of condescension and compassion of Sainte-Beuve's attempts at verse in *Les Rayons jaunes* and *Les Larmes de Racine*, there is again an unmistakable sensation of overlap, the younger literary critic and journalist feeling uncomfortably at one with a colleague from an older generation who perhaps – but only perhaps – produced enough brief creative work to justify his life:

the trifling thing, the trifling yet also delightful and sincere thing that is his poetry . . . demonstrates . . . the lack of significance in his vast, marvellous, ebullient œuvre as a critic . . . Mere appearance, the *Lundis*. The reality, this handful of poems. The poems of a critic, they it is out of all his writings that tip eternity's scales. (*ASB*, 23)

[ce peu de chose charmant et sincère d'ailleurs qu'est sa poésie . . . montre . . . l'absence de signification de toute une œuvre critique merveilleuse, immense, bouillonnante . . . Apparence, les *Lundis*. Réalité, ce peu de vers. Les vers d'un critique, c'est le poids à la balance de l'éternité de toute son œuvre.] (*CSB*, 232)

Is there really such a difference, objectively, between the language of social exchange and the language of literature, or between journalistic discourse and that of the novel? Is Proust not simply involved, in this quarrel, in a typical literary ranking exercise where the preferences and technique of Sainte-Beuve (we might substitute Péguy, Romain Rolland, Musset, Gautier and others) are found to be of lesser value than his own? Quite obviously, Proust *is* determined to set literature – as defined by himself – on a higher rung than what he sees as sub-creative genres, and he is also launched, in *Contre Sainte-Beuve*, in a battle over tastes. Let us examine, for a moment, three other perspectives on the question of linguistic hierarchies.

Assessed from the standpoint of a sociologist such as Pierre Bourdieu, Proust's put-down of Sainte-Beuve's style could be attributed to a class-based clash of tastes. For families like the Prousts, membership in the highest levels of the Parisian haute bourgeoisie meant the maintaining of an active distance from the workaday social world. The exclusive character of such a class means that it refuses to accept social belonging, and its tastes involve an aesthetic distancing from those of individuals on a different social rung. Exalted culture and superior class go together, and thus develops, according to Bourdieu, 'the sacred character, separate and separating, of high culture'. There is no arguing that this world of social distinctions is expertly noted by Proust, and both participated in and disavowed. His condemnation of Balzac and of Sainte-Beuve is undoubtedly linked, at least in part, to the 'vulgarity' and 'impurity' not only of their language, but of the occupations and preoccupations from which their language emanates. Proust is perfectly aware of Sainte-Beuve's economic situation: the author of *Les Lundis* was not financially secure and this was the reason he had to grind out the 'mercenary art' (Bourdieu's expression) – the weekly newspaper columns – that was to make him famous at the same time as it depleted his store of creative ideas. *A la recherche* is consistent in the condescension it shows towards the action-orientated individual – the diplomat Norpois, for example – whose language connects him too closely to practical realities. This insistence on the meaninglessness of external action, and Proust's denial of the value of social language, would thus be linked to and characteristic of an upperclass aestheticism that insists on maintaining a distance from social worlds other than its own. Proust's own aesthetic disposition could be seen as the logical pendant of his life of ease.[26]

Proust's aestheticism does not fit quite so well the next step in Bourdieu's analysis, according to which artistic intention becomes the basis of an 'art of living'[27] for the high culture establishment. Proust very clearly rejects this attitude in Sainte-Beuve, partly because he identifies its seeds in himself. Artistic intentions do not count for much in the world of *A la recherche*, and the novel reserves a special negative lesson for those who believe that a life radiant with an appreciation of art, music and literature can itself serve as an aesthetic object.

In attempting to situate Proust within the artistic aristocracy of his time, one should remember that his critique of Sainte-Beuve is not in the name of some poetic absolute of language that lies only within the comprehension of an elite. When he attacks Mallarmé and the wilful obscurity of the Symbolist poets, in his 1896 article 'Contre l'obscurité' (*CSB*, 390–5), he is immediately condemned himself for having a socialite's relationship to, and a journalist's understanding of, poetic language.[28] But what Proust is truly driving at in this early expression of his aesthetic, is his theory of artistic impression as mimesis: the language of literature should replicate a personal reality, that is, a lived impression of nature or of life. Words read as 'dead allegories' if they cease to be 'living symbols', he writes. He sees the Symbolists as contemptuous of their readers and Mallarmé as defending a movement towards abstraction, no doubt having in mind texts such as the foreword to René Ghil's *Traité du verbe* where Mallarmé speaks of transposing the facts of nature 'into their vibratory quasi-disappearance ... so that, without the bother of a close or concrete reminder, their pure notion is decanted'.[29]

It seems to me that Mikhail Bakhtin's analysis of the discourse of fiction[30] provides the most apposite schema for explaining Proust's struggle with the differentiation between social language and a more authentically personal artistic discourse. Where Bourdieu admits that his theory of taste simply disallows traditional views of philo- sophical and literary aesthetics,[31] Bakhtin, also working from a sociological perspective, is more nuanced. He does not accept claims for the absolute specificity and uniqueness of literary language: 'The idea of a special unitary and singular language of poetry is a typical utopian philosopheme of poetic discourse', he remarks ('Discourse', 288). But he does admit the linguistic dilemma in which the writer finds himself, and the alienating situation from which he must extract language: 'The word in language is half someone else's [...It] exists in other people's mouths, in other people's contexts, serving other people's intentions' (*ibid.*, 294). All objects have already been recognized and qualified verbally, he observes; they do not exist outside a social consciousness. Thus the prose artist sees his task as finding a method of appropriating the word to himself, of forming a personalized verbal image of the objects he describes to set against the background of the heteroglot voices that have already spoken on the subject. Bakhtin does not envision this quest for a purer language as a taste transfer from a class-based cultural ranking system. He admits that the problem of classifying the hybrid genre that is the novel is that it does possess some poetical elements and a certain aesthetic value (*ibid.*, 268). The writer's dilemma is to square the poetic reality of his product with the linguistic means available for its production.

To return to Proust then, what we register in him is an exceptionally exacerbated sense of the potential for alienation in the writer's situation. The habit of 'making judgements without being ourselves', of 'saying what we don't mean', Proust sees as part of a kind of automatic speech that blocks the quest for objects in their unuttered state. This linguistic phenomenon he labels 'oblique interior discourse' (VI, 247) ['l'oblique discours intérieur'] (IV, 469), an interior monologue that instantly disguises novel impressions and experience in stock terminology, clichés or nomenclatures. The hapless Narrator is easily capable of reducing a page of beautiful literature to the blank adjective 'admirable'. Drunk on the Guermantes' reputation and wine, he pronounces them (in a half-voice, to himself, as though it explained his attraction to them) 'exquisite' people with whom it would be wonderful to spend one's life. An outside presence has displaced the Narrator's self, and the world has been rendered bland.

The language of Sainte-Beuve is decried as inferior and unworthy, but it is the mechanism by which it arises that frightens the neurasthenic: this is language not thought out, but language given in to. Sainte-Beuve's words are translations of physical tics of the body, the corporeal remnant of the desire to say something witty. Proust has not forgotten his own obsessive desire to give oral pleasure, and the following text places his Narrator on exactly the same footing as Sainte-Beuve:

Above all I should have to be on my guard against those phrases which are chosen rather by the lips than by the mind, those humorous phrases such as we utter in conversation and continue at the end of a long conversation with other people to address, factitiously, to ourselves although they merely fill our mind with lies – those, so to speak, purely physical remarks, which, in the writer who stoops so low as to transcribe them are accompanied always by, for instance, the little smile, the little grimace which at every turn disfigures the spoken phrase of Sainte-Beuve, whereas real books should be the offspring not of daylight and casual talk but of darkness and silence. (VI, 256–7)

[Plus que tout j'écarterais ces paroles que les lèvres plutôt que l'esprit choisissent, ces paroles pleines d'humour, comme on en dit dans la conversation, et qu'après une longue conversation avec les autres on continue à s'adresser facticement à soi-même et qui nous remplissent l'esprit de mensonges, ces paroles toutes physiques qu'accompagne chez l'écrivain qui s'abaisse à les transcrire le petit sourire, la petite grimace qui altère à tout moment, par exemple, la phrase parlée d'un Sainte-Beuve, tandis que les vrais livres doivent être les enfants non du grand jour et de la causerie mais de de l'obscurité et du silence.] (IV, 476)

The lips choosing words, rather than the mind: the image physically captures the idea of habit, but it contains more, the kernel of the hysteria of body displacing mind. The pleasurable ripple of a muscle, the tendon stretch in a smile, afford sufficient physical gratification to discourage complex mental effort.

One of the central Proustian strategies for dealing with the world of the already verbally recognized and qualified, is to circumvent language entirely, to pass through to language's other side, where words have not yet been uttered. We see this in a sketch for the 'Zut' episode – the moment of inarticulation at Combray (I, 186; I, 153) – where the Narrator's voice appears to shift increasingly towards that of the biographical Marcel Proust as he explains the aesthetic efforts of a lifetime:

I attempted to step back a few seconds in time and to contemplate this idea whose passage had made me so happy that I had shouted and which I had not seen. And since then I have scarcely done anything else, in a certain sense, and as regards a part, at least, of what I have written when I was writing it, than to try to reflect on those happy moments when one cries, 'Gosh, is that beautiful!', and to explain what the happy moment was, which 'Gosh, is that beautiful!' does not express, to try to see what there is beneath the words that everyone says . . .

[Je cherchai à revenir à quelques instants en arrière et à apercevoir cette idée dont le passage m'avait rendu si heureux que j'avais crié et que je n'avais pas vue. Et depuis je n'ai guère fait autre chose en un certain sens et pour une partie au moins de ce que j'ai écrit quand j'écrivais, que d'essayer de revenir sur ces minutes heureuses où l'on crie: 'Zut, que c'est beau', et de dire ce qu'était la minute heureuse, que 'Zut, que c'est beau' ne dit pas, d'essayer de voir ce qu'il y a sous les mots que chacun dit . . .] (I, 836)

An early version of the argument that closes *Le Temps retrouvé* incorporates the 'zut' reaction into reasons for lack of artistic production, identifying the problem as a tendency to utter a 'language of mechanical habit' ['le language de l'habitude machinale'] (IV, 809). In fact, resisting the mechanical, bodily-based language of habit continues to dominate the whole final development of the Narrator's views on contemporary writing, what art should be and what his own work will contain. It is not only that our social interlocutors enter into our discourse through the body. When others are absent, we re-create their reactions, take up the slack, in what Proust calls our 'passionate dialogue with ourselves' (VI, 248; IV, 469). In love, the problem is especially acute, because our self-image is critical to us. If the beloved is not present to listen to our supplications and stratagems, then '[we repeat them] endlessly to ourselves, sometimes aloud in the silence of our room' (VI, 248) ['[nous les disons] sans fin à nous-même, quelquefois à haute voix dans le silence de notre chambre'] (IV, 469).

Proust's argument about authentic art shows sociability encased inextricably in habits, movements and gestures of the body that are, like involuntary muscles, almost beyond our normal control. He resolves the aesthetic dilemma of bodily entrapment in a surprising way: he does not dismiss the body and invest the mind and intellect with all inventiveness and creativity. The body, in fact, remains at the centre of 'word-processing' in Proust; it is the mechanism through which authentic metaphor is created, and bodily simulation is the test of almost all other writers' authenticity. When Proust explains in greater detail what he has said above about the effort to 'relive' experience, he speaks of a physical, mimetic contortion of the body through which we actually reconstruct an impression we have had.

Georges Poulet was the first to point out that the essential mechanism of metaphor in Proust was contained in the Narrator's mimetic relationship to the hawthorn. The effort to reproduce inwardly the gesture of the flower's budding is the primary act of creation:

It seems that here we catch a glimpse of the spiritual operation which is normally the best hidden ... the operation by which, by miming within oneself the external gesture of a tangible object, one imagines, one creates something.[32]

Proust writes, in one important sketch, that we need to be open, to be 'a porous, ductile substance, which itself becomes the impression it wishes to render, *miming it, reproducing it*, so as to be sure that nothing is changed and nothing added' ['une matière poreuse, ductile, se faisant elle-même l'impression qu'elle veut rendre, *la mimant, la reproduisant*, pour être sûr de ne pas l'altérer, de n'y rien ajouter'] (IV, 811; the emphasis is mine).

What seems to be an oblique reappearance of Sainte-Beuve in the aesthetic discussions of *Le Temps retrouvé* (VI, 257; IV, 476) is thus part of a reaffirmation crucial to Proust: he insists that social language, which so dominated much of his own early production, is a prideful hysteria of the body. Sainte-Beuve's writing is not necessarily characterized either by good or bad instinctive judgements. His words come from just beneath his skin, he is (and the Narrator fears he too could be)

the superficial man – the man who retains the sensation of his face and of his tie while he composes, who writes certain words as he would pronounce them for the pleasure of accompanying them with a little shrug of the shoulders and who sees the fullness of the epithet he has chosen expressed not in his style but between his teeth. Instead of substantiating what he has to say in his style via truths, the pleasure that he derives from [his words] completes itself in his cheek in a little grimace that complements the bizarre choice of all Sainte-Beuve's epithets, just like the diatribes against contemporary art of certain of today's writers.

[l'homme superficiel – l'homme qui garde la sensation de son visage et de sa cravate pendant qu'il compose, qui écrit certains mots comme il les prononcerait[33] pour le plaisir de les accompagner d'un petit haussement d'épaules et qui réalise la plénitude de l'épithète qu'il choisit non dans son style mais entre ses dents où le plaisir qu'il en ressent, au lieu de les motiver entièrement dans son style par des vérités, éprouve le besoin de se compléter dans sa joue par une petite grimace complémentaire du choix bizarre de toutes les épithètes de Sainte-Beuve comme des diatribes de certains écrivains d'aujourd'hui contre l'art contemporain.] (IV, 828)[34]

The figure of Sainte-Beuve thus embodies Proust's fear of a hysterical domination by oral language. But the portrait he develops of Sainte-Beuve and Sainte-Beuve's mistakes, however pungent, cannot resolve the writer's fear of orality. Only total absorption in writing could do that. Sainte-Beuve himself almost disappears from the final version of the novel. However, the debate on the oral content of writing continues unabated in *A la recherche*, fictionalized in one of the mini-quests that help the Narrator to come to terms with art. The inquisitive young man, himself destined to become a writer, is given the task of investigating how the writer Bergotte's oral voice and social self are somehow reflected in his prose. The most striking difference, perhaps, between the debate in *Contre Sainte-Beuve* and the analysis of Bergotte in *A la recherche*, is the serenity of tone in the latter. There are suggestions in the portrait of Bergotte that we must not fear any aspect of ourselves, even the terrifying social voice.

VOICING BERGOTTE

Can there be a creativity of the oral voice? Is there a relationship between oral accents and rhythms on the one hand, and rhythm and tone in fiction on the other? Can there be any positive relationship at all between the oral and the written registers?

Proust's absolute condemnation of Sainte-Beuve's writing style seems to suggest such connections are impossible. But this verdict is not necessarily the same as his Narrator's answer regarding the intriguing oral speech patterns of Bergotte. Because of his mimetist's habit of 'voicing' the Other, plus the rather long period of literary impotence that coincided with this period of social voice, Proust struggled with the question of oral patterns. 'Our intonations', declares the Narrator at one point, 'contain our philosophy of life'. Maurice Bardèche saw Proust applying his gift for distinguishing oral voice to prose voice:

the banality or the pretentiousness of an expression are, for him, stylistic tics which reveal a certain mediocrity of the heart or the intelligence as surely as an intonation. Reading and hearing are the same operation. He judges writers by the way they pitch their voice.[35]

Proust seems, in fact, to have been greatly attracted by the idea that the uniqueness of oral tone may somehow incorporate an individual's essential difference.

As we have seen, the speaking voices of Robert de Montesquiou and Anatole France were two of those that possessed Proust, and which he felt obliged to counterfeit. But his instinct was not entirely caricatural. In 1893–4, when he was making the acquaintance of Montesquiou, one sees him attempting to connect voice and artistic potential. In spite of the fawning tone of the correspondence, what percolates through is the sense that Montesquiou's voice captures his individuality, and that the identification of that individuality is essential for Proust. I see in this obsession in Proust's criticism, in particular, a growing recognition, which culminates in *A la recherche*, that speaking in the personal 'I' voice will resolve Proust's own search for creativity. *A la recherche* is both a search for and demonstration of the locus of personal tone and therefore individuality. By my tone I exist.

In early 1894 Proust sends regrets to Montesquiou that he cannot attend the latter's lecture on Marceline Desbordes-Valmore. He speaks – no doubt with irony – about the place the talk may occupy in the history of 'spoken criticism', but there is more than a hint of conviction in another comment in the same letter: 'the «all-powerful» chords of your voice and your diction have a true magic power for me' ['les «tout-puissants» accords de votre voix et de votre diction ont pour moi une vertu proprement magique'] (*Corr.*, I, 269). A few months earlier Proust had written an article on Montesquiou that also focused on his voice, because in it the man's drive and willpower seemed personified: 'From the moment he speaks, one is overcome by a powerful rhythm which is surprising initially, since we are so used to the soft, toneless voices of today' ['Dès qu'il parle, on est dompté par un rythme puissant qui étonne d'abord, habitué qu'on est aux molles voix, sans accent, d'aujourd'hui'] (*CSB*, 407). In a subsequent letter to an editor who is considering the article for publication, Proust insists that if cutting is to be done, the crucial section to remain untouched is that on Montesquiou's voice (*Corr.*, II, 485). Gradually his view became clear that Montesquiou's genius would never transcend the oral register, but Proust still connected the man's hysterical appetite for manipulating words with the revelation of what was essential in his character. In an article that appeared in 1905, Proust imagines the Count as a member of the Académie Française on a day when new words are being vetted for inclusion in the dictionary:

All those who have seen Montesquiou stop and, as it were, rear up as he is about to pronounce a word ... all those who have seen him seize a word, show all its beauties, taste it, almost grimace at its specific, over-strong flavour, pronounce it emphatically, repeat it, shout it, chant it, sing it, serve it up like a theme with a thousand sparkling variations, improvised with a richness that astounds and disconcerts the efforts of the memory to retain them, those people can imagine what marvellous days one would spend, in his company, on dictionary days at the Académie.

[Tous ceux qui ... ont vu [Montesquiou] s'arrêter et comme se cabrer au moment de prononcer un mot ... tous ceux qui l'ont vu saisir un mot, en montrer toutes les beautés, le goûter, faire presque la grimace à sa saveur spécifique et trop forte, le faire valoir, le répéter, le crier, le psalmodier, le chanter, le faire servir comme un thème à mille étincelantes variations, improvisées avec une richesse qui étonne et déconcerte les efforts de la mémoire pour les retenir, celui-là peut s'imaginer quels jours merveilleux seraient, avec lui, à l'Académie, les jours de dictionnaire.] (*CSB*, 507–8)

What Proust finds to praise in an article by Fernand Gregh on Anatole France is an ability similar to the one he demonstrates *vis-à-vis* Montesquiou, 'the explanation of Monsieur France's delivery when he speaks' ['l'explication du débit de Monsieur France quand il parle'] (*Corr.*, II, 477).

Oral tone and prose tone seem to be superimposed in Proust's judgements of writers he admired much more than Montesquiou.

Like Cocteau and Morand, Georges de Lauris remembered the interplay between Proust's oral and written styles, but he also remembered that Proust's assessment of mentor writers such as Chateaubriand seemed to integrate vocal and literary tone. Proust used to read Chateaubriand's prose out loud to Lauris, not only for the quality of his images or the harmonious structure of sentences, but in order to identify, in the tone of this or that phrase, the writer's personal strengths and weaknesses, even his obsessions.[36]

Nowhere is Proust's preoccupation with the connection between oral and written register more evident than in the Narrator's attention to Bergotte's style. And nowhere in other discussions of language are the contradictions more pointed and the conclusion less conclusive.[37] The examination of Bergotte is based, of course, on the relationship between an artist's creations and his material self. Norpois sees no difference between Bergotte the man and his work, condemning *en bloc* his unvirile prose, his affected speech, and his public promenading of his mistress. The Narrator is far more sympathetic but still faces a difficulty: how to reconcile the gorgeous musicality of Bergotte's style with his curlicue nose and annoyingly monotonous diction?

Musicality is the link between that diction and its prose voice. The Narrator is initially struck by the harmonious gathering of forces at certain junctures in Bergotte's writing, as though an internal melodic prelude were building. The young admirer tends to hum those lines, rather than read them: 'And so I would read, or rather sing his sentences in my mind, with rather more *dolce*, rather more *lento* than he himself had perhaps intended, and his simplest phrase would strike my ears with something peculiarly gentle and loving in its intonation' (I, 114) ['je chantais intérieurement sa prose, plus *dolce*, plus *lento* peut-être qu'elle n'était écrite, et la phrase la plus simple s'adressait à moi avec une intonation attendrie'] (I, 95–6).

The first meeting between the young Narrator and Bergotte underlines, perversely, that the tics of speech can connect directly to an artist's creative personality. At that meeting the Narrator is immediately struck by the writer's curious voice, and surprised to observe that the most affected and unpleasant moments in his speech appear to correspond to the most poetic, musical moments in his prose. This contradiction is explained by a maxim-type statement that first appears to separate oral voice from the realm of writing: 'as human speech reflects the human soul, *though without expressing it as does literary style,* Bergotte appeared almost to be talking nonsense, intoning certain words, ... stringing them together uninterruptedly on one continuous note, with a wearisome monotony' (II, 143) ['comme la parole humaine est en rapport avec l'âme, *mais sans l'exprimer comme le fait le style,* Bergotte avait l'air de parler presque à contresens, psalmodiant certains mots, ... les filant sans intervalle comme un même son, avec une fatigante monotonie'] (I, 540; the emphasis is mine). But oral voice impinges and haunts, it is too important in the life/art equation to ignore. And so the Narrator investigates further, claiming that one day the key to the puzzle is given him: by carefully repeating phrases he has heard Bergotte speak, he is eventually able to detect the 'armature' of his written style and connect the elements of the written style back to the very different idiosyncrasies of his speech. There *is* a relationship, then, between oral and prose voice; it is simply coded, not transparent.

This discovery does not in any way exhaust the interest in the special characteristics of oral voice. The Narrator's research continues, taking a curious sideways step into heredity as an explanation of certain aspects of Bergotte's oral inflections: he has inherited many of his speech patterns from his family, for when the Narrator later meets Bergotte's brothers and sisters, he can hear the resemblances. At the same time, we are told – in an apparent contradiction – that Bergotte's conversational style was copied (unconsciously) from a lifetime chum (II, 149; I, 545–6).

But just when things are getting interesting again, when the reader might begin making family connections between the prolix, cliché-ridden, medical voice of Adrien Proust and that of his son,[38] the text primly cuts off discussion and returns to its initial orthodoxy, the mutual exclusivity of oral and written registers. Bergotte is said to have done what few artists had, that is, transpose some of his family's pronunciations into his writing. But it was a one-time experiment:

There are in his books just such closing phrases where the accumulated sonorities are prolonged (as in the last chords of the overture of an opera which cannot bring itself to a close and repeats several times over its final cadence before the conductor finally lays down his baton), in which, later on, I was to find a musical equivalent for those phonetic 'brasses' of the Bergotte family. But in his own case, from the moment when he transferred them to his books, he ceased instinctively to make use of them in his speech. From the day on which he had begun to write – and thus all the more markedly later, when I first knew him – his voice had abandoned this orchestration for ever. (II, 148)

[Il y a dans ses livres telles terminaisons de phrases où l'accumulation des sonorités qui se prolongent, comme aux derniers accords d'une ouverture d'opéra qui ne peut pas finir et redit plusieurs fois sa suprême cadence avant que le chef d'orchestre pose son bâton, dans lesquelles je retrouvai plus tard un équivalent musical de ces cuivres phonétiques de la famille Bergotte. Mais pour lui, à partir du moment où il les transporta dans ses livres, il cessa inconsciemment d'en user dans son discours. Du jour où il avait commencé d'écrire et, à plus forte raison, plus tard, quand je le connus, sa voix s'en était désorchestrée pour toujours.] (I, 544)

Even as, in these heavily reworked passages, the wall is re-erected between writing and speaking, self-contradictory text surfaces. In reflecting on how Bergotte had influenced the vocabulary and sentence structure of younger writers, the Proustian text lends high status to the notion of accent as it relates to individuality and creativity. Certain distortions of syntax and accent in Bergotte's speech are said to exist in a necessary relationship with intellectual originality (II, 149; I, 545).

The texts of some of the *Esquisses* contained in the second Pléiade edition go further, demonstrating that prose style at times simply reflects oral choices:

The habitual choice of certain adjectives seemed to represent, in his prose, only the pleasure he had in pronouncing them. Simply in the way he paused complacently over the consonants, one felt that the pleasure he took in saying them caused him to place them in his books and position them in his sentences in a somewhat unusual, unexpected place which gave them the sort of importance that he gave them in speech by pronouncing them more precisely than the others. I thus found in his style a certain hoarse abruptness of voice when he wanted to say something gay which became in his books a little too short and forceful.

[Le choix habituel de certains adjectifs semblait n'être dans sa prose que le plaisir qu'il avait à les prononcer. Rien qu'à la façon dont il s'arrêtait complaisamment sur les consonnes, on sentait que le plaisir qu'il avait à les dire les lui faisait placer dans ses livres, et mettre dans ses phrases à une place un peu rare, inattendue qui leur donnait cette sorte d'importance qu'en parlant il leur donnait en les prononçant plus précisément que les autres. J'ai retrouvé ainsi dans son style une certaine brusquerie rauque de sa voix quand il voulait dire quelque chose de gai qui devenait dans ses livres un peu trop court et fort.] (I, 1032)

Certain other passages appear to confirm that oral voice reveals the same thing as the written text, the special individuality of its author:

'I saw that with the transposition of voice to literary style, it was essentially the same thing, and that this perpetual reasoning that Bergotte made about everything was precisely the movement, the progression, the living soul of his works' ['je vis qu'avec la trans-position de la voix au style, c'était au fond la même chose, et que ce perpétuel raisonnement que [Bergotte] faisait sur tout était juste-ment la démarche, la progression, l'âme vivante de ses livres'] (I, 1033). This is the oral music of Bergotte's prose, what is essential to it and essential in him, a certain arrangement of words which con-stituted his originality (I, 788). Ralph Waldo Emerson, whom Proust had read like a brother, had said much the same thing: 'A man's style is his mind's voice'.

Beyond the contradictions in these texts, what is apparent is the desire to mix the unmixable, to follow the seam of vocal tone and inflection from social speech to the unconsciously structured pattern of words that is original style. The unremitting nature of the analysis also suggests, in its self-referential way, that to lay bare and understand one's own tone, the 'armature' of one's own indi-viduality, as it somehow extrudes from the oral and written word, is the real search to which the Narrator is dedicated.

There is a further, curious connection between Bergotte's oral voice and writing, and it is once again set within a discussion of imitation versus individual creativity. Once again too, the text attempts to move to safe ground by denying that orality can beget creation, but refuses to shed self-contradicting elements within itself. Like a number of the Narrator's acquaintances, the violinist Morel turns to journalism during the war. Earlier, as has been discussed, he had enjoyed doing oral imitations of Bergotte's speaking voice, but now that he has turned to writing, he writes, to the Narrator's amazement, as Bergotte spoke:

[The style of the articles] derived from Bergotte but in a way which, for the reason that follows, perhaps no one but myself perceived. Bergotte's *writings* had not the slightest influence on Morel. The fertilization had been effected in a most unusual way, which I record here only because of its rarity. I have described earlier the very special manner which Bergotte had, when he spoke, of choosing and pronouncing his words. Morel, who for a long time had been in the habit of meeting him at the Saint-Loups', had at that period done 'imitations' of him, in which he exactly mimicked his voice, using just the words that Bergotte would have chosen. And now that he had taken to writing, Morel used to transcribe passages of 'spoken Bergotte', but without first transposing them in the way which would have turned

them into 'written Bergotte'. Not many people having known Bergotte as
a talker, the tone of his voice was not recognized, since it differed from
the style of his pen. This oral fertilization is so rare that I have thought it
worth mentioning here. The flowers that it produces are, however, always
sterile. (VI, 96)

[[Le] style [des articles] dérivait de Bergotte, mais d'une façon à laquelle,
seul peut-être, j'étais sensible, et voici pourquoi. Les écrits de Bergotte
n'avaient nullement influé sur Morel. La fécondation s'était faite d'une
façon toute particulière et si rare que c'est à cause de cela seulement que je
la rapporte ici. J'ai indiqué en son temps la manière si spéciale que Bergotte
avait, quand il parlait, de choisir ses mots, de les prononcer. Morel, qui
l'avait longtemps rencontré chez les Saint-Loup, avait fait de lui alors des
'imitations', où il contrefaisait parfaitement sa voix, usant des mêmes mots
qu'il eût pris. Or maintenant, Morel, pour écrire, transcrivait des
conversations à la Bergotte, mais sans leur faire subir cette transposition
qui en eût fait du Bergotte écrit. Peu de personnes ayant causé avec
Bergotte, on ne reconnaissait pas le ton, qui différait du style. Cette
fécondation orale est si rare que j'ai voulu la citer ici. Elle ne produit,
d'ailleurs, que des fleurs stériles.] (IV, 347)

Why is it so surprising that orality can actually incite a type of
creativity? In part, no doubt, because this would be to remind us too
crudely that artistic individuality begins with imitation, and that oral
and literary pastiches served quite literally as the trampoline for
Marcel Proust's launching as a writer. The Narrator recognizes
certain aspects of that imitative bent as linked to hysteria, which is
full-scale occupation by the other, Morel's malady. Only a thread
separates this obsessive recitalist, this hysteric capable of waking
trances, from the very symbol of the creative artist, the 'dormeur
éveillé', capable of self-metamorphosis into a work of chamber
music or a church. Self-reference in the Proustian text is not limited
to the more substantive and somewhat more positive 'Charles'
figures, Swann and Charlus. Charlie Morel is a performer, neurotic
pasticher and dabbler in the art of others who deserves consideration
as well.

Proust's concerns about 'finding his own voice' are especially
apparent in the pre-*Recherche* period. In the introduction to *Sésame et
les lys*, he contrasts the febrile excitement of social relationships, the
'agitations of friendship', as he says, with the otherworldly calm one
can attain through reading. In reading we reach beyond words to
make contact with the essence of individuality, and that exercise is

really a twin of writing, the silent seeking of our own self beyond our social words:

The atmosphere of this pure form of friendship [= reading] is silence, which is purer than speech. Because we speak for others, but remain silent for ourselves. So silence, unlike speech, does not bear the trace of our faults or affectations. It is pure, it is genuinely an atmosphere ... The very language of the book is pure (if it is worthy to be called a book), made transparent by the thought of the author, which has removed whatever was not itself to make of it its own faithful image; each sentence, at bottom, resembling the others, because all are spoken with the unique inflection of a personality. (*ASB*, 219)

[L'atmosphère de cette pure amitié [= la lecture] est le silence, plus pur que la parole. Car nous parlons pour les autres, mais nous nous taisons pour nous-mêmes. Aussi le silence ne porte pas, comme la parole, la trace de nos défauts, de nos grimaces. Il est pur, il est vraiment une atmosphère. ... Le langage même du livre est pur (si le livre mérite ce nom), rendu transparent par la pensée de l'auteur qui en a retiré tout ce qui n'était pas elle-même jusqu'à le rendre son image fidèle; chaque phrase, au fond, ressemblant aux autres, car toutes sont dites par l'inflexion unique d'une personnalité.] (*CSB*, 187)

One is reminded here of the constant superposition, in Proust, of tone and musical inflection as definers of individuality. In the unconscious arrangement of notes and chords, of sounds and textures and accents, a musician communicates to us an imprint of his individuality that is at the same time an utterance of the soul's voice:

I do not believe that the *essence peculiar* to the music of Gluck reveals itself in any one of his sublime arias so much as in certain cadences of his recitative, where *the harmony is like the actual sound of the voice of his genius as it drops on an involuntary intonation* on which is stamped all of his artless gravity and distinction, each time one hears him catch his breath so to speak. (*ASB*, 224–5, n.)

[Je ne crois pas que *l'essence particulière* de la musique de Gluck se trahisse autant dans tel air sublime que dans telle cadence de ses récititatifs où *l'harmonie est comme le son même de la voix de son génie quand elle retombe sur une intonation involontaire* où est marquée toute sa gravité naïve et sa distinction, chaque fois qu'on l'entend pour ainsi dire reprendre haleine.] (*CSB*, 192, n.; the emphasis is mine.)

Interpreting language, be it speech or literary texts, as the essential tone of personality is the single most important ability in a critic. Proust and his Narrator have the gift of hearing the 'tune' that is unique and different in every author (*ASB*, 92; *CSB*, 303). It is that same tune that one must identify in oneself in order to write creatively: 'The beautiful things we will write (if we have the talent) are within us, indistinct like the memory of a tune that charms us without our being able to remember its shape' ['Les belles choses que nous écrirons si nous avons le talent sont en nous, indistinctes, comme le souvenir d'un air qui nous charme sans que nous puissions en retrouver le contour'] (*CSB*, 312).

But if social voice may be linked, hesitantly, to the essential inflections of individuality, and therefore to the artist's writing voice, some texts on music and individuality return us to our starting point: the anxiety-ridden language of the nerves. The structure of the individual artistic personality is equated with the structure of the artist's neuroses. One passage on Wagner identifies what is authentic in the composer's production with the repeated twang of his nerve ends:

I was struck by how much reality there is in the work of Wagner as I contemplated once more those insistent, fleeting themes which visit an act, recede only to return again and again, and, sometimes distant, dormant, almost detached, are at other moments, while remaining vague, so pressing and so close, so internal, so organic, so visceral, that they seem like the reprise not so much of a musical motif as of an attack of neuralgia. (V, 174–5)

[Je me rendais compte de tout ce qu'a de réel l'œuvre de Wagner, en revoyant ces thèmes insistants et fugaces qui visitent un acte, ne s'éloignent que pour revenir, et parfois lointains, assoupis, presque détachés, sont à d'autres moments, tout en restant vagues, si pressants et si proches, si internes, si organiques, si viscéraux qu'on dirait la reprise moins d'un motif que d'une névralgie.] (III, 665)[39]

Tensions, anxieties and many unresolved contradictions characterize Marcel Proust's meditation about language. In the preface to *Sésame et les lys*, he draws stark contrasts between everyday human speech and the spiritual and intellectual communication possible through reading. Reading produces an ethereal calm so intense that it allows us, by contrast, to imagine the hysteria the Proustian personality feels when exposed to the Other's presence in conversation. *Contre Sainte-Beuve* addresses the same antinomy, the absolute imbalance between talking about art and creating it, but at the same time a start is made on absorbing orality into art. Part of the work will take the form of a conversation with the mother figure, an intimate exchange no doubt, but a form of talk none the less. In parallel, Proust introduces the notion that style (Sainte-Beuve's, Morel's) can be hysterical when it regurgitates the Other's language unthinkingly.

In *A la recherche du temps perdu*, the dilemma of artistic creativity is partially resolved. Creativity centres more firmly around the idea of voice, and although concerns remain because tone and accent can apply indifferently to speech, writing and music, Proust's earlier intense anxiety about language seems relieved. The idea that speech and writing may not be so qualitatively different remains resident in the text, attached to long-held views about the unique quality and character of the creative person's nervous makeup.

A network of speculations on the neurotic origins of genius and the compulsive content of even creative language underpins Proust's final arguments about artistic individuality. The social words we pronounce are empty, borrowed, meaningless, but the tone in which an artist speaks them, the inflections of his speech, resonate with his individuality and intellectual difference. Voice seen as tone is totally distinctive, unreproducible, and it is especially apparent in music and in prose. But vocal tone is also an expression of an individual set of nerves. The final text of *A la recherche* left to us by Proust points in the direction of reconciliation and reintegration. It juxtaposes excommunicatory remarks about the verbal hysteria of Sainte-Beuve with solid indications that the most compulsive aspects of self-expression are the very ones that define the creative artist. To an artist who had devoted so much time to not-quite-creative writing pursuits, such a reconciliation with self was an internal necessity, so that he might legitimately and self-consciously tap into the deep wellsprings of self where all language originates.

It is time to examine more closely the physical embodiment of Proust's attachment to social language, his lifelong praxis of forms of writing that were less creative than fiction, that often had a strong 'social exchange' quotient, and that, therefore, were placed low on Proust's official ratings system. How did Saint-Beuvian types of writing, Proust's correspondence, journalism, criticism and pastiches, lead him to the realm of literature?

CHAPTER 3

Transitive writing

In spite of his carefully cultivated image as a literary hermit, Marcel Proust was always very much attuned to his social and cultural environment. He wrote frequently about the literary activities of his contemporaries – René de Chantal's *Marcel Proust, critique littéraire*[1] is a monument to his life-long critical activity – and from time to time about societal issues close to his heart. Proust was a social chronicler and journalist, a productive essayist and critic, an inexhaustible (if perpetually exhausted) correspondent, a translator, and a master of the pastiche, before he became the novelist we know today.

Yet, as we shall see, writing to others and about others was, in Proust's view, a malady which required a cure. I have chosen the term 'transitive writing' to describe this Other-orientated part of Proust's production, because it suggests writing with an external object in mind, and a stance of attention and response to an external phenomenon. (Jean-Louis Baudry uses 'intransitive writing' to describe an activity which refers back only to the writing subject.[2]) For Proust, writing about the Other means being filled with the presence of the Other, having the Other predominantly on one's mind as one writes, becoming a sympathetic resonating chamber for the Other's ideas, and I shall include even correspondence under this rubric, for reasons explained later in this chapter. Many critics concur that the quasi-intransitive feel of the beginning of *A la recherche du temps perdu* is one of Proust's great innovations. A man drowses fitfully in a darkened room, immobilized by conflicting impressions and memories. The first-person preoccupation with self in those pages, the imposition on the reader of a creative stasis of mind instead of immediate plot development, was a hard-won victory of technique and form, earned at the expense of much writing about the world exterior to the self. Richard Terdiman's apt formula for this technique is the 'depreciation of the event',[3] while

Leo Bersani views Proust's conscious focus on an inner reality as what differentiates him from nineteenth-century novelists.[4]

It is not unfair, I think, to picture the pre-*Recherche* Marcel Proust in the posture of one of his characters, searching, like Swann, for a literary vocation in a pre-literary form such as an essay on Vermeer, or, like Brichot, in a non-literary form like wartime journalism. Proust always viewed not only literary magazines but newspapers and journals as vehicles for introducing or promoting his fiction and exposing his ideas to the public. It was Proust's image as a habitué of the conservative *Figaro* that at first made him unacceptable to the editors of the avant-garde *Nouvelle Revue Française* such as Henri Ghéon and André Gide. Proust was painfully conscious of the gap between writing from personal inspiration and writing that buries itself in the ideas and style of another writer. On the other hand, writing transitively, about someone or something else, meant that form and structure were to a large extent given.

The practice of non-literary genres refined Proust's view of what his fictional ideal might entail. His experience also set firmly in his mind a hierarchy of writing. In a way, what is most striking about that hierarchy is Proust's adamant stance within it, for few of his fellow novelists would quarrel with the subordinate values he assigns to journalism, criticism, biography, literary history, etc. Proust's anxiety of language translates directly into an anxiety attached to non-authentic writing forms. The author protests so loudly, in fact, against non-authentic genres, that the nettled reader continually wants to assay the purity of Proust's own fictional text against his theoretical statements.

As I examine Proust's correspondence, journalism, literary criticism and his pastiches, there are a number of questions I would like to pose. Are there unifying aspects to his style that are consistent across all his writing, including the non-fiction? Does his correspondence, for instance, provide any key to his literary style? Are the absolute distinctions he makes between certain non-literary genres – journalism, for instance – and fiction, as absolute in Proust's writing practice as he maintains in some of his more rigidly ideological statements? What meaning, if any, can one ascribe to the multiple borrowings from Proust's criticism, social columns, correspondence and pastiches into his fiction? Does such activity not suggest that Proust's real aesthetic belief is that forms and genres are simply surface delineations? Given the intimate connections between his non-fiction and fiction, what do the sub-genres he practises contribute to our understanding of Proustian structure and meaning?

CORRESPONDENCE

An unexpected tension surrounds discussion of letter writing in the Proustian text. In spite of the fact that the object of correspondence seems quite distinct from that of fiction, the letter is seen as a form that competes with literature as a vehicle for expressing an individual's true self. This epistolary anxiety is masked by irony, but quite visible, in the well-known observation (by the unastute comtesse d'Arpajon) that Flaubert's correspondence is much more lively and interesting than his novels:[5]

Have you noticed how often a writer's letters are superior to the rest of his work? What's the name of that author who wrote *Salammbô*? ... How intriguing his correspondence is, and how superior to his books! It explains him, in fact, because one sees from everything he says about the difficulty he has in writing a book that he wasn't a real writer, a gifted man. (III, 565)

[Avez-vous remarqué que souvent les lettres d'un écrivain sont supérieures au reste de son œuvre? Comment s'appelle donc cet auteur qui a écrit *Salammbô*? ... comme sa correspondance est curieuse et supérieure à ses livres! Elle l'explique du reste, car on voit par tout ce qu'on dit de la peine qu'il a à faire un livre, que ce n'était pas un véritable écrivain, un homme doué.] (II, 779–80)[6]

The broader context for this remark, as critics have suggested,[7] is the Narrator's anxiety at his own inability to be artistically productive, and his fear that it is his well-oiled social reflexes which prevent him from getting down to work. A complaint Proust sends off to Jacques Copeau makes exactly the same point as does the observation about Flaubert: how could a contributor to the *Nouvelle Revue Française* have uttered the absurdity that the Emerson–Carlyle correspondence is somehow their masterpiece? How could Emerson's letters, written out of duty and boredom and containing nothing of himself, equal those pages where he had tried to express 'his most precious, most interior essence, an essence which must be so laboriously extracted' (*Corr.*, XII, 157–8)? The subject of a writer's correspondence immediately raises the red flag of distinguishing the man from his work, but there is more to this antagonism than the pat and traditional incommensurability of the personal life and the creative process. It is especially instructive to examine Proust's pre-*Recherche* works in this regard.

Letters did, of course, play a prodigious role in Proust's life. The sheer weight of his correspondence (21 volumes in the Plon edition) is impressive given that he died aged fifty-one. After viewing the pile of envelopes in Proust's out-tray one day in 1896, Albert Flament expressed his disbelief, wondering if Proust did not produce several volumes of letters a year.[8] It was the correspondence of Balzac and Flaubert which intrigued Proust particularly during these formative *Jean Santeuil* years, though his fascination with Flaubert's letters is durable; references to them continue throughout his life, in the *Carnet de 1908*, in *A la recherche* itself and in his late article, 'A propos du «style» de Flaubert'.

The hero of *Jean Santeuil* sees letters as a deviation from artistic purpose, a potentially debilitating extension of the writer's social activity and social voice. Correspondence operates as a double of conversation, always resonating with some selfish desire we want to achieve, and thus never frank:

> The exaltation that causes us to utter beautiful words in order to achieve some self-interested end is the opposite of literature which attempts to express what one feels with sincerity. This is the source, no doubt, of the antagonism that exists between art and life, and people who write too many letters, who have too many objectives related to their personal feelings ..., have less talent, especially those who talk too much.
>
> [Cette exaltation qui nous fait proférer de belles paroles dans un but et pour quelque fin intéressée est le contraire de la littérature qui s'efforce d'exprimer avec sincérité ce que l'on sent. D'où sans doute l'antagonisme qu'il y a entre l'art et la vie, et les gens qui écrivent trop de lettres, ont trop de buts sentimentaux dans la vie ..., ont moins de talent, et surtout ceux qui parlent trop.] (*JS*, 762)

Proust's own problematic talent is at stake in these lines: logorrhoea spills over from the oral into the written domain, and the potential for infecting one's literature is evident. Love letters are cited as the worst; in them, the word 'sincerity' is a synonym for 'lie'. Logically then, the letter must be anathematized and banished, along with talk, to the low end of the writing spectrum. Otherwise, if we judged an author by his letters, we would ignore his ability to reformulate reality and to create the illusion of truth. The flattery quotient in many letters of Anatole France, Alphonse Daudet and even Flaubert, is elevated; the writer of *Jean Santeuil* trembles at the idea that one day his own

insincere correspondence might see the light of day (*JS*, 488). Some
of Proust's adamant stance may derive from the reading of an article
by Maurice Barrès protesting against the publication of Baudelaire's
more banal, workaday correspondence. Barrès insisted that letters
written in order to obtain a specific result were composed as a
reflection of the addressee's character, not of Baudelaire's: '[Baude-
laire's poems] are evidence of what was individual and disinterested
in him. He wrote them when he was reflecting only about himself.'[9]

In his preface to *Sésame et les lys*, the anxiety about insincerity in
letters comes fully to the surface as Proust dissects the idea of
friendship. There is no way to step back, he explains, from the
initial, excessive language with which we deluge an individual we
find sympathetic. And that language is pitched at a level which we
must always match in subsequent communications: he compares it
to a debt we have incurred which must forever be paid back (*ASB*,
219; *CSB*, 186). At the heart of Proustian speech and letters, there is
an agitation about dependency that is calmed only in the act of
reading, or in the activity that is the reading of oneself, writing.

Still, the text from *Sésame et les lys* raises an interesting question
directly: are not letters an aspect of a writer's stance, a sample of the
voice in another register, a component of the 'expressive machine'[10]
that, in an individual, produces all writing? Without seeing in
Proust's letters a full-fledged component of his art, equal to his
fiction, can one identify certain exchanges of expression between the
two, certain parallels in the communicative stance from which all his
writing emanates? Clearly, there are parallels between the way he
pitched his oral voice to people he knew, or had newly met, and the
way letters re-create the linguistic level of his correspondent. Lucien
Daudet speaks of Proust's uncanny gift for finding the exact level of
language of his interlocutors, even if they were strangers; his knack
for locating the perfectly appropriate gift was a pendant to this
linguistic attentiveness.[11] Philip Kolb, editor of the correspondence,
felt that Proust's letters appear to adopt the intellectual stance of his
correspondent, and he recalls a remark of Georges de Lauris who
described Proust's conversation as depending on his interlocutor.[12]
Ramon Fernandez's analysis of the Proustian psyche again comes to
mind: it is almost as though there were no independent spirit at work
in Proust; his actions are a re-action to the object or person that is
before him.[13]

This is not to say that Proust's letters are all slavish reproductions of his correspondents' wishes. In 1906, the year after his mother's death, the tone is much more direct. He criticizes Reynaldo Hahn's writing style (*Corr.*, VI, 80–1), expresses his regret to Bertrand de Fénelon that the latter will never exercise his creative talents (*ibid.*, 266–7), and questions Montesquiou's judgement (*ibid.*, 353). And Proust is fairly open about his own fault of effusiveness: he admits that a princess has slammed down a telephone receiver on him; he tells Reynaldo how he is cooking up an exaggerated letter of praise for the comtesse de Chévigné.[14]

Letters are a gesture of reaching out to the Other, and all letters, it has been said, are love letters of a sort. We have seen, however, the deep need of the Proustian personality to maintain its independence from the Other, and its fear of the language of agreement, of mutual supportiveness, of depersonalized agreement over 'nothing'. Just like a social conversation, the letter threatens Proust with his correspondent's linguistic proximity. What develops in that correspondence, therefore, are various strategies for holding the interlocutor at bay: access is often literally refused, and often agreement or access is made to appear immensely complicated, full of unexpected obstacles.[15] This aspect of his correspondence reminds us, in fact, of a feature of his prose style. Could one not imagine the numerous optional images which Proust offers to explain an idea or a phenomenon as a device designed to delay over-rapid agreement between writer and reader? Ultimate meaning is made to reside not in any single expression or phrase which one might isolate and nail down as such (and perhaps, therefore, appropriate), but in a well-protected, slightly indeterminate, in-between zone. The whole message of *A la recherche* supports this way of interpreting Proustian style: truth is a complex discovery, locatable only 'by comparison', never available in specific statements, or scenes viewed once.

After the publication of *Du Côté de chez Swann*, when Proust became the object of intense scrutiny by domestic and foreign critics, the letter functioned increasingly as a shield. Not a few of Proust's correspondents – among them, Louis d'Albuféra, Jacques Copeau, Albert Thibaudet and Jacques Boulenger – were quoted lines from Sully Prudhomme that neatly combine a sincere idea of friendship with a certain dismissiveness:

> Dear passer-by, take only a small part of me,
> The part that pleased you because it resembles you;
> But let us not hope to meet,

True friendship is in feeling together,
The rest is fragile, let us avoid the adieux.

[Cher passant ne prenez de moi-même qu'un peu
Le peu qui vous a plu parce qu'il vous ressemble;
Mais de nous rencontrer ne formons pas le vœu
Le vrai de l'amitié c'est de sentir ensemble
Le reste en est fragile, épargnons-nous l'adieu.][16]

The poet's lines contain the kernel of a Proustian axiom: the pleasure (and menace) of social relationships is that they are based on what we choose to share with others, and not that part of us which is original and different, which we would not and could not share. Social exchange puts us at risk, the risk of losing our difference and of losing our self to the Other.

In Proust's notes to his friends, and even more pointedly in his letters to individuals enjoying literary prestige or social eminence, he demonstrates the linguistic alienation with which he had to struggle in face-to-face relationships. Between Proust and his correspondent as between Proust and an oral interlocutor, a power dynamic is set in motion, though in letters it appears exacerbated. Under the pressure of social amiability or more personal desires, language is malleable and can expand hysterically. As Flaubert had said earlier, 'Speech is a rolling-mill that always stretches sentiments'.[17]

'Un flatteur hystérique'[18]

Nowhere is Proust's particular ability to flatter – an ability which is, in part, a talent for rearticulating the language and personality of his interlocutor – more evident than in his letters to two early literary acquaintances, Anna de Noailles and Robert de Montesquiou. In the poet Anna de Noailles Proust seems to have identified a kindred spirit, a sensitive, intelligent soul in an aristocratic embodiment, and an individual with a nervous disposition. After reading a few poems from Le Cœur innombrable, just before the collection is to appear in 1901, Proust writes to her in what will become a typical tone, drawing from her work the nature images that their writing shares, speaking of hawthorns, roses, pigeons, roads in sunlight, swans, even noting her image 'the cheeks of the moon', as if to underline the importance of a part of the body that has obsessional attractive force in his own writing (see Corr., II, 422–4). Her inspiration, like his own, Proust suggests, is in the nerves: 'Nervous states and enchanting poems can very well be the inseparable manifestations of the same tempestuous power' ['Des états nerveux et des poèmes enchanteurs peuvent très bien être des manifestations inséparables d'une même puissance orageuse'] (*Corr.*, II, 426). Later, when she is awarded the Archon-Desperouses prize, but must share it with two other writers, Proust's letter seems to lose control completely and ends by comparing her to Jesus Christ, 'crowned between two thieves' (*Corr.*, III, 53).

The entrapment of letters is that of all friendships in the over-gracious Proustian mode. Once excessive politeness has been articulated in an encounter or a letter, one must meet the same level of ceremony in the language of subsequent exchange. Kafka experienced the same phenomenon: the letter – and especially a sequence of letters – created its own fictional characters, that is, an imagined addressee and a constructed writer. Letter-writing, he said, resembled communicating with ghosts.[19] This entrapment and this fictionalization of one's correspondent go a long way to explain the rigid similarity of Proust's letters to correspondents such as Anna de Noailles and Montesquiou. In another letter to her, where he sends along his congratulations on the publication of *Les Vivants et les morts* (*Corr.*, XII, 214), we find Proust caught in a strait-jacket of ascending hyperbole, for he compares the progression in her various poetic collections to ... the development of Wagner's operas. No wonder the embarrassed woman labelled Proust's letters to her 'horrifying'.[20]

Overloaded as it is with exaggerated praise, the Proustian letter must make room within itself for a counterdiscourse. If the letter form forces me to use the Other's language, I must somehow make a place within it for my own words. This is the linguistic manifestation of the dynamic of attraction and repulsion we have seen at work in Proust's social relationships. Proust's 1907 review of Mme de Noailles' collection *Les Eblouissements* (*CSB*, 533–45) appears to maintain his standard adulatory fervour, with comparisons to Voltaire and Chateaubriand and a section picturing her as the living stem of the Saint-Simon family. But the article begins with a quotation from Sainte-Beuve (not one of Proust's favourite critics) who is speaking to the Goncourt brothers about the genius of Voltaire (not one of Proust's favourite writers). Mme de Noailles is said to have earned her title as genius just as much as Voltaire did. The lameness of the remark, and the devalued voice that utters it, undermine the article by framing it in what one takes to be unconscious irony. One sees precisely this same pattern of flattery equipped with its own counter-discourse in some of the prefaces Proust was persuaded to write for literary friends, writers in whose genius he may not have had full confidence. There is the oddly combative introduction to 'Propos de peintre' by Jacques-Emile Blanche (where Sainte-Beuve is again invoked and Blanche's essays on artists are equated to '*les causeries du lundi* of painting'), and the tangential foreword to Paul Morand's *Tendres Stocks*, in which the last lines hint at the inadequacy of Morand's images and allude to Charles Péguy, a poet Proust warmly disliked. Proust's critique of *Les Eblouissements* recoups, if in particularly gentle style, the tribute that his normal effusiveness demands in return.

Proust's correspondence with the haughty and easily irritated Robert de Montesquiou is almost, in itself, a novel by letters.[21] One of the early chapters was written during the first year of their acquaintanceship, when Proust received Montesquiou's collection of poems, *Les Chauves-souris* (1893). The text sets the hyperbolic tone which subsequent letters had to match:

For a long time now I have been aware that you are far more than the typical exquisite decadent according to whose features (never as perfect as your own, but still rather ordinary in these times) you are described. You alone, in these days without thought and without will, that is, at bottom, without genius, excel by the dual power of your meditation and your energy. And I believe that this is quite unheard of, this supreme refinement with this energy and this creative force of ages past, this intellectuality which is almost of the seventeenth century, so little has there been since then. (I believe, in fact, that for Baudelaire and yourself, one could show how you belong – and this is not to flirt with a paradox – to the seventeenth century. The taste for maxims, the habit – now lost – of thinking in verse...) And I believe that this is what has kept so pure, in you, that generosity which is now so rare – which has enabled the most subtle of artists to write the most forcefully thought-out of verse, verse which would take its place in a very thin anthology of philosophical poetry in France – which has made of the Sovereign of things transitory the Sovereign of things eternal – and which prevents us from predicting how the rest of your work will continue, as in all situations where there are spontaneous outpourings, springs, true spiritual life, that is, freedom.

[Il y a longtemps que je me suis aperçu que vous débordiez largement le type du décadent exquis sous les traits (jamais aussi parfaits que les vôtres, mais assez ordinaires pourtant à ces époques) duquel on vous peint. Seul de ces temps sans pensée et sans volonté, c'est-à-dire au fond sans génie, vous excellez par la double puissance de votre méditation et de votre énergie. Et je pense que jamais cela ne s'était rencontré, ce suprême raffinement avec cette énergie et cette force créatrice des vieux âges, et cette intellectualité du dix-septième siècle presque, tant il y en a eu peu depuis. (Je crois, du reste, que pour Baudelaire et pour vous, on pourrait montrer comme vous tenez – et pas pour s'amuser à un paradoxe – du dix-septième siècle. Le goût des maximes, l'habitude – perdue – de penser en vers...) Et je crois que c'est ce qui a gardé si pure chez vous cette générosité si rare maintenant – et qui aura permis au plus subtil des artistes d'écrire aussi les vers les plus fortement pensés et qui resteraient dans une bien mince anthologie de la poésie philosophique en France – qui a fait du Souverain des choses transitoires le Souverain des choses éternelles – et qui enfin nous empêche de prévoir ce que sera la suite de votre œuvre comme partout où il y a jaillissement spontané, source, vie spirituelle véritable, c'est-à-dire liberté.] (*Corr.*, I, 220–1)

Over time, Proust's letters to the irascible count introduce a note of balance. Proust pays him the following compliment on the publication of his *Têtes couronnées*: 'with you the vein is never exhausted, nor the talent for metamorphosis ever limited' ['avec vous la veine n'est jamais tarie, ni l'aptitude à la métamorphose jamais limitée'] (*Corr.*, XV, 176). It is certainly possible to read the first phrase as suggesting that Montesquiou continually recycles the same material, and also that it is impossible to shut him up, while the second might be read as a comment on Montesquiou's fickleness and unpredictability, rather than on his versatile creative nature.

Proust's language seems least forced when he attempts to console. Be it an acquaintance who has lost a loved one,[22] or an André Gide who has emotional hurts and doubts about the qualities of *Les Caves du Vatican* (*Corr.*, XIII, 118–20; 138–40), Proust's ability to write from the Other's emotional position is impressive. But compensation will be exacted. When Proust thanks Gide for a copy of a new edition of *Les Nourritures terrestres*, his letter contains a not-so-kind pastiche of Gide's style and an ambivalent reference to a writer who can suffer, like Gide, from artificiality of tone, Paul Claudel (*Corr.*, XVI, 239).

Montesquiou chose, in public at least,[23] to be mollified by the lavish praise he often received, and his explanation of it was not without insight. In his memoirs he would describe Proust as 'in no way servile, simply a seductive charmer',[24] although this comment misses the compulsiveness of Proust's behaviour. Gide did not miss it. The great diviner of sincerity, whose journals show his irritation that Proust refused to write about homosexuality in the first person,

was appalled by Proust's toadying letters, sensing a manic element in
their desire to please:

I see in his shameless flattery less hypocrisy than a maniacal need to serve
up to each person whatever he might find most pleasant, without the
slightest concern for truth, only opportunism; above all, it is a desire to
delight and to encourage the self-abandonment of the person he is trying to
melt.[25]

When it cajoles, Proust's correspondence does in fact often show a
loss of control, and the expression 'hysteric flattery' does not seem
far off the mark. Flattery has its own irresistible internal dynamic, as
a text from *Jean Santeuil* (*JS*, 488) shows. We verbalize our praise of
an author's work so persuasively, even when we are unmoved by it or
have not even read it, that the author is deeply touched; the approval
our own praise reaps is a powerful incitation to provide more. Out of
itself the text builds a mimed image of what the Other might see as
most perfect in himself. Much of Proust's 'worst' correspondence is
that most typical of his psychological stance *vis-à-vis* others: in his
attraction to the other personality, his language attempts to become
them. From here there is but a small step to self-elimination.

   Some of Proust's observations about good manners show him
casting about for a positive explanation of an innate tendency to
flatter. The Narrator feels a certain affinity for the ingrained, though
mannered amiability of the *grand seigneur*:

Even with certain personages of the court of Louis XIV, when we find signs
of courtesy in letters written by them to some man of inferior rank who
could be of no service to them whatever, these letters leave us astonished
because they reveal to us suddenly in these great noblemen a whole world
of beliefs which they never directly express but which govern their conduct,
and in particular the belief that they are bound in politeness to feign
certain sentiments and to exercise with the most scrupulous care certain
obligations of civility. (III, 482)

[Même chez tels personnages de la cour de Louis XIV, quand nous
trouvons des marques de courtoisie dans des lettres écrites par eux à
quelque homme de rang inférieur et qui ne peut leur être utile à rien, elles
nous laissent surpris parce qu'elles nous révèlent tout à coup chez ces
grands seigneurs tout un monde de croyances qu'ils n'expriment jamais
directement mais qui les gouvernent, et en particulier la croyance qu'il faut
par politesse feindre certains sentiments et exercer avec le plus grand
scrupule certaines fonctions d'amabilité.] (II, 710)

A letter to Louis Martin-Chauffier reinforces this self-congratulatory
view that social communication must leave room for some courteous

blurring of the facts, as long as one's art remains scrupulously honest. 'When one is being polite, one cannot be too ceremonious', says Proust, 'but one always shows too much ceremony if it appears in one's descriptive writing' ['On n'est jamais assez cérémonieux dans la politesse. On l'est toujours quand on décrit'] (*Corr.*, XX, 97).

Closeness is ransomed by distance in almost all the major epistolary exchanges in Proust's life, including especially the later ones, with correspondents as different as Proust's financial adviser Lionel Hauser and his editor Jacques Rivière.

Let us return to Mme d'Arpajon's benighted comment about Flaubert and to Proust's article on Flaubert's style. In his energetic and not totally convincing dismissal of Flaubert's letters as second-rate, Proust insists that inspired writing can result from only one writing posture: '[the writer] has to model himself on a tyrannical reality in which he is not permitted to change anything whatsoever' (*ASB*, 267) ['il doit se modeler sur une réalité tyrannique à laquelle il ne lui est pas permis de changer quoi que ce soit'] (*CSB*, 592). Fiction involves mimetism just as a letter does; thus the letter *does* compete with fiction to express the self. As impossibly ornate and servile as they may seem, at a closer glance one recognizes Proust's letters as mimetic exercises in which he feels under the tyrannical domination of an object external to the self. But that object speaks, has its own language, appears to dictate the discourse that will be allowed with it, even though that discourse is mostly the letter-writer's creation. No longer do we obey an inner ideal; we obey an external thing, a construct partly of our own making whose impurity is absurdly evident. The letter is thus the consummate vehicle for the writer's alienation. When that writer's object becomes an impression he wishes to translate into literature, it is not the profusion of his language that changes. The incredible effusiveness and creativity of Proust's literary style, the ornate images and comparisons, the scientific often juxtaposed unexpectedly with the rollickingly funny, these are the signs of the same giddy linguistic involvement in the object (but the object now domesticated and 'tranquillized' within the self) that we see across his writing production.

The pattern of acceptance and disavowal, of admiration and aggressiveness in Proust's letters, has as its parallel within *A la recherche* a dynamic of proximity and distance, compassion and cruelty, with regard to individuals to whom the Narrator is attached: the taste for blasphemy of Mlle Vinteuil's female friend is redeemed by her later patient devotion to the musician's memory; the Narrator's admiration for Swann is paired with the ignorant, hurtful treatment Swann receives when he announces his impending death to the duc and duchesse de Guermantes; sadistic descriptions of Charlus's drag-queen walk and voice are set against the Narrator's appreciation of his talent and sensibility; and a mixture of grief and extravagant comedy is attached to the episode of the grandmother's death. As if to underline the crossover of emotional patterns from correspondence to fiction, that death had already been inscribed in a letter to a correspondent who needed a taste of reality to counterbalance the flattery she almost always received. Anna de Noailles mentions a lost letter from Proust in which he described his mother's death agony so vividly, and so clinically, that she was angered. But she admired him for his ability – an ability that both the letter and his subsequent fiction reveal as part of a basic writing stance – to look unswervingly at events even in the midst of great emotion.[26]

That letter to Mme de Noailles is far from unique. It represents a dual tendency in Proust's writing, a tendency which asserts itself ever more forcefully after the publication of the first volume of *A la recherche*. Not only are many of Proust's letters transposed, or absorbed, into his fiction, but the letter can also be the initial point of inscription of important episodes that appear in *A la recherche*, as though personal correspondence were not the devalued and impersonal genre Proust paints it to be, but an important staging area, or an *avant*-textual waystop, in the process by which fictional writing evolves. The fact that material from letters has been transferred wholesale into Proust's fiction has raised critical eyebrows, and the thought that important text from the novel *began* its life within a letter has been even more disturbing for some.

Already at the time of *Jean Santeuil*, Proust was borrowing language from correspondence to reinforce the emotional symbolism of an important fictional episode. After a bitter dispute with his parents, Jean deliberately shatters a piece of Venetian glass. In a letter to her son, Jeanne Proust forgave him for a similar outburst, saying, 'The broken glass will be simply what it is in the temple, the symbol of indissoluble union' ['Le verre cassé ne sera plus que ce qu'il est au temple, le symbole de l'indissoluble union.'] This sentence appears in *Jean Santeuil* as 'Ce sera comme au temple le symbole de l'indestructible union' (*JS*, 423).[27] Many such loans have been identified in *A la recherche*. Insults which Proust directed to

Albert Nahmias in a letter show up in Swann's mouth as he criticizes Odette for refusing to go alone to the theatre (I, 349–50; I, 285–6)[28] and certain phrases in a Nahmias letter to Proust may have been inserted in a letter from Albertine to the Narrator.[29] A description of Paris from a 1914 letter to Louis d'Albuféra is used in *Le Temps retrouvé* (VI, 137; IV, 380, and *Corr.*, XIV, 71).[30] The head and face of the ageing duc de Guermantes are described in terms that recall a passage depicting the comte d'Haussonville in a letter to Mme Strauss (VI, 410–11; IV, 594, and *Corr.*, XIX, 257). The Narrator reproduces a letter drafted by a footman working for Françoise. The misspelling and trite literary references are partly inspired by correspondence between Robert Ulrich, a nephew of the Proust family cook, and his mistress (III, 655–6; II, 854–5). There is, as well, the celebrated letter of 30 May 1914 to Alfred Agostinelli (*Corr.*, XIII, 217–21), never received by its addressee because he died the same day. Fragments from it are used in a letter the Narrator sends to Albertine (V, 520–1; IV, 39, and n. 1), and fragments of a conversation between Agostinelli and Proust are spoken by Albertine and the Narrator (V, 534–5; IV, 50–1). It is good speculation that Proust may have made a number of Agostinelli's letters Albertine's letters to the Narrator.[31]

In one letter, to Mrs John Work Garrett (*Corr.*, XVIII, 181–3), Proust describes very openly to his correspondent how he will use certain of her gestures and her voice in a portrait of the princesse de Luxembourg. Elyane Dezon-Jones sees this kind of rotation of text outward from fiction into correspondence and then back into the manuscript or novel as a testing device: Proust tries out his drafts on various readers before transforming them into the definitive text.[32] It is as if letters, like private notes on the manuscripts that were never intended to be seen by a literary audience, can become an offshoot of the work, a proving ground for new ideas or, if they are not included in the final text, a version of what Gerald Prince has called the unnarrated or denarrated.

What does the process of using real letters in fiction suggest about the sanctity of the creative work, composed as its author supposedly focuses on an interior reality? How does this practice square with Proust's horror (evident in the passage below) at the way Balzac's real life and personal correspondence invaded his fictional world?

There is no need to distinguish between his correspondence and his novels ... There was no dividing-line between real life (the one which is not so, in my opinion) and the life of his novels (which is alone real for a writer). In his letters to his sister ... not only is the whole thing constructed like a novel, but all the characters are set out, analysed, deduced, just as in [his] books. (*ASB*, 59)

[Il n'y a pas ... à séparer sa correspondance de ses romans ... Il n'y avait pas de démarcation entre la vie réelle (celle qui ne l'est pas à notre avis) et la vie de ses romans (la seule vraie pour l'écrivain). Dans ses lettres à sa sœur ..., non seulement tout est construit comme un roman, mais tous les caractères sont posés, analysés, déduits, comme dans ses livres.] (*CSB*, 266)

We must not forget that Proust's ideology regarding genre distinctions lives side-by-side, and comfortably, with a less well articulated writing practice at the heart of which are iteration and recursiveness. That is, all of Proust's major ideas and essential scenes are recurrences. That an idea be written about more than once seems essential for its inclusion in the Proustian text, and this means that self-quotation (to be discussed at greater length in chapter 4) takes precedence over concerns about the context from which text is being quoted. There is a 'glissement' in Proust, a slipping backwards and forwards between written reflections about the novel, its developing text, and the perpetual state of change and exchange in which his manuscripts evolved. As his life and work progressed, especially as they telescoped into the single task of completing and publishing the successive parts of *A la recherche*, his work and his speculations about it seem to become one, with the result that in practice, if not in theory, the notion of Proustian 'text' takes on great elasticity.

Jean-Louis Baudry believes that many important Proustian themes were first inscribed in letters, though an important example he cites, that of a mother's suffering at the knowledge of her child's sin, seems to appear in fiction (in 'La Confession d'une jeune fille') before it resurfaces in a number of letters written after the death of Jeanne Proust.[33] And Alain Buisine contends that Proust's habit of corresponding with his own mother, even while they were in the same house, establishes, literally, the tone of his novel. *A la recherche* is the interminable nocturnal monologue to the mother, a huge 'post-scriptum' to Marcel's correspondence with Jeanne Proust.[34] A more pertinent observation, I believe, is Baudry's remark that Proust's 'writing position' dictated the form and content of his work: if he wrote a long monologue-confession, it was because he composed prone, in the early hours of the morning, and from the equivalent of the psychiatrist's couch. It is a position of revelation by association of ideas, of proximity to dream and fantasy, of borderline rationality, a fence-rail between the real and the imagined.

Perhaps the most important gift of Proust's correspondence is the re-creation of his 'voice'. One cannot recover the actual tone or delivery – he was never recorded – but some of the profusion of sentiment and language that sparkles in his prose and marked his social interchange with many who knew him remains in Proust's letters. Mme de Noailles used a musical metaphor to characterize this movement towards hyperbole, speaking of 'the shifting upwards of tone, the transposition of the middle range into a high, heavenly song, which was his natural vocalization'.[35] Does floridness of social/epistolary voice simply equate with profusion of literary style? Fernand Gregh was one of those who thought so:

Proust sometimes exaggerated this grace in simpering ways that were always witty, just as he exaggerated his civility in flattery that was always intelligent ... People have tried to explain the length of his sentences, and the explanation is very simple: they are incomparable Proustifications. We write with our character just as much as we do with our mind.[36]

The Proust who spoke of the complex oral origins of Bergotte's style – the secret, contradictory correspondences between vocal and prose tone – would have dismissed this remark. In the last part of this study, I will return to the relationship between the social and the creative voice, and discuss the practices and strategies which allow Proust to engage all his several voices in fiction itself.

JOURNALISM

In Proust, the word journalism inevitably invokes the name of Sainte-Beuve, but there is another reason for the negative overtones attached to it. Much of Proust's production in the 1890–1907 period was destined for newspapers.[37] In the post-World War I period, as the project of re-editing his pastiches and some of his more important essays came to fruition, he speaks with equanimity of the link between his articles and the rest of his work.[38] In 1913, however, as *A la recherche* is being launched and success is far from sure, Proust asserts that, strictly speaking, he has never published a newspaper article (*Corr.*, XIII, 175). In the same year, in the famous Elie-Joseph Bois interview that appeared in the newspaper *Le Temps*, he again contradicts himself, recalling with gratitude that it was Gaston Calmette of *Le Figaro* who published his first article.

As a working journalist Proust contended that the journalistic activity represents an attitude towards writing that involves a much more focused attention to audience than does literature. A French journalist of our own time sees a similar distinction:

To write articles, whether they be good or bad, you have to live with your antennas directed to the outside. To write a book you must, on the contrary, direct them to the inside. These are two very different psychological attitudes ... I can only practise them alternatively.[39]

Proust actually wrote true society columns, where like some latter-day journalist version of Saint-Simon, he would rhyme off graciously the names and get-up of the prominent, titled and wealthy with whom he attended a myriad of high-society events. One of his earliest ventures is an article that appeared in *Le Gaulois* of 31 May 1894, titled 'Une Fête littéraire à Versailles', in which he reviews a party given by Robert de Montesquiou. The Bibliothèque Nationale has an invitation to this affair, included with the manuscripts of Proust's letters to Pierre Lavallée, on the back of which Proust noted the names and dress details of the most prominent ladies.[40] The piece is done by a professional; it is gracious, chatty and astute in recording the presence of a great many noblewomen, such as comtesse Greffuhle, who will lend parts of their persona to characters in *A la recherche*.

Between 1901 and May 1905, Proust wrote six elaborate social columns describing some of the literary and aristocratic salons that he frequented, those of the comtesse Aimery de La Rochefoucauld, the princesse Mathilde (Napoleon's niece), Madeleine Lemaire, the princesse de Polignac, the comtesse d'Haussonville, and the comtesse Potocka.[41] It is upon such worldly chronicles that Proust may retrospectively have looked with most distaste, for by their nature they concentrate on surface elegances, flatter, cajole, send coded messages to an in-crowd, and frequently refer back to their author in self-congratulatory style. And yet, the same borrowing characterizes the social columns as the letters: many visual snapshots and humorous exchanges are appropriated from the latter for later use in *A la recherche*, as well as a few much more extensive scenes.[42] Proust was actively exercising his talents as a social chronicler at the same time as he was elaborating a much more 'important' text, the preface to *Sésame et les lys* (published in 1906), where in a few pages he sketches his theory of creative reading, delineates his quarrel with Sainte-Beuve, and serves up an early version of what will be his Narrator's childhood in Combray. In fact, Proust's relations with *Le Figaro* and its literary supplement were almost as regular, particularly in the five years that preceded *Contre Sainte-Beuve,* as were Sainte-Beuve's with *Le Constitutionnel.*[43]

Journalism is a key representative of unauthentic writing in *A la recherche,* but its weaknesses are not confronted head-on in the novel. It has a special, more submerged and integrated role to play, in large part because the fictional developments in *Contre Sainte-Beuve* over-took and quickly overshadowed Proust's attack on Sainte-Beuve's journalistic approach to writing. The central episode in *A la recherche* that reflects on journalism is the publication in *Le Figaro* (V, 649–54; IV, 147–52) of an article which the Narrator has submitted some time ago. He seems almost to have forgotten its existence when the newspaper arrives with the mail. To some, it may seem surprising that Proust's Narrator should make his literary debut via an article in a newspaper, given the high literary ideals to which he aspires. Yet the appearance of the article in *Le Figaro* was part of Proust's earliest plan for the opening of *Contre Sainte-Beuve.* This event was to serve as the 'entrée en matière' for the conversation with his mother about Sainte-Beuve. Several manuscript variants of the article episode, first reproduced by Bernard Brun,[44] demonstrate this clearly.

The essay would commence with the morning mail delivery. Included with the letters that his mother places on his bed is *Le Figaro* in which he discovers his article. What followed then was to be 'the morning of the conversation with mother'. Instead of spinning out the morning conversation (although numerous traces of it do exist in the *Cahiers*), the manuscripts show the writer becoming fascinated with what morning represented for him. His hero's attention is inexorably commanded by the physical sensations of the early dawn hours, by sleeping and awakening, and by the repetitions of sleeping and awakening in his life. In a word, rather than move forward with the attack on Sainte-Beuve and then a reasoned presentation of his own aesthetic theories, Proust is drawn back-wards and inward by association of ideas and absorbed by what had at first been but a pretext: morning itself.

What strikes one at a first reading of the article episode in *A la recherche* and, to a lesser extent, the version of the episode in *Contre Sainte-Beuve,* is the sensorial apparatus set in place around it: this segment has the potential overtones of a moment of illumination like an involuntary memory. The incident is an early-morning one. It takes place in the waking hours of a dank, misty winter day in Paris against the backdrop of a rose-coloured sunrise. The experience of reading the article in *Le Figaro* is bathed in that kind of illumination of happiness and hope reminiscent of the feeling which accompanies tasting the madeleine and several other privileged moments in *A la recherche*. But the references to sunlight immediately take a trivial turn. The pink dawn arouses sexual thoughts in the Narrator – memories of the pink-cheeked milkmaid, 'la laitière aux joues roses' – and in the *Contre Sainte-Beuve* variant leads to an image of egocentric domination:

And just when the sun, having swollen and filled and brightened, has leapt above the purple of the horizon with the brief impulse of its dilation, [the author of the article] sees, at that same moment, triumphing in each mind, his thought rising like a sun to imbue it all through with its colours. (*ASB*, 18)

[Et comme le soleil s'étant gonflé, rempli, illuminé, a sauté par le petit élan de sa dilatation au-dessus de l'horizon violacé, l'auteur de l'article voit, triomphant dans chaque esprit, sa pensée, à la même heure, monter comme un soleil et le teindre tout entier de ses couleurs.] (*CSB*, 227)

The newspaper is presented as a kind of spiritual bread, warm and moist like the real bread one eats with morning coffee,[45] and it is also remindful of another pastry, familiar from Combray, that is dipped like the madeleine in one's coffee or tea: 'thousands of newspapers …, more nourishing and appetizing than the hot brioches that will be crumbled into the *café au lait*, around the still-lit lamps' (*ASB*, 18) ['des milliers de journaux …, plus nourrissants et plus savoureux que les brioches chaudes qu'on brisera, autour de la lampe encore allumée, dans le café au lait…'] (*CSB*, 227). The ingestion of the newspaper article is accompanied by a powerful sensation of pleasure and a need to get to the bottom of the impression. What follows is an exercise in decoding that duplicates the Narrator's attempts to understand other vivid impressions:

To appreciate exactly the phenomenon which was occurring at this moment in other houses, it was essential that I read this article not as its author but as one of the readers of the paper; what I was holding in my hand was not only what I had written, it was the symbol of its incarnation in so many minds. (v, 650)

[Pour apprécier exactement le phénomène qui se produit en ce moment dans les autres maisons, il faut que je lise cet article non en auteur, mais comme un des autres lecteurs du journal; ce que je tenais en main, ce n'était pas seulement ce que j'avais écrit, c'était le symbole de l'incarnation dans tant d'esprits.] (IV, 148)

And so the Narrator concentrates his intellectual forces. He attempts to clear his head of all self-importance and prejudice and to assess his article as an average reader would. He is intensely conscious, however, that the article is not simply a piece he has written. Now that it has appeared in print, its status has changed: it is an article written by him and already admired by thousands of readers.

What strikes him immediately is the vivacity of the images in his text. They seem to explode directly into his consciousness. But he understands as well that the unprepared reader will reflect differently on his ideas and that, not being their author, the reader will never experience the direct communication of the author's thought. But here too the Narrator's ego interposes itself. He reckons that there will be an admirer for each part of the article somewhere among the newspaper's readership. The parts that the literate Bloch may dislike will likely be found witty by the duc de Guermantes. The Narrator's diffidence disappears. He slips easily from one role to another, replacing reader with author as needed: if the author detects a weakness in his presentation, he can always count on the reader being thick-headed enough to miss it: 'Bah! how could a reader possibly notice that? There may well be something lacking there, but good heavens, they ought to be pleased! There are enough good things in it to be getting on with, more than they usually get' (V, 653) ['Bah! comment un lecteur peut-il s'apercevoir de cela? Il manque quelque chose là, c'est possible. Mais sapristi, s'ils ne sont pas contents! Il y en a assez de jolies choses comme cela, plus qu'ils n'en ont d'habitude'] (IV, 151). Proust would have it that the journalist's confusion with his role springs from the nature of journalism itself. Because the newspaper article is specifically designed for mass consumption, it is only complete when one takes into account the impressions it produces on the reader. Journalistic writing serves mostly the social purpose of connecting:

So did his articles seem to him like a sort of arch, the beginning of which certainly was in his own mind and his prose but whose other end plunged into the minds and admiration of his readers, where its curve was completed and received its final colouring. (*ASB*, 18)

[Et ainsi ses articles lui apparaissaient comme une sorte d'arche dont le commencement était bien dans sa pensée et dans sa prose, mais dont la fin plongeait dans l'esprit et l'admiration de ses lecteurs, où elle accomplissait sa courbe et recevait ses dernières couleurs.] (*CSB*, 227)

It is not so much that the reader determines the sense of what the author writes, eliminating the author from the text in a neat, structuralist gymnastic, but that a certain type of writing seems to seek out its audience's approval, to pander after that approval. The style and therefore the content of journalistic writing are influenced by audience expectations, and the author's personal taste and judgement are often clouded by the reader's anticipated reaction. The excessive 'prettiness' of Sainte-Beuve's style is an example:

Thus Sainte-Beuve, on a Monday, could imagine Mme de Boigne in her four-poster bed reading his article in the *Constitutionnel*, and appreciating some pretty sentence which he had taken a long delight in composing and which might never, perhaps, have flowed from his pen had he not thought it opportune to stuff it into his article in order to make a more far-reaching impression. (V, 652)

[Ainsi Sainte-Beuve, le lundi, pouvait se représenter Mme de Boigne dans son lit à hautes colonnes lisant son article du *Constitutionnel*, appréciant telle jolie phrase dans laquelle il s'était longtemps complu et qui ne serait peut-être jamais sortie de lui s'il n'avait jugé à propos d'en bourrer son feuilleton pour que le coup en portât plus loin.] (IV, 150)

The pleasure of egotism stroked is everywhere at hand in this episode, beginning at the most basic, childish and humorous level: the Narrator has a physical need to buy extra copies of *Le Figaro* so that he can experience opening and handling each new copy, and thus repeat the pleasure of encountering himself in print! The instant multiple impact of the daily newspaper is another measure of the journalist's power, and appealing to that power is the artist's downfall. At about the same time as he is working on the earliest versions of the *Figaro* article episode, Proust lifts this idea from his manuscript and sends it, unframed by any explicit irony, to Maurice Barrès whose novel *Colette Baudoche* has begun to appear in serial form: 'this publication in a journal must make you sense the impact you have made on the hearts of a thousand readers all at the very same moment' ['cette publication dans une revue doit signifier pour vous l'ébranlement communiqué par vous à une même heure dans des milliers de cœurs'].[46]

Each type of satisfaction experienced by the journalist appears chosen for its base origin. Part of his pleasure comes from the simple realization that his name will be in every household, even if his

readers do not possess the intellectual accomplishments to understand what he wrote. Condescension and vulgarity are built into his
feelings about the impact the article will have: 'I thought of some
female reader into whose room I would have loved to penetrate and
to whom the newspaper would convey, if not my thought, which she
would be incapable of understanding, at least my name, like a eulogy
of me' (V, 654) ['Je pensais à telle lectrice dans la chambre de qui
j'eusse tant aimé pénétrer et à qui le journal apporterait sinon ma
pensée, qu'elle ne pourrait comprendre, du moins mon nom, comme
une louange de moi'] (IV, 151). In fact, the article will be a socially
recognized mark of his superiority, both the symbol and the means
of his dominance of others: 'I saw at that same hour my thought, or
... an embellished evocation of my person, shine on countless
people, colour their own thoughts in an auroral light which filled me
with ... strength and triumphant joy' (V, 652) ['Je voyais à cette
même heure pour tant de gens, ma pensée ou même ... une
évocation embellie de ma personne briller sur eux, colorer leur
pensée en une aurore qui me remplissait de ... force et de joie
triomphante'] (IV, 150).

The newspaper article is so dependent on the audience for whom
it is written that it makes the Narrator/journalist want to consult
that audience on how well he did. His trip that day to refresh his
acquaintanceship with the Guermantes will become a mission to
find out what they think of his article. Journalism thus enables the
Narrator to maintain his relationships and contacts within aristocratic society; he appears almost ready, based on his newspaper
success, to put aside his search for an artistic vocation and settle for
journalism as a way to keep in touch (V, 654; IV, 152). This stance
echoes Sainte-Beuve's definition of the literary *galant homme*, quoted
earlier, lines that had sent Proust into a paroxysm of contempt at the
notion that society relations and solid friendships could play such a
significant role in the creation of art.

As we accompany the Narrator through this brush with literary
notoriety, it becomes clear that we have been walked through a
gradual exposure to the weaknesses of a journalistic approach to
serious writing. The episode of the article in *Le Figaro* is in fact a
Contre Sainte-Beuve in miniature. But what is interesting is the presentation: Proust has integrated his argument into a mini-drama. The
segment shows his remarkable gift for 'writing-through-physical-
mime', the uncanny ability to adopt the attitude of the object or

person – here the concept – he is describing, and to reproduce in words a physical impression of it. Instead of arguing out his objections to journalistic writing, the Narrator acts them out in a pantomime of the writing process. He becomes at once the vain author of an article and a would-be objective reader. In this way, we have a demonstration of Proust's view that the prime flaw of journalism is excessive participation of the reader in the writing process.

At the same time, the allusions to creative experiences such as tasting the madeleine – the sensorial references, the atmosphere of joy and discovery, the attempt to 'read' the deep meaning of the impression – take on an ironic tone because they are accompanied by crass reflections about the Narrator's social position and social successes. Although it has most of the paraphernalia of a privileged moment, the *Figaro* episode reads instead like a self-pastiche, a send-up of the creative experience and thereby an effective symbol of the nullity of the journalist's approach to writing and literature.

All the while that the Narrator contemplates journalism as a glorified type of correspondence with his social acquaintances, and a medium for staking out a certain position for himself and attracting consideration, he understands clearly that the writing process and the pleasure derived from it are not social or sociable. They have an opposite, more forceful dimension, a centripetal attraction that draws one away from others and into the self. Although the notoriety he derives from being known and read as a journalist gives him pleasure, the Narrator designates the pleasure itself as interior and spiritual. It is not produced by conversing with his friends, but by writing far away from them. The result is that even though he may initiate writing with a social intent, the satisfaction of the solitary writing process may make him wish to opt for solitude when he fully realizes that the pleasure is in literature itself.

At the end of the *Contre Sainte-Beuve* sketches of the *Figaro* episode, Proust leaves the subject of the novice writer to make a comment which underscores the overlay of the relationship between the journalist and the Narrator as social beings: 'Sainte-Beuve [believed] that the salon life which he enjoyed was indispensable to literature' (*ASB*, 19) ['Sainte-Beuve [croyait] que la vie de salon qui lui plaisait tant, était indispensable à la littérature'] (*CSB*, 228). At the time he composed *Contre Sainte-Beuve*, Proust seems to have been particularly affected by the threat of the writer's involvement in society, the temptation that writing could be viewed as, and effectively become, a society rite no more significant than the witticisms one exchanges over cocktails at a reception.

It is not only the Narrator of *A la recherche* who tries his hand at journalism. The temptation to report affects the literate and intellectual class in general. Alongside the Narrator is a motley crew of salon creatures who make the transition to journalist or social chronicler with little effort. Characteristically, these individuals simply transfer their oral skills into their columns, for journalism, notes Proust, seems to flower in wartime when cultural values recede and 'reality' becomes all-important. The stilted Norpois writes frequently about the war (VI, 113–18; IV, 361–3), and his oral clichés on international politics find their way, word for word, into his articles.[47] The pedant Brichot has a regular column in *Le Temps*, which he whips off with the same alacrity as one of his lectures (VI, 123–6; IV, 369–71). Verdurin, the author of a critical study on Whistler, has written on art for *La Revue des Deux Mondes* (or perhaps *La Revue Bleue*, the text is undecided on the question), and Morel obtains an assignment in the military press office (VI, 94–6; IV, 346–7), where he writes derogatory articles about Charlus. In a manuscript variant not included in the final text of *A la recherche*, Bergotte himself, the representative of Art for Art's sake, takes on a newspaper column during the war (IV, 785–6). Patriotism is a convenient replacement for his waning inspiration. The journalistic function is itself so clichéd, and the number of would-be writers in *A la recherche* so considerable, that Proust's text sometimes makes the characters interchangeable, confusing one individual's activities with another's.

It is in the metaphor of the Narrator's journalistic efforts that Sainte-Beuve's literary theories and practices are most effectively taken to task. The little episode of the article in *Le Figaro* is at once journalism in action, a pastiche of a Proustian epiphany, an almost submerged reflection of an article once published in reality, and a mini-*Contre Sainte-Beuve*. All of these aspects make of the article episode a richly stuffed intertext and, as such, an apt symbol of the attainments of the mature Proustian technique.

LITERARY CRITICISM

Criticism was an object of perilous attraction for Proust. Potentially, of course, it had a creative aspect. In reacting to another writer's text, a budding novelist is led naturally to articulate his own ideas about writing and to measure his own technique against another model. But in an individual so permeable to language, so impressionable and so lacking in drive, there was also the potential for arrested development, for never being more than a critic. The partly fictional introduction to *Sésame et les lys* and the hybrid mix of novel and essay that is *Contre Sainte-Beuve* demonstrate that Proust's early creative effort seems imprisoned by the juxtaposition of a critical element. The essay on aesthetics in *Le Temps retrouvé* and the frequent theoretical discussions of writing throughout *A la recherche* suggest, moreover, that without analytical, if not polemical, discussion of its own tenets, Proust's fiction would have an inner sense of incompleteness.

Proust went so far as to contemplate literary criticism as a career, especially at times when success in prose fiction seemed unattainable or insufficiently lucrative. In late 1903 we find him pondering an offer from Constantin de Brancovan, Anna de Noailles' brother, to be the drama critic at *La Renaissance Latine*; the offer is withdrawn in January 1904, to Proust's great frustration (*Corr.*, IV, 35). In early 1914, after some disastrous stockmarket speculations, he proposes his writing services to Robert de Flers, then director of *Le Figaro* (*Corr.*, XIII, 195–6). In 1918, after the death of Francis Chevassu who headed *Le Figaro*'s literary supplement, Proust expressed surprise and disappointment that the job fell to Abel Hermant. He had assumed it was coming to him (*Corr.*, XVII, 239). And in 1919 he discusses with Jacques Rivière a proposal that Proust review fiction for the *Nouvelle Revue Française* (*Corr.*, XVIII, 437).

As self-assured as Proust may sound in his ridicule of Sainte-Beuve for misjudging Stendhal, Baudelaire, Balzac and others, it is clear he felt awe before the writers he admired. His critical writings, then, are a chosen locus for his struggle to find himself and to be himself, and this explains, in part, why some of his critical texts metamorphose into fictional pieces. But there is also the fact that, from three different points of view, the stance Proust naturally adopts as a critic is a replica of his creative stance. First, criticism is for him the science of sensing recurrence, and recurrence reveals personal essence. It is also, as Proust practises it, a mime of the writer under study through physical identification with him. Third, criticism, as discovery through reading, is a rehearsal for the 'reading' of the self that is the basis of creative writing about the self.

It is in his writings about Ruskin, particularly in the translation prefaces, that Proust tried his hand at criticism as a means of approaching art, and of approaching the type of communication that comes through art. His introduction to *La Bible d'Amiens* lays out some essential aspects of the critic's role. The objective is to identify the specifics of a writer's deep personality.[48] Proust's approach to Ruskin will be to alert the reader to important, recurring aspects of his thought by a carefully designed set of footnotes that highlight other instances where Ruskin treats the same or a similar idea. And this is the critic's task: to supply the reader with what he calls an instantly improvised memory:

In placing a note beneath the text of the *Bible of Amiens* each time that the text awakened through analogies, even distant ones, the memory of other works by Ruskin . . ., I have attempted to enable the reader . . . to recognize what is, in his writings, permanent and fundamental.

[En mettant une note au bas du texte de la *Bible d'Amiens*, chaque fois que ce texte éveillait par des analogies, même lointaines, le souvenir d'autres ouvrages de Ruskin . . ., j'ai tâché de permettre au lecteur. . .[de] reconnaître ce qui est, chez lui, permanent et fondamental.] (*La Bible d'Amiens*, 10)

The reason for activating a reader's memory is to provide him with a framework for interpretation. Moreover, the same laws of memory can be applied to art or to life, and if we are attentive to the periodic revelations, the deep structures, of each, we can make art of an individual's life, be it our own or that of an author read. The creative part of the Narrator's first encounter with the writings of Bergotte – before he begins to treat him as an idol, searching out his opinions on worldly issues – is the moment he deduces, from the repeated resonances of Bergotte's writing, a kind of 'essential Bergotte', the spiritual bones on which plots, stories and philosophical reflections are hung.

The network of reminiscences with which Proust footnotes both *La Bible d'Amiens* and *Sésame et les lys* resemble quasi-involuntary memories, though in a slightly different register. The critic insists that they are not just a set of rational notations. The reason they have enormous prestige is that they appear with the sudden inevitability of a spark from the unconscious:

These comparisons . . . are essentially individual. They are only a flash of the memory, a glow of one's sensibility that suddenly illuminates two different passages simultaneously. [They well up] from the deepest reaches of my self.

[Ces rapprochements...sont essentiellement individuels. Ils ne sont rien qu'un éclair de la mémoire, une lueur de la sensibilité qui éclairent brusquement ensemble deux passages différents. [Ils jaillissent] du plus profond de moi-même.] (*CSB*, 794).

Proust compares his annotation of Ruskin's text to the creation of a resonating chamber ('une caisse de résonance'), a formula that also aptly describes the structural casing that is *A la recherche*, with its multiple layers of harmonics and harmonies. With musical themes, understanding comes from the intuitive shock of recognition.

Proust does not yet draw a full parallel between criticism and personal art, however. Still, the lyricism of his style accelerates as he notes the gap between the two, and we feel that art is close at hand, like a shimmering image barely occluded by the surface of consciousness:

[The echoes of other words of Ruskin] will not be obliged, in order to join up with the present word whose resemblance has attracted them, to traverse the soft resistance of that intervening atmosphere which has the breadth of our life and which is all the poetry of memory.

[[Les échos d'autres paroles de Ruskin] n'auront pas, pour venir rejoindre la parole présente dont la ressemblance les a attirés, à traverser la résistante douceur de cette atmosphère interposée qui a l'étendue même de notre vie et qui est toute la poésie de la mémoire.] (*La Bible d'Amiens*, 10)

The images attached to memory in this passage – attraction, movement upwards, resistance – look forward to the madeleine text in *A la recherche*. Memories from the distant past are attracted by similar experiences in the present, but a middle ground, that of our intervening life experiences, resists their passage:

I feel something start within me, something that leaves its resting-place and attempts to rise ... I can feel it mounting slowly; I can measure the resistance, I can hear the echo of great spaces traversed. (I, 53)

[je sens tressaillir en moi quelque chose qui se déplace, voudrait s'élever ... cela monte lentement; j'éprouve la résistance et j'entends la rumeur des distances traversées.] (I, 45)

Truly, we find ourselves here less at the heart of a critical approach, than at the essential argument of a handbook about creative technique. We are witnessing the analysis that a later synthesis will reconstruct. It is Proustian narration that operates on the basis of 'quotation', 'repetition', and the creation of an 'improvised (i.e., fictionalized) memory'. The Narrator of *A la recherche* will 'quote' himself endlessly, in the countless repetitions of life events and patterns by which he will 'recognize' permanent, fundamental aspects of his own deep personality. And the writer/Narrator will equip *A la recherche* with an endless set of critical notes – the constant quotations from, and allusions and references to, other writers – in order to create a resonating chamber which demonstrates the resonance of his own ideas within the outside world of artists, writers and musicians.

A second important aspect of Proust's literary criticism is its physicality. His criticism often seems to begin with the gesture of physically measuring himself against the other writer. We saw in chapter 1 how Proust slips into Flaubert's body while reading his *Lettres à Caroline*, revisiting Concarneau with him, awaiting the same book delivery, sharing his desire of a beautiful ending for his fiction. We have seen how Proust impersonates Balzac, lustily tying into his dinner and caressing his women. Surprisingly, Proust even identifies with Sainte-Beuve; both are trapped in the role of journalist and critic while harbouring a deep need to devote themselves to their poetry and fiction.

Of course, the basis for this superposition of critic upon the artist, of this criticism by identification,[49] is a recognition of certain resemblances, often a feeling of shared ideas and ideals. These earlier versions of the self are viewed as precursors and can be subject, as Harold Bloom has said, to a set of manipulations, one of the most complicated of which he calls apophrades (the Return of the Dead), which he defines as

the triumph of having so stationed the precursor, in one's own work, that particular passages in his work seem to be not presages of one's own advent, but rather to be indebted to one's own achievement, and even (necessarily) to be lessened by one's greater splendour.[50]

Before a writer like Proust develops the assurance to speak from his own voice, he begins by finding strength and support in the convergence of his own ideas with those of mentor artists. In describing Schopenhauer's habit of quoting at great length from other authors in support of his arguments, Proust claims that these references are not at all indications that Schopenhauer was inspired by others, they simply confirm the philosopher in his own thought. Proust makes another claim which seems especially strange: Schopenhauer's citations have an *unconscious* relationship to his own argument: 'one has the feeling that for [Schopenhauer] the texts he cites are merely examples, unconscious or anticipatory allusions in which he likes to discover a few features of his own thought' (*ASB*, 217) ['On sent que les textes cités ne sont pour lui que des exemples, des allusions inconscientes et anticipées où il aime à retrouver quelques traits de sa propre pensée'] (*CSB*, 185).

In these individuals, whom one might call mimetic writer–critics, there is identification with actual text, and it is interesting to note that Baudelaire, with whom Proust felt deep affinities of sensibility, also experienced discovering his own lines in the writings of a precursor. He defended Manet for having pastiched Goya and El Greco, and redefined the pastiche in an explanation of his own relationship with Edgar Allan Poe:

people accuse *me* of imitating Edgar Poe! Do you know why I translated Poe so patiently? Because he resembled me. The first time I opened a book about him, I saw, with horror and delight, not only subjects about which I had dreamed, but SENTENCES imagined by myself and written by him twenty years earlier.[51]

Proust is subject to the same effect in reading Senancour. Whole lines from the text appear lifted from his own works: 'a sentence that could have been written by me: «But at least I will be attuned to certain accidents of light and several affinities of plants»' ['une phrase tout à fait de moi: «Mais du moins nous serons sensibles à q.q. accidents de lumière et de plusieurs convenances végétales»' (*CSB*, 568). It is natural that intensely mimetic writers insist, at some point, on distancing themselves from their precursor figures. Proust immediately observes how his own thinking differs from the ideas of Senancour that he cites. But Proust may represent a special case in denial, for he goes so far as to say that *no one ever influenced him*, with the exception of his philosophy teacher Darlu (*Le Carnet de 1908*, 101).

Proust's practice of literary criticism as a physical identification with certain preferred writers who appear to quote ideas he will later develop has important consequences for the structuring of *A la recherche*. The novel appears to ingest and redeploy what Proust the critic discovers: Balzac's retrospective discovery of the unity of his work, Wagner's leitmotive, Baudelaire's sense-based reminiscences, Nerval's involuntary memory in 'Sylvie'. A pair of remarks on the structure of Ruskin's work, which Proust included in the original notes to his translation of *Sésame et les lys*, demonstrate how close the critical function could bring him to the launching of creative ideas. In the first note to the translated text of *Sesame and Lilies*, a note that is two pages long, Proust comments on the themes in Ruskin's work. His observations so strongly foreshadow the thematic structuring of *A la recherche* that we instantly recognize a moment of important self-discovery.[52] The attraction of Ruskin's works is the writer's after-the-fact discovery of links and resonances between them:

there are, between the ideas in the same book, and between his various books, links which he does not reveal, which he causes to appear barely for a moment, and which he may in fact have woven in after the fact.

[il y [a] entre les idées d'un même livre, et entre les divers livres des liens qu'il ne montre pas, qu'il laisse à peine apparaître un instant et qu'il a d'ailleurs peut-être tissés après-coup.] (*Sésame et les lys*, 61, note 1)

Proust also reflects on the seven-theme conclusion to Ruskin's lecture on reading, a gathering of ties that imposes retrospective order and meaning on the work. As readers, we are bound to hear the Vinteuil septet in the wings, reflect on the obvious drawing together of major themes in *Le Temps retrouvé*, and anticipate its theoretical revelations:

I see, in the note placed at the end of the lecture, that I believe I have noted as many as seven themes in the final sentence. In point of fact, here Ruskin is arranging one beside the other, mixing together, manœuvring, and dazzling us with all the principal ideas – or images – which have appeared in non-ordered fashion throughout his lecture ... The caprice that leads him on follows his own deep affinities which impose on him, in spite of himself, a superior logic. The result is that, at the end, he finds that he has obeyed a kind of secret plan which, unveiled at the end, imposes a sort of retrospective order on the whole and makes it appear to rise in magnificent stages to the final apotheosis.

[Je vois que, dans la note placée à la fin de la conférence, j'ai cru pouvoir noter jusqu'à 7 thèmes dans la dernière phrase. En réalité Ruskin y range l'une à côté de l'autre, mêle, fait manœuvrer et resplendir ensemble toutes les principales idées – ou images – qui ont apparu avec quelque désordre au long de sa conférence... [L]a fantaisie qui le mène suit ses affinités profondes qui lui imposent malgré lui une logique supérieure. Si bien qu'à la fin il se trouve avoir obéi à une sorte de plan secret qui, dévoilé à la fin, impose rétrospectivement à l'ensemble une sorte d'ordre et le fait apercevoir magnifiquement étagé jusqu'à cette apothéose finale.] (*Sésame et les lys*, 62-3)

The plan, which becomes explicit only at the end, imposing order retrospectively, and his notion of ending as apotheosis, these are techniques that are put to work both in *Contre Sainte-Beuve* and in *A la recherche du temps perdu*.

One of Proust's comments on Flaubert is equally revelatory of the intimate relationship between criticism and creativity. He is deeply intrigued by Flaubert's transfer of action away from characters into the physical components of the environment, by his passivization, as it were, of narrative. The quasi-stasis that marks the overture of *A la recherche*, the presentation of a main character who is a passive conscience more than an actor, and the absence of direction in the Narrator's life recall Proust's own verdict on Flaubert's masterpiece: '*L'Education sentimentale* is a long account of an entire life, without the characters taking any active part so to speak in the action' (*ASB*, 265) ['*L'Education sentimentale* est un long rapport de toute une vie, sans que les personnages prennent pour ainsi dire une part active à l'action'] (*CSB*, 590). Reflections about Flaubert's novel clearly played some role in the weakening of event-based narrative that characterizes Proust's fiction.

Much has been written about Proust's ideas on reading, and especially about the paradigm that is developed in detail in *Le Temps retrouvé*: reading as a model for extracting the material of art from one's own life.[53] But reading sets the stage for creativity in another way. If social relationships produce a kind of hysteria of de-centredness in Proust – the 'agitations of friendship' (*ASB*, 219; *CSB*, 186) – reading restores a sense of protectedness and wholeness that is healing. There is a true hallucinatory quality about some of Proust's comments on reading in his preface to *Sésame et les lys*:

the pure and peaceful form of [friendship] that is reading ... The atmosphere of this pure form of friendship is silence, which is purer than speech ... So silence ... is pure, it is genuinely an atmosphere ... The very language of the book is pure ..., this tranquil mirror. (*ASB*, 219)

[cette amitié pure et calme qu'est la lecture ... L'atmosphère de cette pure amitié est le silence, plus pur que la parole ... Aussi le silence ... est pur, il est vraiment une atmosphère ... Le langage même du livre est pur ..., ce calme miroir.] (*CSB*, 186–7)

The language of these pages – which are not a casual sketch but an important preface revised for a second publication – is obsessional. What has been 'purified' out of the written word is the physical existence of the Other. The outlines of the author's thought remain, the flavour of his personality, and with these communication is possible. But his presence is of another order. The space is freed and the Proustian personality can occupy it. And there is no talk.

'Silence, contact with oneself', says Proust in a notebook (*Le Carnet de 1908*, 71).

This is the important aspect of communicating with a written text: rather than imposing its existence on us, it allows us to expand and grow, to strengthen our own personality by co-opting and absorbing elements of the Other. And no doubt Proust's sensation of fusion with the Other's ideas explains why some of those ideas become attached, in the form of quotations and allusions, to the Proustian text:

When we read, we receive another individual's thought, and yet we are alone, our thoughts actively at work, aspiring, *in full personal activity*: we receive another person's ideas in spirit, that is, in truth, and one can thus link up with them, we are that other person and yet *we are simply developing our self* with more variety than if we were reflecting on our own, *we are urged along our own paths by another person.*

[Quand on lit, on reçoit une autre pensée, et cependant on est seul, on est en plein travail de pensée, en pleine aspiration, *en pleine activité personnelle*: on reçoit les idées d'un autre, en esprit, c'est-à-dire en vérité, on peut donc s'unir à elles, on est cet autre et pourtant *on ne fait que développer son moi* avec plus de variété que si on pensait seul, *on est poussé par autrui sur ses propres voies.*] (*Sésame et les lys*, 70, n. 1; the emphasis is mine.)

There is a rawness in these lines, a hunger to empower the self by absorbing the Other. Proust's choice of the term 'aspiration', which suggests inhalation as well as desire, is revealing. The spoken words of the Other have the opposite effect: they smother Proust. Even in a more polished version of the same thought (*ASB*, 208; *CSB*, 174), the text retains references to the social power dynamic which haunts passive personalities, but which reading can reverse.

The critic Marie Miguet has provided a neat description of the way criticism can be linked to the creative function. 'Critique/autocritique/autofiction' is the phrase she uses,[54] as though the detection of essential themes in a writer we have under close observation necessarily brings to the surface our own personal thematic framework, and provides the material to establish a personal fiction. Swann and Verdurin are authors, or near-authors, of critical studies on painters they admired. In this, they are incarnations of a creative potential that was never realized. But Proust's literary criticism, as Proust actually practised it, led him to a position of identification/emulation where the most nourishing creative ideas of the writer under study could be absorbed as one's own. In the end, Proust did not need to reject criticism, as he had letter-writing and journalism, because it showed him the way from preoccupation with the Other back into the self.

THE PASTICHE: 'NOTRE VOIX INTÉRIEURE'

Mimicry is Proust's native mode of reacting to the personality of the Other. A social conversation, a letter, are opportunities to say what an interlocutor wants to hear, in the way the latter would want to hear it. Not only is Proust attuned to style, tone and emphasis in the language of others, his own stylistic obsessions are well known to himself, and he is perfectly capable of self-pastiche. Corresponding with his financial advisor Lionel Hauser, he concocts a full-blown parody of his own syntax, a sentence complete with four parentheses and a self-mocking, climactical 'chute' wherein he regrets, vapidly, that he did not catch his friend at home on a recent visit:

Just a line (though I've wanted to speak to you for some time about many other things) to tell you (I have no doubt, in fact, that your concierge communicated the message) that about two weeks ago (I believe it was two weeks ago Thursday or Saturday), I took advantage of being able to get up (which happens to me about every three years) in the late afternoon, feeling that it would be my great pleasure and my most urgent duty, to drop in on you and say hello.

[Une seule ligne (j'aurais pourtant à te parler depuis longtemps de bien d'autres choses) pour te dire (je ne doute pas du reste que ta concierge ne se soit acquitté[e] du message) qu'il y a environ une quinzaine de jours (je crois il y a eu jeudi ou samedi quinze jours) ayant pu me lever (ce qui m'arrive à peu près une fois tous les trois ans) à la fin de l'après-midi, j'en ai profité, trouvant que ce serait mon plaisir [le] plus grand et mon devoir le plus impérieux, pour aller te serrer la main.] (*Corr.*, XVIII, 88)

The exuberance of this language is part of what Sheila Stern sees as the conversational effusiveness of Proust's lavish metaphorical passages, and his habit of the 'conceit', with its oral origin.[55]

Proust authored scores of written pastiches. Many of them are in his letters, rapid sketches composed for the amusement of correspondents like Reynaldo Hahn. Sometimes a pastiche formed part of a book dedication (the Goncourt pastiche in an album Proust offered to the wife of his friend Georges de Lauris[56]). But the pastiche is an integral part of his earliest literary efforts, beginning with stories published in *Le Banquet* and sections of *Les Plaisirs et les jours* such as 'Mondanité et mélomanie de Bouvard et Pécuchet' and the Baude-lairian 'Portraits de peintres'. Proust was well attuned to the literary market of his day, and it is likely that the very successful launching, in December 1907, of *A la manière de...*, a collection of pastiches by Paul Reboux and Charles Müller, was part of the impetus he needed to write a series of his own.[57] Basing his texts on a real-life diamond manufacturing hoax perpetrated by an engineer named Lemoine, Proust published a set of seven pastiches in *Le Figaro* in early 1908 (an eighth appeared in March 1909).

It is clear that his work on the pastiches and on the beginnings of *A la recherche*, in its *Contre Sainte-Beuve* phase, overlap.[58] References in the correspondence[59] make it clear that Proust thought of publishing critical essays on each of the pastiched authors as analytical pendants to the instinctive parodies. Indeed, from all accounts it would appear that some of the critical material in *Contre Sainte-Beuve* (sections of the essay on Balzac, for example) was intended to form part of the essays. In Proust's own mind the pastiche was a form of intuitive reflection on another writer, 'literary criticism in action' as he called it (*Corr.*, VIII, 61).

Although apparently derivative as a genre, Proust's pastiches became a quasi-creative exercise, not because of any novelty in the pastiches themselves, but because writing them made him dissect his own personal drive to mimic others and to identify the mental processes that are fundamental to any writing that tries to represent reality. André Malraux, who was equally conscious of the influence of other writers on his prose, spoke openly of the movement from pastiche to personal style.[60] In a search for voice, the pastiche represents the ultimate abandonment of self, and yet at the same time the ultimate exhibition of control, the re-creation of an author's style from the inside. To want to pastiche an author suggests an attraction to his writing and just as often a profound irritation with it. Proust spoke of being positively 'intoxicated' by Flaubert, and of the 'debauched' fun he had had with Sainte-Beuve's 'bad music'. The *pasticheur* clearly experiences a kind of domination by the other writer. Just as the Narrator talks to himself after a social event, still resonating with the voices of other guests, Proust's internal voice continues to mimic the rhythm of Balzac's or Flaubert's prose when he puts down one of their novels. The pastiche is thus a cleansing, cathartic exercise:

Above all, the whole thing was for me a question of hygiene; one must purge oneself of the natural vice of idolatry and imitation. And instead of doing deceitful versions of Michelet or Goncourt (here we might add the names of one or the other of our most amiable contemporaries), to do it openly in the form of pastiches, so as to be able to retreat and simply be Marcel Proust when I write my novels.

[Le tout était surtout pour moi affaire d'hygiène; il faut se purger du vice si naturel d'idolâtrie et d'imitation. Et au lieu de faire sournoisement du Michelet ou du Goncourt (ici les noms de tels ou tels de nos contemporains les plus aimables), d'en faire ouvertement sous forme de pastiches, pour redescendre à ne plus être que Marcel Proust quand j'écris mes romans.] (*Corr.*, XVIII, 380)

There is a measure of revenge in the pastiche, getting back at dominance by redoing the original in an act of creation that can be a negation of the original model. At times, Proust makes this attraction-idolatry-exorcism movement conscious, as when he mentions parodying the style of Théophile Gautier, an author whose stories the Narrator reveres as a child. The *pasticheur* works by accumulating the naggingly obsessive expressions of an author into a concentrated whole. In Gautier's case, Proust identifies certain archaic expressions and precious epithets as the 'beauties' that he has fused into one (*ASB*, 209, n.; *CSB*, 175 n.).

Stylistic tics are the match that lights the *pasticheur*'s fuse, and it is instructive to observe Proust identifying irritants of style in letters to two contemporaries whose writing affected him, Henri de Régnier and André Gide. A Régnier pastiche was actually published; a parody of Gide's style is provided in the letter itself. Each letter identifies a dubious stylistic device but, outright criticism of a literary lion seeming impossible, Proust's tone takes on its special blend of deference and partially veiled disapproval. Proust was much attracted to Henri de Régnier's novel *La Double Maîtresse*, published in 1899. In a letter to the author, Proust praises Régnier's style, as though having him realize that Proust understands and appreciates that style is the key to their communicating as artists. At the same time, Proust is clearly irked by aspects of Régnier's writing:

I believe I feel the beauty of this style with particular violence, what recurs and takes strength from the style of the other books and what, in it, is different from them, and certain peculiarities of syntax that I had not seen to date which are perhaps reserved by you for works that are vast in their liberty and working-class negligence, like the use of pronouns instead of repeating a noun, the use of crude, popular terms, of everyday types of expression.

[Je crois ressentir avec une violence toute particulière la beauté de ce style, ce qui s'y retrouve et s'y fortifie de celle qui était dans les autres livres et ce par où il s'en distingue, et certaines particularités de syntaxe et de manière que je ne vous connaissais pas encore et qui sont peut-être réservées par vous aux œuvres vastes, en manière de liberté et de négligence populaire, comme l'emploi des pronoms au lieu de répéter un nom, l'usage de termes grossiers et populaires, des façons courantes de dire.][61]

The criticism of Régnier's syntax here is made even more explicit in a 1909 letter to Georges de Lauris (*Corr.*, IX, 61) where Proust speaks of the writer's habit of mixing up pronouns and repeating himself.

The same attraction/irritation surfaces in a note to Gide. Proust's congratulations to Gide for having 'nourished' a generation of readers are juxtaposed with a deflected critique of his style. With apologies, Proust reports that his otherwise ignorant housekeeper, Céleste Albaret, has begun to do impersonations of Gide after reading parts of his novel out loud to her employer. She now prefaces her criticisms of Proust's lifestyle with classic Gidian apostrophes:

Nathaniel, I shall speak to you of the friends of Monsieur. There is the one who had him go out after years of interval, taxi to the Ritz, pages, tips, fatigue . . . I know the lady, etc.

[Nathanaël, je te parlerai des amies de Monsieur. Il y a celle qui l'a fait ressortir après des années, taxi vers le Ritz, chasseurs, pourboires, fatigue. . . . Je sais la dame, etc.] (*Corr.*, XVI, 239)

Every comment surrounding this mini-pastiche (including a telltale reference to the artificiality of accent in some of Claudel's free verse) suggests that it is intended to poke fun at the engorged lyricism of *Les Nourritures terrestres* and, no doubt, at its author's personal rigidity.

Proust's attentiveness to his own propensity to mime eventually led him to differentiate between instinctive style and intellectual style, to see that he parodied the manner of other writers in an instinctive reaction but that that same instinctive miming of physical impressions was the basis of his own creative writing. The ability to counterfeit another writer's prose was the ability to re-experience tone and rhythm directly and intuitively, without the benefit of any elaborate intellectual analysis. When the Narrator attempts to see further into aesthetic sensations, as with his blind attraction to the hawthorn, he has recourse to this same mimetic gift and attempts, as he says, to copy to himself the action of their efflorescence (I, 133; I,

111). The exercise is productive, for equivalents are created, a series
of metaphors is born, and the essential creative movement of writing
is brought to the surface of the Narrator's conscience.

What Proust learned from the 1908 pastiches was a lesson about
intelligence and intuition that flowered into a more developed
argument in *Contre Sainte-Beuve*, an argument which begins with the
phrase 'Daily, I attach less value to the intellect'. It is also evident,
from his editorial notes in the manuscript sketches for *Du Côté de chez
Swann*, that he consciously related his mimetic writing to the creative
process. In a passage where the Narrator is struggling to understand
the childhood happiness of a sunny day in Combray, and where he is
frustrated by his initial, inarticulate reaction (all he can utter is the
words 'zut, zut'), Proust steps into the fictional decor to make the
following observation:

In this order of ideas, even the little pastiches of mine that people have read
are but the continuation of the effort that begins on the old bridge, on the
Méséglise Way, and instead of saying, reading Renan or Flaubert, 'Gosh, is
that ever beautiful!', I attempt to relive exactly what we express in such an
inadequate and confused fashion.

[Dans cet ordre d'idées, les pastiches qu'on a lus de moi ne sont que la
continuation de l'effort qui commence sur le pont-vieux, du côté de
Méséglise, et au lieu de dire devant Renan ou Flaubert zut que c'est beau
de tâcher à revivre exactement ce que nous exprimons d'une façon si
inadéquate et confuse.] (I, 836)

Miming the gesture of the hawthorn's flowering equals reliving (that
is, internally replicating) the tone of Renan's or Flaubert's prose.
Creation begins with a stretching outward towards the object, and a
mimetic rehearsal of its movement. When we practise that movement of analogy, we can then articulate the images, or metaphors,
that reproduce the kinetic analogies we found. In a second, related
note Proust describes the pastiche as a descent beyond the surface of
language, that is, a voyage beyond words to the shapes and objects
that are the other writer's pre-conscious:

pastiche is, essentially, this same perception in literature, for whereas
someone else will say 'that's delightful' I descend beneath and make
contact with the pure theme ... whereas others speak of the beautiful
language of Renan I descend lower still, to the things that are intertwined
in the depths of his prose.

[le pastiche est au fond cette perception en littérature car là où un autre dit
c'est délicieux je descends au-dessous et je prends connaissance du thème

clair … q^d d'autres parlent de la jolie langue de Renan, je descend[s] plus bas, jusqu'aux choses qui s'enlacent au fond de sa prose.][62]

This second text reinforces an important point: the strategy of the *pasticheur*/creator is designed to delay a linguistic response both to the language of the text and to the immediate suggestion of an impression. Proust descends beyond the conscious surface of Renan's language, as it were, in order to make contact with the interwoven structures of personality on which articulation will be based. This, Proust suggests, is the realm of the pure theme, the recurring materials that structure a writer's style but which may be obscured by the ornamentation of that style. The gift of mimetism is the ability to pass through the other writer's language to the semi-conscious staging-ground that is its other side. The act of re-living, or of re-creating within oneself the impression made upon us by a text, happens initially in a pre-linguistic zone. Proust's immediate need is not for a word or phrases – they would mask or convert the impression before it fully took shape – but for a sense of contact with substance, and a subsequent refiltering of that material through himself, a bodily simulation of it. This need recalls Proust's quarrel with Mallarmé and the Symbolists, mentioned earlier. He sees the tenuous connection between Mallarmé's language and the physical impressions it describes – in other words, the borderline abstraction of his language – as the reason for its obscurity.

Proust's notes to himself on his manuscripts reveal a hesitation between criticism and pastiche, between the role of reason and that of intuition, that is at the centre of his wavering over creative writing in the *Contre Sainte-Beuve* period. As his new edition of *Pastiches et mélanges* is appearing, much later, in 1919, Proust's remarks on the pastiche as form are more tranquil in tone,[63] suggesting that he found an equilibrium between the intuitive and the intellectual through the long process of composition that produced *A la recherche*.

Part of the productivity of the 1907–9 period is due, I think, to Proust's increasing consciousness of the mental processes that underlie his writing. As he began to articulate these processes to himself, it was clearer to him that truly creative writing was a process of 'self-pastiche'. When the writer realizes that the stuff of his novel is the impressions and memories of his own life, re-experienced with new awareness through a more attuned consciousness, then he is free to 'write himself', and to write endlessly. As he had said of his pastiche of Renan, so he might henceforth say of his own self-nurturing novel: 'I had set my interior metronome to his rhythm and I could have written ten volumes like that' ['J'avais réglé mon métronome intérieur à son rythme et j'aurais pu écrire dix volumes comme cela'] (*Corr.*, VIII, 67). When one understands that Proust sees writing as mimesis of personal impression, and therefore copying of the self, this comment about the connection between finding the rhythm of a style and not being able to stop the flow seems, in its simplistic way, to explain entirely the prolixity of Proust's style and the length of his novel.

If Proust always hesitated about literary form, pointing with evident relief to writers like Baudelaire and Nerval who had told the same story in prose and poetry, it is because the deep structure of his fiction, and of his psyche, is a hesitation between two forms of articulation of the same idea, one an intellectual analysis (criticism), the other mimetic. When finally he had uncovered for himself this process of slipping from one pole to another, he was already free and launched on the creative path.

Hesitation over form, the duplication of messages (one explicit and analytical, the other which we must intuit) and the pastiche are all brought together in a curious and often discussed feature of Proust's novel, the bogus pages from the Goncourts' journal. The pastiche is placed right at the beginning of *Le Temps retrouvé*, as though it were an initiation – a negative one, of course – to the hero's ultimate creative effort. The excerpt shocks the Narrator with its highly decorative, artful presentation of a reality (the Verdurin salon) he knows to be dishearteningly insipid. But I would contend that there is something of the primordial apparition about the Goncourt pastiche, as though it constituted an earlier form bobbing to the narrative's surface from a time in the writer's life when, with characteristic inarticulation, an imitation of a writing stance that is wrong is presented as a substitute for an explanation of what is right. Proust instinctively juxtaposes mimetism and pastiche with the creative act, and his Narrator/writer is made to live out this juxtaposition, presenting us with an unavowed copy of a famous writer of the day as a prelude to the composition of a novel of his own.

The idea for embedding a pastiche into the Narrator's search for a vocation may well have lain dormant in Proust's mind for years. Although the Goncourt pastiche was probably composed in 1917–18,[64] a 1909 letter to Robert Dreyfus appears to prefigure the physical stage-set that Proust will construct in *Le Temps retrouvé* for the resolution of the Narrator's doubts. The letter concludes with a short pastiche of Taine which explains why pastiches are beginning to bore Proust; they end where real literature begins, in a pre-literary vestibule:

One willingly accepts one or two caricatures in the waiting-room, before entering the library. But it's a bore to remain indefinitely in the waiting-room.

[Vous voulez bien d'une ou deux caricatures dans un vestibule, avant d'entrer dans la bibliothèque. Mais il est ennuyeux de rester indéfiniment dans le vestibule.] (*Corr.*, IX, 135)

Proust actually constructs this vestibule and library in *Le Temps retrouvé*, at the home of the prince and princesse de Guermantes. Still plagued by writing doubts after experiencing the caricature of reality that the Goncourts present, the Narrator is asked to await the end of a musical interlude in the Guermantes' library. Here, a series of involuntary memories inform him of his own uniqueness, liberating him in a location symbolic of his previous dependency. The library itself is a vestibule preceding real action. It is a highly charged locus of Otherness for the Narrator, its shelves packed with works of writers that have engrossed him, some of them writers who for a time imprisoned Marcel Proust's energies and originality in literary criticism and the pastiche. The library is revealed, ironically, as the ultimate vestibule, for even though it opens on to a social gathering, the Narrator is already seeing far beyond it to the creation of his own world.

CHAPTER 4

Form: from anxiety to play

The shift in Proust's activity, in the 1907–9 period, from non-fiction to fiction, from what I have called transitive writing to the more personal mode of the novel, brought with it some of the uneasiness associated with writing in pre-creative forms. In this chapter I wish to investigate how certain Proustian anxieties about language, voice, literary genre and fictional structure become embedded features of the novelistic form he finally adopted. In spite of the intellectually satisfying closure of *Le Temps retrouvé* – it provides us with a newly enlightened Narrator fully equipped with a methodology for inscribing his life into art – there are many aspects of *A la recherche* that make of it more a work in progress than a fully completed whole. I am not thinking so much of the structural anomalies which the work certainly does display, as of the polemical nature of the Proustian text: it often attempts to reconcile warring elements within itself that remain both visible and visibly irreconcilable.

My objective is not to deconstruct the artistic values presented in Proust's text, but to complete some of the writer's aesthetic stands by pointing to the tensions that underpin them. Proust rails, for example, against the incursion of orality into literature and campaigns to discredit Sainte-Beuve's oral style. Yet the argument has to be made that many aspects of Proust's style are oral, that the vestiges of oral performance and the anxieties of Proustian speech patterns seem anchored in his prose, and explain certain elements of it. Moreover, Proust's early doubts about his ability to find a novelistic form for his ideas are obviously still resident in what becomes his novel's final form. I will examine some of these preoccupations by exploring the notions of closure and openness in *A la recherche*.

It appears to me, however, as it has appeared to many other readers, that it is repetition, recursiveness and iteration that are most central both to Proust's use of language and to the way his novel structures experience. Before *A la recherche* is launched, Proust demonstrates a fair amount of concern about repetitions in Baudelaire and Nerval. Later, he slams Charles Péguy's unproductive use of poetic repetition (for example, *ASB*, 285; *CSB*, 616). His own novel invests this concern in a dazzling variety of repeats, reprises and reuses of material; certain repetitions suggest that the Proustian text is, at times, a prisoner of iteration, rather than an active artisan of it. There are patterns of quotation and self-quotation in Proust that appear obsessive, as though the reinscribing of text were a kind of preliminary structuring exercise for him. Another aspect of iteration that deserves more exploration is the idea of self-contemplation, which Proust invokes in discussing the aesthetic successes of Michelet and Balzac. Some of the creative artist's richest insights arise when he muses and comments upon his own work. The effect of this self-observation is capital, for it invites author and reader alike to see an author's production as a continuum and to view not only discarded fictional drafts but also the non-fictional as organic offshoots of the final work.

There are two essential aspects of the Proustian text which work towards ensuring the novel's integrity and 'completeness', even as they bear within them the seeds of ancient anxieties. One is the voice of the ubiquitous narrating 'I', and the other what one might call the 'faith in fragments', that is, the conviction that the unity of tone and substance resident in the diverse fragments of an artist's work may supplant the traditional notion of form. Early in his career, Proust argues against confusing the writer's personal voice and the voice of his fictional protagonists. The theoretical canon of today insists that we separate Proust's voice from that of his Narrator, and even that we subdivide the subject of enunciation, the first-person narrating 'I' of *A la recherche*, into a subset of voices. I would argue that there is an opposite tendency at work in Proust's writings: the text of all those writings stresses their connectedness and the unity of a variety of Proustian voices, Proust the correspondent commenting on his work, Proust the author/Narrator in his manuscripts and marginal notes, and Proust the author/Narrator in *A la recherche* itself. The movement towards fusion of these enunciators is an important aspect of the self-contemplation essential to the Proustian aesthetic experience.

In chapter 2, it was observed that from the point of view of language, *A la recherche* is the Bakhtinian novel par excellence. 'The word', notes Bakhtin, 'is shaped in dialogic interaction with an alien word that is already in the object'.[1] In the brief moment of self-articulation that is the Martinville spires episode, and in the scene on the Guermantes Way where he can utter only an exuberant but meaningless 'zut', the Narrator is depicted locked in a struggle to find a personal language. The narrative would have us believe that, for the longest time, the alien words swirling about him win the day. The novel is an immense compendium of languages competing for truth: the voice and language of a duke and duchess, of a pedantic diplomat, of lesbians and gays, of beloved family members, of servants and chauffeurs. In a hundred ways, the polyphony of meaning in society is asserted, and the dialogic two-wayedness of a language which for the speaker and receiver always has a different sense.

What one may deduce from chapter 3, and from Proust's use in fiction of inserted forms such as the letter, social columns, journalism, literary criticism and the pastiche, is that he saw the novel as a dialogic genre, a meeting place of all forms. He mixes genres in a special way, of course, for many of the inserted materials have been carefully vetted: they are lifts from Proust's own earlier production. Some of the tension that arises in the Proustian text derives from the fact that it describes a search for unitary meaning – the real meaning of life as seen in the Narrator's life search – within what the writer discovers, progressively, to be a non-unitary form. It is as though Proust were making the same discovery, in the writing process, that Bakhtin did as he marvelled at the unstoppable evolution of the novelistic form. As one critic has put it,

[N]ovel is the name Bakhtin gives to whatever force is at work within a given literary system to reveal the limits, the artificial constraints of that system. Literary systems are comprised of canons, and 'novelization' is fundamentally anticanonical. It will not permit generic monologue. Always it will insist on the dialogue between what a given system will admit as literature and those texts that are otherwise excluded from such a definition of literature.[2]

I believe increased emphasis should be placed on the ways in which the Proustian text insists on its own insecurities about the novel as a genre through a praxis of generic gamesmanship. As Proust triggers our laughter at the trickery of language, at the multiple meanings it conveys – the classic example is the duc de Guermantes' telegram, 'Impossible venir, mensonge suit' – his text

begins to mock some of the rule-setting about genre incommunic-
ability in which he himself had been involved. Anxieties about form
are subsumed to a noticeable degree by a feeling of play and
bravado which this chapter will attempt to explore.

CLOSURE

Some years ago, René Girard defined the novel as that narrative that
has an ending, as opposed to the more contemporary 'story' which –
in Kafka's hands, for example – is interminable. Girard saw the act
of concluding as an invasion of the flow of normal reality, a
conversion that was an act of quasi-religious faith, even a symbolic
acceptance of death. 'One must think of the conclusion', he wrote,
'as a movement beyond the impossibility of closure.'[3] Before him,
Sartre had criticized the coherence and knowledge of outcome that
were obvious in the retrospective narration of the traditional novel.
Reality was entirely contingent, and beginning and ending were thus
a betrayal of reality, part of 'the absurd dishonesty of all prefabri-
cated patterns'.[4] Barthes takes up this theme in *Le Degré zéro de la
littérature*: the novel structures experience in a false way, introducing
order and connection into life which is always a jumble and always
lived in the present.[5] The idea of closure has been further challenged
by deconstructionists who label it an ideological intervention in the
'freeplay' of literary language.[6] Umberto Eco has defined the truly
modern work of art as a 'work in motion', in which certain
constituent elements are assigned their place by chance or by the
consumer.[7] From one perspective, Proust seems leagues from this
modernity, yet as we shall see, in Proust the tendency towards
openness fights against closure, and the attraction of incompletion –
'the enchantment of not ending', as Valéry called it[8] – undermines
the notion of conclusion.

For Proust, closure is certainly ideological. He was elated when an
observant reader, Jacques Rivière, recognized the first volume of his
novel as the beginning of a demonstration (*Corr.*, XIII, 98). Yet the
term ideological does not quite do justice to the visceral need which
Proust felt to demonstrate closure. He seems to have begun to reflect
upon structures of ending quite a few years before he actually began
A la recherche du temps perdu, during the precise period he was declaring
himself devoid of inspiration as a writer. We have seen his deep
fascination with the seven-theme conclusion of Ruskin's *Sesame and*

Lilies. In fact, it is in Proust's introduction to this translation that he articulates the basic structure of all his major works, a structure that is ideological. That introduction is clearly an early rehearsal, in simplified, miniaturized format, of *A la recherche.* The first part is an excerpt from the author's youth in Illiers, stocked with the familiar sensuousness of flowers, food and reading, the second an essay on the aesthetics of reading. The essay draws together the ideas launched implicitly in the 'life-portion', and makes them understandable retrospectively. At its core, the form deemed natural to the exposition of Proustian thought is this bipartite entity, life-fiction-completed-by-aesthetic; it is like a musical genre native to his mind, to which the introduction to *Sésame et les lys, Contre Sainte-Beuve* and *A la recherche* are scored. Of *Contre Sainte-Beuve* he wrote:

I am finishing a book which, in spite of its provisional title, *Contre Sainte-Beuve, Souvenir d'une matinée,* is a genuine novel and a very indecent novel in certain parts ... Sainte-Beuve's name is not mentioned by chance. The book ends with a long conversation about Sainte-Beuve and about aesthetics (like *Sylvie,* if you will, ending with a study of popular songs) and when the reader has finished the book, *he will comprehend (this is my intention) that the entire novel is simply the implementation of the artistic principles expressed in this final part, which is a kind of preface, as it were, but placed at the end.*

[Je termine un livre qui malgré son titre provisoire: *Contre Sainte-Beuve, Souvenir d'une matinée* est un véritable roman et un roman extrêmement impudique en certaines parties ... Le nom de Sainte-Beuve ne vient pas par hasard. Le livre finit bien par une longue conversation sur Sainte-Beuve et sur l'esthétique (si vous voulez, comme *Sylvie* finit par une étude sur les Chansons populaires) et quand on aura fini le livre, *on verra (je le voudrais) que tout le roman n'est que la mise en œuvre des principes d'art émis dans cette dernière partie, sorte de préface si vous voulez mise à la fin.*] (*Corr.,* IX, 155–6; the emphasis is mine.)

Fictional narrative is seen as necessarily complemented by a statement of literary ideology that draws its lessons from an initial story. The structure of *Le Temps retrouvé* clearly reveals, in spite of the fusion of the *Matinée chez la princesse de Guermantes* and *Le Bal de têtes,* this polemical aesthetic as both the final plank in the structure of the mature novel, and its final explanation.

And yet Proust's notion of overall fictional structure is amazingly fluid. Two documents bring striking testimony to bear on this point. One is a letter to Gaston Gallimard of October 1917, the second a 1921 note to Jacques Rivière. In the Gallimard letter, faced with problems of an overlong second and third volume, Proust proposes various structural scenarios to his editor. In one, two *cahiers* would be inserted, as a story told retrospectively, into *Le Côté de Guermantes*; the title of *A l'ombre des jeunes filles en fleurs* would be changed; and references to Albertine would be inserted in the story of his hero's first visit to Balbec. The reason for these transformations, admits Proust, is that since the publication of *Du Côté de chez Swann*, the balance and weight of the various sections have changed, and the story of Albertine has become the 'active principle and the true centre of the work' (*Corr.*, XIX, 765). Yet in another context, when he is attempting to defend the unity of his novel to the critic Paul Souday, he relegates this same Albertine episode to the status of an 'intermezzo' (*Corr.*, XVIII, 536).

An even more intriguing discussion, this one with Jacques Rivière, concerns the editing of an extract of *Sodome et Gomorrhe* for its appearance in the *Nouvelle Revue Française*. In giving Rivière instructions, Proust shows a curious openness to resituating portraits, descriptions and episodes in his novel; he almost seems to invite the reader (though of course the reader is the benevolent Rivière) to participate in the exercise. There is no admission that randomness is a part of this constructed world, but there is apparently easy acceptance that other arrangements of the same material are quite possible, because the same message will result. Proust seems to take delight in demonstrating how natural he finds the rearrangement of text and episode, and one senses at the same time his serene confidence at how the parts fit into a much larger whole:

Eliminate the Cambremer visit; remove the Norwegian scholar (I had in fact put him there to beef up your extract, but in the book he is with the Verdurins – and he'll only take a few lines); remove, as well, the lover of Le Sidaner (it's very easy to put him in the little tram). Finally, remove the salivation of old Mme Cambremer. Don't put her in the little tram, simply evoke her memory when the faithful, in the tram, recount how the young couple is going to dine that very evening at La Raspelière, saying that she used to go to the Cambremers' place, and add: 'Let us observe for the moment in her regard this single peculiarity. When art is the subject, etc.' In this way you will have a coherent whole, not at all scattered, which I find tempting for the book version.

[Supprimez la visite Cambremer; extrayez-en le savant Norvégien (que du reste je n'avais placé là que pour nourrir votre extrait, mais qui dans le livre va chez les Verdurin – et qui ne vous prendra que quelques lignes); extrayez-en également l'amateur de Le Sidaner, il est très aisé de le mettre dans le petit tram. Extrayez-en enfin la salivation de la vieille Cambremer.

Celle-là, ne la mettez pas dans le petit tram, mais tout simplement, au moment où les fidèles racontent dans le tram que le jeune ménage va dîner le soir même à la Raspelière évoquez son souvenir en disant qu'elle allait autrefois chez Madame de Sainte-Euverte et ajoutez: 'notons à son sujet pour l'instant cette seule particularité. Quand on parle de chose d'art, etc.' De cette façon vous aurez un tout cohérent, point éparpiller [*sic*], qui me fait envie pour le volume.] (*Corr.*, XX, 510)[9]

Perhaps there is a hint, here, of a work in motion. A discussion of what is relevant about episodes and their order in the text suddenly unveils a measure of arbitrariness in all fixed structures.

As I have noted, one aspect of Proustian anxiety about form centres around the importance connected to the idea that the opening of his novel be viewed as seamlessly attached, in a single writing flow, to its conclusion. He stressed this point with a variety of correspondents in the 1919–20 period. A 1909 comment to Mme Strauss concerning *Contre Sainte-Beuve* confirms that this connected overture and closure was Proust's earliest conception of his novel's structure, even before it had fully developed into *A la recherche du temps perdu*. Proust says in that letter,

I have just begun – and completed – quite a long book. Unfortunately, the departure for Cabourg interrupted my work, and it's only now that I'm getting back to it ... I really would like to finish, to get to the end. Even though everything is written, there are many things left to be revised.

[je viens de commencer – et de finir – tout un long livre. Malheureusement le départ pour Cabourg a interrompu mon travail, et je vais seulement m'y remettre ... je voudrais bien finir, aboutir. Si tout est écrit, beaucoup de choses restent à remanier.] (*Corr.*, IX, 163)

The anomaly of completion and incompletion is captured in these phrases. The book that has been finished is particularly long, as though length alone were a not unimportant achievement.[10] More remarkable, the work has been both begun and terminated, as though in the same moment; the text seems concerned with stressing that completion came right at the beginning. Beginning and ending are a continuum, and the writer appears to suggest that to truly begin is to have found one's completion. But the text also seems to posit that 'to finish is to contemplate further change'. Of course writing implies, in any professional sense, reworking or re-writing, and Proust was adamant that rewriting produced a superior product (*Corr.*, XVII, 69). Julia Kristeva and others have made the distinction between 'compositional completion' ['achèvement compositionnel'] and 'structural finishedness' ['finition structurelle'].[11] But there is an evident obsession in the Proustian text regarding closure that appears to have, at its core, a fear of losing the sense of openness.

When one examines the models of closure that a variety of critics have identified in traditional narrative, one is struck by the fact that *A la recherche* appears to exhibit most, if not all of them.[12] The novel as quest ends when the object sought (a vocation, the revelation of essential reality, lost time) is found. Proust's ending in *Le Temps retrouvé* is at one and the same time a *coup de théâtre*, the resolution of an enigma, the revelation of a secret.[13] It is 'a plenitude regained', as Barthes characterized the ending of Balzac's *Sarrasine*.[14] It is also an ending that constitutes a conversion, in René Girard's sense,[15] a repudiation of one's former life that at the same time allows a reconciliation between the individual and the world.

The Proustian ending corresponds to four of the five models discussed by Armine Mortimer in her study *La Clôture narrative*. The dramatic appearance of Mlle de Saint-Loup, the fusion of the Guermantes and the Swann lines, fits the pattern of an ending that Mortimer has called 'une fin-fils' (in this case 'fille'), a denouement in which the appearance or birth of a child crowns the work. *Le Temps retrouvé* is also a classic ending-as-beginning. At the same time, it is the archetype of the novel which ends with art resolving life (like *Les Faux-Monnayeurs*, *La Nausée*, *La Modification*). It even participates in a fourth type of ending, the return to the present (Mortimer's example is the statement about Homais, 'Il vient de recevoir la croix d'honneur'). In *Le Temps retrouvé*, retrospection ends as the Narrator recognizes that all his past experience is the fuel he can now use in the present to fire his artistic endeavour. Even Mortimer's last model, the epigrammatic closing, or tagline ('C'était Augustin', in *Dominique*; 'A nous deux maintenant!', from *Le Père Goriot*) is replicated, in Proust's inimitable, prolix fashion, in the structuring of the last lines of the novel so that they will end in a rather ponderous *chute* that connects the last phrase in the text, 'dans le Temps', to the opening word of the narrative, 'longtemps'.

There is a tendency towards incompletion in Proust's earlier works (the unfinished *Jean Santeuil*, the partially abandoned *Contre Sainte-Beuve*) for which the climactical structure of *A la recherche du temps perdu* serves as evident compensation. *Le Temps retrouvé* suffers from an overdetermination of closure, and an endless set of what Frank Kermode has called 'end-effects', that supplement the conclu-

sion in advance.[16] The text is extremely self-conscious, even neurotic, where closure is concerned. One might turn against Proust
some of his own comments about the self-consciousness of other
writers in ending their works. Proust admitted irritation at the forced
climactical effects of some of Hugo's poems:

In my opinion, Hugo is even too skilful in retaining for the end, for the
brilliant, supreme rocket, the image that might not necessarily have come
at the end,
   'the sickle of gold in the field of stars'.

[A mon avis, [Hugo] a même trop d'habileté à garder pour la fin, pour
l'éclatante et suprême fusée, l'image qui ne serait pas forcément venue à la
fin,
   'la faucille d'or dans le champs des étoiles'.] (*Corr.*, XIX, 156)

One epiphany at the home of the princesse de Guermantes is not
enough. Three successive insights are proposed to the reader, each
arising from a different sensation, the kinetic experience of the
uneven stones, the touch of the rough-textured napkin, the sound of
a spoon clinking on a plate. It is as though an effort were being
made to square the circle of the taste-and-smell madeleine experience. The symbolism of the two Ways (which certain readers have
labelled 'forced'), and the manner in which they are brought
together geographically and in human form (Mlle de Saint-Loup),
these are similar efforts. The reader understands: the author is
capable of completing a major work and of bringing a complex
thought process to a conclusion.

   The idea of ending is a natural source of anxiety for an author
whose major work is so clearly, as in the case of Proust, his life's
work. Still, the aesthetic lessons and the joyous discovery of vocation
that arise from the involuntary memories experienced in the
Guermantes library seem to provide an ideal ending to the Narrator's search. However, Proust appears to have had doubts about that
ending, just as he remained concerned until the end of his life about
the unwieldiness of the book's structure as a whole. He writes to one
correspondent in 1921 that the only reason some acquaintances find
his work remarkable is that they are reading short extracts of it in
the *Nouvelle Revue Française* (*Corr.*, XX, 558). From the Ruskin years
forward, when he observed that, like Henri de Régnier, his ideas did
not fit the novel form, Proust's question remains, 'Do I possess the
novelist's craft?' As if to echo René Girard's idea that the novel
equals closure, he questions in particular whether the periodic,

intermittent architecture of revelation he has set in place actually functions as fiction. There exists in his manuscripts a startling alternative schema for the end of *Le Temps retrouvé* (dating from about 1915), a concentrated, rapid conclusion where revelations about characters would be much less gradual. It would be another novel completely,

> a second novel ... if I imagine the story told here to be a novel, where what appears here and there at random would, on the contrary, be compressed and would appear all in one stroke to the reader, who would be expecting it no more than I would: the pages on the Goncourts, the real life of Charlus, of Albertine, the genius of Vinteuil and of Elstir, in a lightning-quick, condensed accumulation.

> [un second roman ... si je suppose l'histoire racontée ici comme un roman, où ce qui apparaît ça et là, serait au contraire resserré, et [apparaîtrait] au lecteur qui n'en soupçonnerait pas plus que moi, tout d'un coup la page des Goncourt, la vraie vie de Charlus, d'Albertine, le génie de Vinteuil et d'Elstir, en une accumulation foudroyante et condensée.][17]

This nostalgia for a savage ending is no doubt a nostalgia for Balzac. Proust felt at home in the notion of his own work as a sweeping, Balzacian-style human comedy, a structure on an impressive scale, 'writ with compass-angle wide' ['à large ouverture de compas'], as he said. But he also greatly appreciated Balzac's gift for the brutal conclusion: 'Bring out in Balzac (*Fille aux yeux d'or, Sarrazine, La Duchesse de Langeais*, etc.) the slow preparation, the theme that is slowly bound tighter, then the lightning strangulation of the ending' (*ASB*, 80) ['Bien montrer pour Balzac (*Fille aux yeux d'or, Sarrazine, La Duchesse de Langeais*, etc.) les lentes préparations, le sujet qu'on ligote peu à peu, puis l'étranglement foudroyant de la fin'] (*CSB*, 289).

Another chapter in this nostalgia for rapid closure is the extraordinary story of the possibility of alternative endings for *Albertine disparue*.[18] In 1986 a typescript of *Albertine disparue* was unearthed in Suzy Mante-Proust's papers; it was a copy of the typescript on which the first publication of *Albertine disparue* was based. However, this particular copy had been considerably edited: Proust had excised almost 300 pages of text[19] and made changes to the story of Albertine's death, and he had very probably carried out these changes in the last month of his life. Of the two parallel possibilities, was this enormously condensed 'ending' to the Albertine affair therefore not the authentic one? Some of Proust's very late letters to the *Nouvelle Revue Française* speak of *Albertine disparue* as brief and full of dramatic action,[20] as though this telescoped option – like the second novel ending Proust imagined in 1915 – were in fact the one he preferred. There is no answer to this dilemma, except to remark that a considerable anxiety about length, tempo and closure accompanied Proust until his death.

Proust's need to physically record closure is itself recorded in his manuscripts on more than one occasion. In all editions of *A la recherche*, the last word printed is FIN, a word which Proust wrote into his text, underlined twice, and completed with a period. That period thus comes not as a completion of the last sentence, after the expression 'dans le Temps', but after the word 'fin'.[21] If one is to trust the memory of his housekeeper Céleste Albaret, it was only some six months before his death, in the spring of 1922, that Proust actually appended the word 'end' to his novel.[22] However, the last sentence of *A la recherche* – marked with the word FIN or not – is itself not finished, according to the editors of the second Pléiade edition (I, p. lxx), and perhaps this a fitting representation of the ambiguity Proust felt about closure. Apparently Proust wrote FIN for the first time in December 1910, above and as a title for the text he called 'L'Adoration perpétuelle', which was to serve as the conclusion for the version of the novel projected at that time.[23] For Proust, the end-word is, in large part, a self-directed signal that anxiety may now end, and that the work of eternal completion may continue, for it may be placed before a concluding section that has finally been imagined, or after an ending that is not quite complete.

It is interesting to note, in concluding this section, how conservative is Proust's praxis of closure compared to that of Flaubert. As we have seen, they share a diffident attitude towards spoken language which migrates, at least partially, into their writing. But the Flaubertian sense of ending is ironic, even confrontational;[24] he insisted that the desire to conclude was 'inept'.[25] And after 1850, though still concerned with the architecture of his works, Flaubert focused much energy on making his endings more inconclusive. His efforts seem to have been directed at draining his texts, via ellipses, cuts and the removal of connections and explanations, of the logic of their closure.[26] While Proust may have been tempted, as we have seen, by a foreshortening of parts of his novel and by a fierce ending that would have revealed all the narrative's secrets in one brutal stroke, he finally opted for the notion of ending as apotheosis. Because he had struggled through an early literary career marked by a series of interrupted or partial works, and perhaps because he accepted that the neurasthenic's great challenge was to master the completion of projects, he approached the crowning work of his life intent on making transparently clear that on this occasion his thoughts had been fully and completely developed.

OPENNESS AND INCOMPLETION

At the same time as *Le Temps retrouvé* celebrates the idea and the modes of closure so triumphantly, sections of the same text admit that large-scale works are inevitably incomplete:

In long books of this kind there are parts which there has been time only to sketch, parts which, because of the very amplitude of the architect's plan, will no doubt never be completed. How many great cathedrals remain unfinished! (VI, 431)

[Et dans ces livres-là, il y a des parties qui n'ont eu le temps que d'être esquissées, et qui ne seront sans doute jamais finies, à cause de l'ampleur même du plan de l'architecte. Combien de grandes cathédrales restent inachevées!] (IV, 610)

While the editors of the second Pléiade edition prefer to stress that Proust left twenty *Cahiers* which contain, sequentially, the manuscript of the novel from *Sodome et Gomorrhe* to the end of *Le Temps retrouvé* (see Pléiade notes, IV, 1176), there are *Cahiers* destined for the conclusion that are simply marked, 'To be added to the last part'.[27] As Luc Fraisse has put it,

the aesthetic meditation in the library realized the dream of the theoretical piece which would be without end; ... this long text, which was not revised by its author, has the aspect, at least in part, of a file full of additions. The aesthetic meditation is thus a quintessential collection of marginal notes which suddenly appear to be self-sufficient, the triumph of the theoretical margins over the central story.[28]

Reflections of a philosophical and aesthetic nature stand outside the flow of narrative time, and outside the rules of fiction. Such observations and insights may well be fragments, but juxtaposed, they defeat the idea of fragmentation because they invite the addition of more of their kind. The theoretical statement remains ever open.

The idea of incompletion as structural openness has drawn thought-provoking commentary from a number of Proustians. Luc Fraisse, both in *Le Fragment expérimental* and *L'Œuvre cathédrale*, has shown the relationship between fragment and unity in Proust's thought. If openness is not a defect but a quality in the works of Hugo and Balzac, for example, it is because the unity of art resides in the deep, constant essence of the artist's personality: each of the author's works radiates an aspect of that essence, but is never a definitive statement of it. Each poem of Baudelaire represents but a fragment of a homeland that is his genius (*ASB*, 47; *CSB*, 255).

At least one feature of Proust's discussion of the incompleteness of nineteenth-century artistic masterpieces deserves more attention. This is the particular twist he gives to the idea of 'self-contemplation'. In an often-quoted discussion in *La Prisonnière* (V, 176–7; III, 666–7), Proust argues that though Balzac, Hugo, Michelet and Wagner at first considered their individual works as free-standing, separate statements, they all experienced subsequent intuitions about the thematic unity of what they had created, and the fact that this understanding came only retrospectively meant that their work always remained 'open':

these works partake of that quality of being – albeit marvellously – always incomplete, which is the characteristic of all the great works of the nineteenth century, that century whose greatest writers somehow botched their books, but, watching themselves work as though they were at once workman and judge, derived from this self-contemplation a new form of beauty, *exterior and superior to the work itself*, imposing on it a retroactive unity, *a grandeur which it does not possess*. (V, 176)

[ces œuvres participent à ce caractère d'être – bien que merveilleusement – toujours incomplètes, qui est le caractère de toutes les grandes œuvres du XIXᵉ siècle; du XIXᵉ siècle dont les plus grands écrivains ont manqué leurs livres, mais, se regardant travailler comme s'ils étaient à la fois l'ouvrier et le juge, ont tiré de cette auto-contemplation une beauté nouvelle, *extérieure et supérieure à l'œuvre*, lui imposant rétroactivement une unité, *une grandeur qu'elle n'a pas*.] (III, 666; the emphasis is mine.)

The beauty of the craftsman's instinctive insights about his craft is *superior to the creation itself*. Hence, Michelet's genius is less to be found in his *Histoire de France* or *Histoire de la révolution* than in the prefaces to these two works, just as the insights of Proust's own *Contre Sainte-Beuve* were to radiate from its conclusion, described as a kind of preface placed at the end. Similarly, Balzac's greatest achievement, his intuition about the links in his works that would make of them a single world, was inscribed in the 1842 foreword to *La Comédie humaine*, and the ultimate charm of Ruskin's *Sesame and Lilies* was made to reside outside the text, in epigraphs added in the later editions.

A subversive aspect of this analysis is that an artistic work is incomplete (and perhaps not even fully capable of appreciation by its audience) without its author's reflections upon it. This idea reinforces, of course, our earlier comments about the deep, bipartite structure of Proust's works, each constructed of a life-portion completed by a set of artistic principles. But more important, this unexpected view of incompletion invites us to read literature in a radically different manner. The fictional text is not closed. Not only is it open to new episodes, its author's reflections about it are part and parcel of it, and the reader must compare the work and those reflections to apprehend the highest level of the author's accomplishments. Without perhaps wanting to open that door, Proust asks us to read in parallel his own fiction and what he has to say about it 'from within' and 'from without'. His 'notes de régie' (that is, his production notes, many of them the repository of intuitions about the work underway), his manuscript drafts and sketches, his essays, articles and letters all reflect on his central treasure, the Work. The self-contemplation which Proust's text proposes as a pathway of self-discovery and readerly discovery is played out in many ways in the Proustian text, but I believe it is especially evident in some of the iterative practices that are so characteristic of Proustian composition, the habit of rewriting one's own text repeatedly, of constantly quoting and requoting other authors, and that special Proustian habit of quoting from one's own writings. It is these features of the Proustian text that I now wish to examine.

STRUCTURE AS ITERATION: REPETITION AND QUOTATION

As Gérard Genette has observed, no other novelistic work has made greater use of iteration – in quantity and complexity – than *A la recherche*.[29] The contrast between iterative and singulative time has been identified as the initial wellspring of narration in Combray, while recurrence – be it the unpredictable intermittence of memory or poetic impression, or the highly constructed repetition of event and situation – is the basic structuring device in *A la recherche*. One type of iteration, the copying and repeated rewriting of text, has been viewed as an unhealthy aspect of Proust's writing practice, a habit that identifies a limitation, or an aporia. It was Proust's first few workbooks, the *cahiers* for *Contre Sainte-Beuve*, that influenced early critical opinion on this point. The repetitions led one reader to speak of 'endless groping' and 'desperation at the inability to move forward'.[30] More recently, it has been said that Proust's text 'reformulates indefinitely, with a stubbornness that borders on obsession, «the same things»'.[31] The second Pléiade edition of *A la recherche*, with its numerous but not exhaustive selection of sketches for the definitive text, demonstrates that re-reading and rewriting were part of the Proustian writing process till the very end. For Flaubert, re-reading often meant, in fact, recopying,[32] and it is interesting to envisage Proust's system of repeating fragments as also, in part, exercises in copying.

It is in the act of recursiveness that the Proustian text finds its forward momentum. To copy one's own words is to remake contact with the self, to employ the impetus and weight of the material copied like a refrain that imparts movement to the new text. One of the effects of rewriting in Proust is also to superimpose new text on old, to set episodes and descriptions on top of older ones with which they reverberate and resonate. Repetition does not denote a dead-end in the manuscript, but a beginning of the layering process that gives the Proustian text its luxury. Moreover, rewriting generally brings a new perspective to already produced text, just as the idea of thematic variations is a generator of new episodes and descriptions in Proust's novel. Anne Simon has argued that the simple act of seeing a draft text a second time reorientates Proust's gaze and elicits additional descriptive material.[33]

I see little distinction in Proust between copying one's own text into one's own 'new text', and copying other writers' words – when they are felt to be fraternal. The fact that the text in question has already been noted down once by Proust, whether in notes with a literary destination or in a letter, provides a stamp of special authenticity. It is as if, as Antoine Compagnon observes, only words already committed to paper came to Proust's mind and were acceptable under his own pen.[34]

How is quoted text integrated into Proust's fiction?[35] Such fusion is of special interest in a writer who spoke so determinedly about avoiding the infection of the Other's discourse. It would seem logical that the habit of quoting other writers is related to the porosity of personality we have seen in chapter 2, the openness of the Proustian individual, and hence his text, to the language of the Other.

Although borrowing the text of others takes place at a quasi-obsessional level in *A la recherche*, if we consider mere frequency, it is evident as well that the anxiety such dependency would generate in a social relationship has been absorbed in the fictional discourse. In fact, the opposite of anxiety is present: quotation, allusion and reference clearly appear to add positive energy to the text, to swell it with extra significance. At the same time, an anomaly is present: a quotation is an impurity in the text and an admission of reference to authority. Moreover, there is a potential for idolatry in the attraction to quotation. Is there not a certain febrility in the way the Narrator is drawn to quotations spoken by the duchesse de Guermantes, and an unappetizing materialism in the way he connects certain lines of poetry and the real-life situation in which they were cited?

by thus quoting an isolated line ... one multiplies its power of attraction tenfold. The lines that entered or returned to my mind during this dinner magnetized in turn, summoned to themselves ... the poems within which they were normally embedded ... I read these volumes from cover to cover and found peace of mind only when I suddenly came across, awaiting me in the light in which she had bathed them, the lines which Mme de Guermantes had quoted to me. (III, 635-6)

[en citant ainsi un vers isolé ... on décuple sa puissance attractive. Ceux qui étaient entrés ou rentrés dans ma mémoire, au cours de ce dîner, aimantaient à leur tour, appelaient à eux ... les pièces au milieu desquelles ils avaient l'habitude d'être enclavés ... Je relus ces volumes d'un bout à l'autre, et ne retrouvai la paix que quand j'aperçus tout d'un coup, m'attendant dans la lumière où elle les avait baignés, les vers que m'avait cités Mme de Guermantes.] (II, 838)[36]

In a social setting, the Other's language is invasive and alienates Proust's speech to the point that the foreign words replace his own: either he replicates the other person's viewpoint in an effort to find agreement, or he mimics that speech, at times hysterically. How then does written discourse from foreign sources become native and innocuous within the Proustian text? The most obvious technique for domesticating imported text is to recontext it, so that its meaning turns playful, ironic or even grotesque. This approach is taken with classical authors like Molière and Racine.

A second tactic lies in the often narrow selection Proust makes in quoting from another author. If Racine is welcome in the Proustian text, it is because Proust creates his own Racine, interpreting and reinterpreting only a few lines from within two or three plays until, in a sense, Racine has been both rewritten and co-opted.[37] Still, an essential aspect of quotation and reference, I believe, is that they support the recursive movement of the Proustian text, they underline recognitions and embody the self-contemplation that, as we have seen, is at the heart of Proust's 'plaisir du texte'. For Proust, as for Paul Valéry, there is rapture in iteration.

Proust makes a number of direct references to art that quotes other art. In a letter to Jacques Rivière, he condones the act of quoting, but in strictly controlled conditions, insisting that it has a creative aspect if carried out by a sensitive writer:

I grant you that sometimes, when it is cited by a writer, an unusual quotation can become a kind of invention. It belongs as much to him, because of the felicitous meaning he draws from it, as to the writer who is quoted.

[Je reconnais que parfois une citation rare quand elle a été faite par un écrivain devient une espèce d'invention. Elle lui appartient autant à cause du sens heureux qu'il en tire, qu'à l'écrivain cité.] (*Corr.*, XIX, 386)

The notion of proprietorship is strangely distorted here. The award for reuse of the Other's language, if the result has more wit than the original, is shared ownership of the idea. Proust's overall strategy for defending the quoting or reworking of other artists' ideas is quite elaborate. We have seen how peremptorily he dismissed – citing his philosophy professor as the sole exception – the suggestion that his own thinking may have been affected by others. And in a sketch from the original 'Adoration perpétuelle', the Narrator (sounding very much like Marcel Proust) assures us that he will leave no traces of other writers' thoughts in his literary work (IV, 811). On the other hand, various Proustian texts contentedly focus on the notion of the precursor text, that is, the feeling that an insight recorded by another artist may be an anticipation of our own ideas, like a phrase of the writer Montesquieu that seems entirely Flaubertian, and therefore quite charms Flaubert (IV, 248; III, 211). Proust identifies Schopenhauer as the supreme quoter, a writer who substantiates each thought with scores of references to similar ideas in other writers:

Schopenhauer never puts forward an opinion without at once supporting it by several quotations, but one has the feeling that for him the texts he cites are merely examples, unconscious or anticipatory allusions in which he likes to discover a few features of his own thought. (*ASB*, 217)

[Schopenhauer n'avance jamais une opinion sans l'appuyer aussitôt sur plusieurs citations, mais on sent que les textes cités ne sont pour lui que des exemples, des allusions inconscientes et anticipées où il aime à retrouver quelques traits de sa propre pensée, mais qui ne l'ont nullement inspirée.] (*CSB*, 185)

Quotation as unconscious self-quotation: this is a capital moment of self-assertion and self-defence in Proust, and a moment when his reader may have to bite his tongue. Proust refuses to allow that the inspiration he has felt in reading other writers is fully external. Racine's *Phèdre* seems to 'quote' his Narrator's entire life. It is almost as though the author of the predecessor work were somehow ourself.[38] By calling quotations anticipations of one's own work, Proust prepares them for integration, literally, into his own discourse. By calling quotations unconscious, that is, touched with the spark of intuitive recognition, he brings them into the same pool of potentially inspiring phenomena as the madeleine or the Martinville spires. What all of these phenomena trigger is a semi-conscious recognition; the artist's mission becomes, in *A la recherche*, the elucidation of the joy that these recognitions release.

At the edge of the practice of bringing quotation into literature is that of applying situations from literature, or from other writers' lives, to one's own circumstances. When Proust notes down a phrase from a letter Carlyle sent to his mother, 'Je ne suis pas si souffrant que je vous le dis' ['I am not as sick as I have been telling you'] (*Le Carnet de 1908*, 47), he creates a one-line synopsis of his own brooding about his delicate health and the effect that it may have had on his mother's life.

In an early note that anticipates the Narrator's last visit to a Guermantes salon, where old age disguises many of the Narrator's social acquaintances beneath wrinkles and white hair, Proust connects a scene from Chateaubriand's old age to the ageing of an acquaintance, Camille Plantevignes. The writer's imagination seems to gain substance and momentum from three separate literary echoes that immediately overlay one another: '«Milord, do you recognize me?»' (old age, Plantevigne's old age, the scene in *Education*) Short story by Thomas Hardy and Chateaubriand's flight' ['«Mylord me reconnaissez-vous?»' (vieillesse, vieillesse de Plantevigne, Scène de l'*Education*) Nouvelle de Thomas Hardy et la fuite de Chateaubriand'] (*Le Carnet de 1908*, 59). The juxtaposition of Plantevigne's old age and the idea of non-recognition looks forward to the surprising appearance of so many aged guests at the reception which closes *Le Temps retrouvé*. The allusion to *L'Education sentimentale* appears to refer to the scene of separation between Frédéric and

Mme Arnoux, while the reference to Hardy may relate to a story called, in translation, 'Deux ambitions'.

There is, at least to some degree, an anxiety of worthiness embedded in this type of literary allusion. Citation embodies the need for reassurance that Proust's own situation, inspiration and eventual production are at a level that permits comparison with noble models. To borrow again from the stockbroker's terminology with which Proust was so conversant, ideas and writerly behaviours that anticipate Proust's own are secure havens for his own investments. One wonders whether there are instances in which the other writer's language actually displaces Proust's, moments when, semi-consciously or unconsciously, Proust's own discourse co-opts other language which later it cannot recognize as foreign. The case of two lines of poetry by Leconte de Lisle is of some interest in this regard.

In *Jean Santeuil* the student hero is presented as enamoured of Leconte de Lisle and Verlaine, desperately bored with Racine, and amenable to almost any opinion of his modish literature teacher Rustinlor. He is said to be exalted by even the most superficially philosophical reading. The last lines of Leconte de Lisle's poem 'La Maya' are ones that Jean would like to set as an epigraph to the literary work to which he senses he will devote his future: 'The life of antiquity is made inexhaustibly / From the endless eddying of vain semblances'[39] ['La vie antique est faite inépuisablement / Du tourbillon sans fin des apparences vaines'] (*JS*, 237). Many years later, in his article on Baudelaire, as Proust sketches a rapid critique of nineteenth-century poetry, the lines from 'La Maya' are again cited (*ASB*, 306; *CSB*, 636). This time, Proust's judgement is outwardly more transparent: Leconte's somewhat abstract spiritualism and idealism have become a bit insipid.

In *A la recherche* the last line of 'La Maya' – disguised slightly – becomes one of the signature phrases of Bergotte, the writer who marries a highly poetic style with cosmic statements, a combination the young Narrator finds luscious. Any ironic feelings about the verse are largely hidden from the reader, and the line is no longer attributed to Leconte de Lisle, although it is placed within quotation marks. Among a series of four typical Bergottian phrases it appears as 'the inexhaustible torrent of fair semblances' (I, 110–11) ['l'inépuisable torrent des belles apparences'] (I, 93).[40] Another variant of the phrase attributed to Bergotte is 'the eternal torrent of semblances' (II, 145) ['l'éternel torrent des apparences'] (I, 542), and two other versions are provided in a manuscript sketch, 'the endless flow of vain semblances' ['l'écoulement sans fin des vaines apparences'] and 'the torrents of eternal Illusion' ['les torrents de l'eternelle Illusion'] (I, 789).

In a sense, not much has changed since *Jean Santeuil*. The young Narrator's blind adoration of Bergotte continues to provide an ironic framework for this poetic line. But a parallel operation takes places as well. Proust also brings Leconte's line, or at least variations on the line involving closely similar phonic, rhythmic and semantic elements, into the most charged and evocative moments in his text, the involuntary memories at the beginning and the end of *A la recherche*. And the line is now part of the Proustian text, co-opted and, in a sense, plagiarized. One variant that is not part of the published text was destined for the 1910 version of 'L'Adoration perpétuelle', where the hero stumbles on the uneven steps in the Guermantes' courtyard:

I stood with one foot on one of the paving stones, the other on another, repeating the same step already accomplished so that it would re-create once again the *elusive touching of indistinct visions* which urgently proposed to my mind the enigma of their happiness.

[je restais un pied sur un des pavés, un pied sur l'autre, refaisant le même pas que j'avais fait pour qu'il fît renaître encore une fois *l'insaisissable frôlement des visions indistinctes* qui proposaient impérieusement à mon esprit l'énigme de leur bonheur.] (IV, 804; the emphasis is mine.)

It is clear what original text Proust has in mind because the editors provide the variant 'once again [the eddyings *crossed out*] the elusive' ['encore une fois [les tourbill<ons> *biffé*] l'insaisissable'] (IV, 804, n. a).

In the published text of *A la recherche*, Proust embeds the Leconte/Bergotte line in the madeleine episode. As the Narrator struggles with the visual images the madeleine sets off in his mind, he speaks as follows:

But [the struggles of the visual memory] are too far off, too confused and chaotic; scarcely can I perceive the neutral glow into which *the elusive eddying of stirred-up colours is fused.* (I, 53)

[Mais [le souvenir visuel] se débat trop loin, trop confusément; à peine si je perçois le reflet neutre où se confond *l'insaisissable tourbillon des couleurs remuées.*] (I, 45–6; the emphasis is mine.)

It seems unlikely, given the careful reworking of this phrase which we have seen in other contexts, that it is an unconscious echo of Leconte de Lisle. One's instinct is to see this redeploying of Leconte's

line in a supremely evocative moment of Proust's text as a sign of
linguistic anxiety; the writer lacks faith in his own abilities, and
borrows a lyrical phrase to supplement his own forces. Or is the
quotation a sly self-parody, a statement that Proust's style is
Bergotte's, that 'Bergotte's tic is my tic'?[41] Yet the context does not
appear ironic.

This is not the only occasion on which the signature phrases of
another writer are stitched into the fabric of Proust's prose. Proust's
epigraph to 'Les Regrets, rêveries couleur du temps', in *Les Plaisirs et
les jours*, borrowed from Emerson, is reused in the same way. It reads,

The poet's habit of living should be set on a key so low that the common
influences should delight him. His cheerfulness should be the gift of a ray of
sunlight; the air should suffice for his inspiration, and he should be tipsy
with water.[42]

[La manière de vivre du poète devrait être si simple que les influences les
plus ordinaires le réjouissent, sa gaieté devrait pouvoir être le fruit d'un
rayon de soleil, l'air devrait suffire pour l'inspirer et l'eau devrait suffire
pour l'enivrer.] (*JS*, 104)

The sun is everywhere in 'Les Rêveries', especially in the initial
pieces, and one of its appearances mirrors Emerson's lines fairly
exactly: 'the sun is like an inspired and prolific poet' ['le soleil [est]
comme un poète inspiré et fécond'] (*JS*, 107). The same type of sun
reference is frequent in *Jean Santeuil* as well. There we read that the
poet's room should be bare, 'so that he may carefully collect the
palest ray of sunlight' ['pour que le poète puisse y recueillir attentive-
ment le plus pâle rayon de soleil'] (*JS*, 436).

Proust thus deploys a number of related strategies to asepticize
foreign quotation so that it can be absorbed with impunity into his
own fictional discourse and generate additional layers of meaning
there. And all these strategies operate under the sign of self-
contemplation, the organizing imperative in Proustian aesthetics.
Another author's line becomes our own if, in appropriating it, we
draw as much meaning as he did from it. (Of course, part of the new
meaning is its original meaning.) As for a quotation being an
anticipated reminiscence of our own thought, Proust's strategy is to
extend this rule from single lines to individual works to the entire
œuvre of another author. Wagner's operas, Hugo's *Légende des siècles*,
Balzac's *Comédie humaine* are designated as anticipatory allusions to
Proust's complete aesthetic system. The attraction towards the
Other's language, and the fear of it, are transformed in this process.

Proustian quotation acknowledges that communication with the Other, and even openness to the Other's language, are possible, in calm, controlled conditions. And, in a sense, quotation provides a way out of a trap. Quotation allows us to escape singular individuality and a singular view of truth into a more universal realm where our originality encounters that of others. Our individual monad, the Leibnitzian unit of being, can fraternize with our universal monad (*ASB*, 101; *CSB*, 311). Communication through art is, first, a recognition – a recognition of quotation in a sense – but its second aspect is a feeling of joyous liberation from the solitude of individual language and individual forms and of access to a universal language:

One of these passages of Bergotte, the third or fourth which I had detached from the rest, filled me with a joy to which the meagre joy I had tasted in the first passage bore no comparison, a joy that I felt I was experiencing in a deeper, vaster, more integral part of myself, *from which all obstacles and partitions seemed to have been swept away.* (I, 111)

[Un de ces passages de Bergotte, le troisième ou le quatrième que j'eusse isolé du reste, me donna une joie incomparable à celle que j'avais trouvée au premier, une joie que je me sentis éprouver en une région plus profonde de moi-même, plus unie, plus vaste, *d'où les obstacles et les séparations semblaient avoir été enlevés.*] (I, 93; the emphasis is mine.)

Paradoxically, quotation seems to neutralize anxiety about the language of the Other. Why? Because quotation functions within the reassuring mechanics of a system of iteration. In the Proustian text, quotation is experienced as a comforting and fruitful recognition. And the very act of acknowledging shared ideas indicates that there is a shared communication *beyond words* to which words can only point.

Self-quotation

The use of the Other's words seems to point backwards towards an anxiety of influence, but what of the delectation in reusing one's own words? The practice of self-quotation is a most intimate and enigmatic type of iteration in which the Proustian text is particularly rich. We have seen in chapter 3 the range of Proust's borrowings from personal sources, especially his own correspondence. It has even been proposed that *A la recherche* becomes a kind of 'occasional work' in the 1914–22 period,[43] for autobiographical material of every kind is patched into the still evolving narrative during these years. It was Luzius Keller who pointed out what is the most striking form of this self-citation: on occasion, Proust actually imports his own *already published text* into *A la recherche*.[44]

The famous 'Guermantes salute' is a marvellous example of this literary recycling. This ambiguous gesture of greeting figures twice in social columns Proust published in January 1904. The language differs somewhat, but the two bows involve the same basic mechanics. The movement is first attributed to the comtesse d'Haussonville:

All admire the magnificent bow with which she greets people, full of both affability and reserve, which bends her whole body forward in a gesture of sovereign civility, and, in a fluid, gymnastic motion that disappoints many, repositions it backwards the exact same distance as it had been projected forward.

[Chacun admire le salut magnificent dont elle accueille, plein à la fois d'affabilité et de réserve, qui penche en avant tout son corps dans un geste d'amabilité souveraine, et par une gymnastique harmonieuse dont beaucoup sont déçus, le rejette en arrière aussi loin exactement qu'il avait été projeté en avant.] (*CSB*, 486)

Just two weeks later, also in *Le Figaro*, and under the same pseudonym of Horatio, Proust ascribes a similar body salute to Robert de Montesquiou, this time in the parodied style of Saint-Simon (*CSB*, 710–11).

The earliest version of the salute was set in a fictional context in *Jean Santeuil*, and attributed to the duchesse de Réveillon. The backward spring of her body is mechanical rather than gymnastic, but the text is clearly the basis of the Haussonville description: 'she ... drew her [body] quickly back in a rapid, mechanical movement, and her spine executed ... a backward movement that extended at least as far as had her forward bow' ['elle ... retira [son corps] vivement en arrière par un mouvement rapide et mécanique, et son dos exécuta ... un mouvement de recul au moins aussi étendu que l'avait été le salut en avant'] (*JS*, 444). In *Le Côté de Guermantes* the bow is attributed to the duchesse de Guermantes (III, 226; II, 497), though shortly thereafter it is revealed as a gesture common to all the Guermantes ladies (III, 514; II, 737).

From unpublished fiction into a published social column, then into a published pastiche of a social column, and finally back, largely unchanged, into various fictional contexts: the social import of the bow is too piquant, the need to mime the gesture too strong, to allow room for any qualms about reuse. No authorial compunction prevents the fictionalization of an excerpt from a journalistic piece. This would be repetition without resolution, were it not for one further scene where the correct manipulation of a body salute shows that the Narrator has interiorized not only the Guermantes gesture, but its moral lesson. He re-enacts a version of the bow, creating wonderment among the aristocrats present, at a reception organized in honour of the Queen of England. As the duc de Guermantes approaches with the monarch on his arm, he sends repeated warm signals to the Narrator that he may approach. The first half of the salute is thus offered. The Narrator responds with its other half, a deep, but unsmiling inclination of the body, signalling his own understanding of his place in the social order. What the Guermantes salute embodies, of course, is a dual message of apparent friendliness covering a knowledge of superiority: 'that one should discern the fictitious character of this affability was what they called being well-bred; to suppose it to be genuine, a sign of ill-breeding' (IV, 72) ['[démêler] le caractère fictif de cette amabilité, c'est ce que [les Guermantes] appelaient être bien élevés; croire l'amabilité réelle, c'était la mauvaise éducation'] (III, 62). Not only is the Guermantes salute a witty observation from real life, it is reintegrated into Proust's fiction in the most meaningful way possible. Like the copying of the hawthorn's movement as it flowers, the Narrator's bow is at the edge of metaphor itself, the physical mime of hidden meaning, but social meaning on this occasion. The attraction of the meaning this gesture holds transcends any concern about damaging fiction with impurities.

Two of the most significant texts in *A la recherche*, structurally and aesthetically, are self-quotations set within quotation marks, and the two episodes are related. One is the well-known description of the Martinville spires (I, 217–18; I, 179–80), the other the Narrator's despairing exhortation to a line of sunlit trees as his train stops in the countryside (VI, 202; IV, 433–4). The text on the church steeples first appeared in a newspaper article in 1907,[45] was reused in *Du Côté de chez Swann*, and then appeared a third time when Proust republished the 1907 article in 1919 in *Pastiches et mélanges*. The passage on the trees was probably first set to paper in Proust's notebooks in 1908,[46] then reused in sketches before turning up in the final version of *Le Temps retrouvé*.

The resuscitation of text that is given a special status via quotation marks is a practice that began with Proust's earliest writing, and it happens first with a lyrical nature description Proust lifted from 'Avant la nuit', published in *La Revue Blanche* in 1893, and inserted in 'La Mort de Baldassare Silvande', composed in 1894–5.[47]

The successive copying of texts, and the placing of them within quotation marks each time, give them anteriority and obvious prestige. They are bracketed as though retrieved from a previous writerly incarnation. If the Proustian novel is, in one sense, 'un jeu de pièces détachées',[48] that is, more a game involving the successful arrangement of individual parts than a coherent whole, then it seems that some of the most important signifying parts in the assembly come from outside it, as though there were a larger structure, beyond the novel's text, which supersedes the somewhat aleatory form the novel takes. The architect, or construction super-intendent, in Proust has a weakness for underscoring the ambiguity of his enterprise – the real aspects of his fiction and the fictional aspects of reality – by setting previously inscribed text, sometimes non-fictional text, in positions of special importance.

The supreme ambiguity of text as independent fragment is seen in the passage on the Martinville spires, which is made to serve both as pure literature and pure journalism. The Narrator reworks his youthful prose poem and submits the piece – in vain, he thinks – as an article to *Le Figaro*.[49] When it finally is published, the journalistic context seems to rob it of its magic qualities. The ambiguity surrounding this text is increased several-fold by Proust's decision to reprint it in the 1919 edition of *Pastiches et mélanges*. He clearly had some qualms about duplicating himself, but his editorial explanation opens wide the question of crossovers between fiction and non-fiction and seems to stress that Marcel Proust the journalist, social columnist and critic must be viewed as a continuum of Marcel Proust not only as author, but also as hero and Narrator of *A la recherche*:

I have naturally avoided reproducing in this volume the many pages I published on churches in *Le Figaro*, for example, 'L'Eglise de village' (although it is, in my view, superior to many others that the reader will find here). However, they had been included in *A la recherche du temps perdu* and I could not repeat myself. If I have made an exception for this one, it is because in *Du Côté de chez Swann* it is only partially cited, in quotation marks, as *an example of what I wrote in my youth*. And in the 4th volume (not yet published) of *A la recherche du temps perdu*, the publication in *Le Figaro* of this revised page is the subject of almost an entire chapter.

[Je me suis naturellement abstenu de reproduire dans ce volume les nombreuses pages que j'ai écrites sur des églises dans *Le Figaro*, par exemple: 'L'église de village' (bien que très supérieure à mon avis à bien d'autres qu'on lira plus loin). Mais elles avaient passé dans *A la Recherche du Temps Perdu* et je ne pouvais me répéter. Si j'ai fait une exception pour celle-ci, c'est que dans *Du Côté de chez Swann* elle n'est que citée partiellement d'ailleurs, entre guillements, comme *un exemple de ce que j'écrivis dans mon enfance*. Et dans le IVe volume (non encore paru) de *A la Recherche du Temps Perdu*, la publication dans *Le Figaro* de cette page remaniée est le sujet de presque tout un chapitre.] (*CSB*, 64; the emphasis is mine.)

Implicit in these lines, I believe, is the assertion that fiction is not, in Proustian practice, a hermetically sealed reservoir of purified language, but rather a central pool connected to the individual's total linguistic reserves. There is, in fact, no separation of writing genres in Proust and no hierarchy between them. Text, even inspired poetic text, is chameleon-like and versatile. What counts is the retrospective view on to our former self, the retrospective view on to a series of our written self-expressions, and it is this gaze that is the arbiter of aesthetic correctness.

Proust finds tranquillity in the self-reflection of reading, an activity in which the Other's words are silenced as they are incorporated into the silent discourse of the reader. The text of the Other becomes a calming, reflecting mirror for the self, and in his preface to *Sésame et les lys*, Proust connects directly the process of reading to that of the neurasthenic being counselled by the psychotherapist. The role books play is one of inciting the patient to creative activity, and they do this by providing an image of their author in a 'calm mirror' that clearly reflects both the author's thought and at the same time leaves room for the reader's self-reflection. If reading the self becomes, in *Le Temps retrouvé*, the metaphor for creative activity, small wonder that the writer finds 'quotations' that interest him, and reproduces them when he recognizes them in himself. A writer who has already written is reading his previous experiences as well as his previous interpretations of them. Self-contemplation through quotation and self-quotation appears to be the linguistic antidote, in Proust's mature writing, to the hysteria of language he felt as a social individual.

MARCEL'S VOICE: THE RECURRING AUTHOR

In the very last years of his life, there is a movement in Proust's prose – closely connected to his practice of self-quotation and his insistence on self-contemplation as an active aesthetic principle – to acknowledge his pre-*Recherche* writing, and to reintegrate former selves – the translator, the story writer, the critic – into his fiction and into the character of the Narrator-as-author. It is as though an imperative of identification were at work, strong enough almost to override the final conceit of the novel, that is, the emergence of a Narrator now equipped to produce the great work of fiction he always knew he had within him. At the time of *Jean Santeuil* and in the *Contre Sainte-Beuve* period, Proust had distanced himself from any notion of compatibility of the fictional and social voice. But when *A l'ombre des jeunes filles en fleurs*, the new edition of *Du Côté de chez Swann* and *Pastiches et mélanges* appear together in 1919, there are visible signs in Proust's writing of a desire to reclaim his total writing output as part and parcel of his individuality and his voice.

Certain ambiguities of voice are characteristic of Proust's writing. One is the struggle between first and third person which the reader encounters in sections of *Jean Santeuil* and which migrates into *A la recherche* via the insertion, in Proust's first volume, of the largely third-person episode *Un Amour de Swann*. Maurice Bardèche discussed some of the crisscrossing between 'I' and 'he' in early versions of that volume; at times the Narrator is the protagonist, at times Swann.[50] In one fragment of *Jean Santeuil* (later to be transformed into the episode where the Narrator feels he is being held nude in the speaker's mouth when he hears his name pronounced), Marcel, not Jean, is the hero's name (*JS*, 830–1). In the early cahiers of *Contre Sainte-Beuve* this practice continues: the hero is identified as a Marcel who has a brother named Robert, just as the real-life Proust did. In one sketch, for example, the article published by the Narrator in *Le Figaro* is signed Marcel Proust (IV, 675); in another, the child who insists on his bedtime kiss is Marcel (I, 675).[51] In notes about the earliest known version of *A la recherche*, Proust mentions having written pages about a character who is apparently his brother Robert (*Le Carnet de 1908*, 56), though the latter disappears completely by the time *Combray* becomes a typescript (*Recherche*, I, 1061 and n.).

Is the much-discussed reappearance of the name Marcel in *La*

Prisonnière simply a holdover from this early ambivalent pattern? Not at all, in fact. The two texts in which the Narrator is thus identified are both quite late additions to the manuscript, as are other namings not included in the published text (see *Recherche*, III, 583, n. 1). One of the references is at once so playful and so brazen that it alone justifies all the ink that has been put to paper separating the first person of *A la recherche* into sets of sub-voices. It is Albertine who speaks: 'Then she would find her tongue and say: «My –» or «My darling –» followed by my Christian name, which, if we give the narrator the same name as the author of this book, would be «My Marcel», or «My darling Marcel» (V, 77) ['Elle retrouvait la parole, elle disait: «Mon» ou «Mon chéri», suivis l'un ou l'autre de mon nom de baptême, ce qui, en donnant au narrateur le même prénom qu'à l'auteur de ce livre, eût fait: «Mon Marcel», «Mon chéri Marcel»'] (III, 583).

It was when *Du Côté de chez Swann* first appeared in 1913, at a time when Proust feared that the work might be seen as a collection of memoirs, that he categorically disconnected himself from his Narrator. His interview with Elie-Joseph Bois in *Le Temps* states that the character who says 'I' is *not* himself. Later this distinction is deliberately blurred: writing in 1919 and 1920 in almost identical terms to critics André Chaumeix and Jean de Pierrefeu, Proust speaks of the 'narrator (or character) who says "I"' and is not always myself' (*Corr.*, XVIII, 524; XIX, 78). These late efforts, within the fiction and in public dialogue with a cultured readership, to highlight the relationship between self and protagonist, are paralleled by two other practices, one part of the narrative, the other barely external to it, that have the effect of expanding the notion of the narrating 'I' of *A la recherche*.

Much of the analysis of the first-person voice in *A la recherche* has had the effect of fragmenting the 'I' into discrete voices. For Leo Spitzer there were two voices (the 'erzählende Ich' and the 'erzählte Ich'), for Brian Rogers three, for Louis Martin-Chauffier four, for Marcel Muller nine.[52] These subdivisions shock all the less, given the text's explicit argument about the fragmentary or intermittent nature of the self. It should not be provocative, however, to point out that the essential characteristic of the 'I' is its oneness,[53] and that the prime effect of creating a consciousness that speaks as 'I' is to integrate and unite. Still, the 'I' is an expanded notion in Proust. One would almost want to claim, for it, Benveniste's suggestive expression 'the dilated I'[54] to take full account of the effort in the Proustian text to bring all selves under one self.

A number of textual and paratextual indications demonstrate Proust's desire to challenge the notion of a purely fictional first-person Narrator and to identify himself both as Narrator and as the author of a series of works that lead up to (or are, in fact, part of) *A la recherche*. Maurice Bardèche was one of the first to remark that in reusing at least one episode from *Jean Santeuil* in *A la recherche* Proust inadvertently wrote Françoise and Jean instead of Odette and Swann.[55] Of course this was simply a slip and remained consigned to the manuscripts. Another early text suggests that the ending of the 1910–11 version of *A la recherche* was to include a reference to *Les Plaisirs et les jours*, a totally unexpected meshing of the lessons the Narrator learns about the social life and those Marcel Proust (as the writer of 'Violante et la mondanité') had attempted to draw in 1896. The earlier short story is hauled into the present narrative in the same way Balzac might have referred to a second novel in the work at hand:

In the same way as, when I was living too much as a social being, I had been tempted to see in the sociability of young Violante, and some others, the true sin against the mind, and to attach to the solitude I did not possess a value which, since then, I have recognized it does not have, in the same way was it not the perhaps premature ageing of my nervous strength that caused me to seek desperately in solitude the sole source of all truth?

[De même que quand je vivais trop de la vie du monde, j'avais été tenté de voir dans la mondanité d'une jeune Violante, et de quelques autres, le véritable péché contre l'esprit, et d'attacher à la solitude que je ne possédais pas une valeur que j'avais reconnue depuis, qu'elle n'avait pas, de même n'était-ce pas le vieillissement, peut-être un peu prématuré, de ma force nerveuse qui me faisait désespérément chercher en elle la source unique de toute vérité?] (IV, 902)

This allusion was not included in the published text of *A la recherche*, but many other references to Proust's published works are.

The reader learns, for instance, that the Narrator is the author of a story about Swann's jealous love affair with Odette (V, 418; III, 868). In addition, there are two references in the published text of *A la recherche* to Proust's work on Ruskin, and other allusions in the *avant-textes*. During his stay in Venice, the Narrator takes notes for a study on Ruskin (V, 741; IV, 224); later, Jupien graciously compliments him on the Ruskin translation *Sésame et les lys* which he has sent to

Charlus (VI, 175; IV, 411). A draft text from 1910 brings the Ruskin studies into the fiction even more directly:

As an example of a style that is quite clearly without value, in the preface of *Sésame et les lys* I speak of certain Sunday cakes, I speak of 'their idle, sugary smell'. I could have described the shop, the closed houses, the fine fragrance of the cakes, their pleasant taste, but that wouldn't have constituted 'style'.

[Pour prendre un exemple dans un style précisément sans valeur, dans la Préface de *Sésame et les lys*, je parle de certains gâteaux du dimanche, je parle de 'leur odeur oisive et sucrée'. J'aurais pu décrire la boutique, les maisons fermées, la bonne odeur des gâteaux, leur bon goût, il n'y aurait pas eu style.] (IV, 818, n. 1)

And in another discarded draft, one of the *jeunes filles* is very impressed when she learns that the Narrator has translated Ruskin's works (IV, 666).

Many of these allusions in unpublished materials are early ones, but some of the most significant and perplexing self-references in the novel are of later date. In a note added to the manuscript of *Le Temps retrouvé*, where it is mentioned that Bergotte had seen great promise in the Narrator's adolescent writings, Proust observes that this is 'an allusion to the author's first work, *Les Plaisirs et les jours*' (VI, 442; IV, 618).[56] Then there is the disconcerting invocation to Charles Swann (which the Pléiade editors feel was added in 1922), who is directly identified with the real-life Charles Haas and spoken of as the hero of one of the Narrator/author's published novels:

And yet, my dear Charles Swann, whom I used to know when I was still so young and you were nearing your grave, it is because he whom you must have regarded as a young idiot has made you the hero of one of his novels that people are beginning to speak of you again and that your name will perhaps live. If, in Tissot's picture representing the balcony of the Rue Royale club, where you figure with Galliffet, Edmond de Polignac and Saint-Maurice, people are always drawing attention to you, it is because they see that there are some traces of you in the character of Swann. (V, 223)

[Et pourtant, cher Charles Swann, que j'ai si peu connu quand j'étais encore si jeune et vous près du tombeau, c'est déjà parce que celui que vous deviez considérer comme un petit imbécile a fait de vous le héros d'un de ses romans, qu'on recommence à parler de vous et que peut-être vous vivrez. Si dans le tableau de Tissot représentant le balcon du Cercle de la rue Royale, où vous êtes entre Galliffet, Edmond de Polignac et Saint-Maurice, on parle tant de vous, c'est parce qu'on voit qu'il y a quelques traits de vous dans le personnage de Swann.] (III, 705)

These words, along with the note from the 1919 publication *Pastiches et mélanges* that identifies Marcel Proust as the author both of the fictional text on the Martinville spires and the version of the same episode that appeared as an article in *Le Figaro* in 1907, reinforce the sensation that the acknowledgement of the 'real' author's productivity and artistic evolution, that is, of the oneness of his intellectual production, have become preoccupations of his fictional text. It appears important that the text eschew authorial anonymity in the end, and recuperate writing – even writing that is at a lower level of interiority – which demonstrates the continuity and the unity of voice that identify the complete Marcel Proust.

There is a peculiar use of first-person voice, on the edges of the Proustian text, that reinforces the connection established formally in his fiction between a Marcel/Narrator and Proust the working author. This is Proust's habit of speaking about his novel from inside and outside the narrative in the same breath. Two of the earliest examples are recorded in the *Carnet de 1908*:

After my grandmother's death, apparitions etc. – somewhere: Félicie unaware that I have taken trional.

[Après la mort de ma g^d mère, apparitions etc. – q.q. part Félicie ne sachant pas que j'ai pris du trional.] (108)

In the second part of the book the girl will be ruined, I will keep her without trying to possess her out of an inability to be happy.

[Dans la deuxième partie du livre la jeune fille sera ruinée, je l'entretiendrai sans chercher à la posséder par impuissance du bonheur.] (49)

In these editorial notes to himself, Proust places himself within the evolving fictional text as a first-person hero/Narrator. Of course, as I have suggested, Marcel Proust may indeed have been the hero of the novel at this early stage. But this practice expands considerably over the period 1908–22. It is no doubt most fully developed, and easiest to consult, in his notes for *Le Temps retrouvé*, where often Proust is both the writer to whom a memorandum is being left, and the hero who will carry out the action set out in the note.[57] The practice is also visible in editorial communications with the *Nouvelle Revue Française* and in letters to friends and acquaintances about the progress of his work.

Within the manuscripts there are literally endless examples of a dialogue about form, structure and order which takes place, as it were, *between* a first-person writer who is organizing that action and the first-person protagonist who will carry it out.

Capitalissimum (if I don't use it for Mme de Guermantes I will use it for Mme Swann). In the context of describing forgetting my grandmother (in reality it is Albertine's death which gives me the idea but it would be better, I think, to use it for my grandmother); the persons that we love die. In death they leave us a certain stock of memories...

[Capitalissimum (si je ne le mets pas pour Me de Guermantes je le mettrai pour Me Swann). A propos de l'oubli de ma grand'mère dont je parlerai (en réalité c'est la mort d'Albertine qui m'en donne l'idée mais il serait mieux je crois le mettre pour ma grand'mère); les êtres que nous aimons meurent. En mourant ils nous laissent une certaine provision de souvenirs...][58]

No doubt it would be better to place the whole passage of Cahier IV bis, where I compare the hotel in Balbec to the era of Solomon, in the mouth of M. de Charlus, for example when I chat with him at the home of the princesse de Guermantes when he says to me...

[Il serait sans doute mieux de mettre tout le morceau du Cahier IV bis où je compare l'hôtel de Balbec au temps de Salomon dans la bouche de M. de Charlus par exemple quand je cause avec lui chez la Princesse de Guermantes quand il me dit...][59]

Publicly too, Proust is insisting on being identified as an intermediate self, productive of and an actor within his own writing. In applying itself to this median space, the 'I' attains a certain self-assurance and independence, as though screened from attack by the very mixed nature of its identity. And in this bundling of component selves into one voice, Proust clearly moves close to the multiple but integrated identity to which he aspires. These organizing notes often provide, as well, the opportunity for yet another type of self-quotation. The quoting of self is marked, in the prose, by a measurable upswing in prosodic momentum, as though a new voice, a kind of biblical voice, were taking over from the stand-in editor:

I can, no doubt, when I have understood the reality that resides in the shared essence of memories, and understood that it is this which I would like to preserve ... say that I hear a quartet by Vinteuil through the door ... And I shall say something like this: 'As in times past at Combray ... I saw on the rising path ...'

[Je pourrai sans doute quand j'ai compris ce qu'il y a de réel dans l'essence commune du souvenir et que c'est cela que je voudrais conserver ... dire que j'entends à travers la porte un quatuor de Vinteuil ... Et je dirai à peu près ceci: 'Comme jadis à Combray... je vis dans le chemin montant...'][60]

In letters to Jacques Rivière, the consolidation of writer and Narrator into a single 'I' may appear as a handy short form for involved discussions on organizing manuscript material, but on other occasions, the practice seems to contain a supplemental pleasure of 'inhabiting the text' that exceeds the simple function of exchanging editorial practicalities:

You [= Rivière] would go directly to my arrival at home when I find in my pocket the card showing the name of the person I was supposed to escort, my parents' regrets that I'm not working, the idea of Mme Swann that I learn things by dining with Bergotte, and this would lead immediately to my quarrel with Gilberte.

[Vous [= Rivière] passeriez directement à ma rentrée chez moi quand je retrouve dans ma poche le carton où était le nom de la personne à qui je devais donner le bras, le regret de mes parents que je ne travaille pas, l'idée de Me Swann que je m'instruis en dînant avec Bergotte et cela conduirait immédiatement à ma brouille avec Gilberte.] (*Corr.*, XVIII, 184–5)

The writer appears extremely pleased with his own fictionalization, though for the reader there is a dizzying feeling of swinging back and forth between identities within identity. This same blurring of voices is not restricted to privileged correspondence between Proust and his editors. When Proust instructs René Blum in 1913 on the content of his work, so that Blum can present it to the staff of the *Nouvelle Revue Française*, again Narrator/protagonist and author are assimilated into one:

Thus part of the book is a part of my life which I had forgotten and which I suddenly regain as I eat a bit of madeleine that I have dipped in some tea ... Immediately my whole former life is restored and, as I say in my book ...

[Ainsi une partie du livre est une partie de ma vie que j'avais oubliée et que tout d'un coup je retrouve en mangeant un peu de madeleine que j'ai fait tremper dans du thé ... Aussitôt toute ma vie d'alors ressuscite et comme je le dis dans mon livre ...] (*Corr.*, XII, 296)

Marcel Muller cites, in the same vein, the example of a letter to Jacques Boulenger where Proust begs not to be considered a snob. As proof, Boulenger need only read Proust's fiction to see the modest situation he and his family occupy there.[61]

Let us now review briefly the concerns about the purity of art and literature that Proust expressed before the writing of *A la recherche du temps perdu*. His quarrel with Sainte-Beuve centred, in part, around the latter's social conception of literature: if one wrote in order to be appreciated by a few tasteful friends, then the product would always have the tone of an elevated society column. Proust condemns Sainte-Beuve not only because he believes his own tastes and purpose to be superior, but because Sainte-Beuve's preference for the social led him away from the more meaningful fiction and poetry of his youth. Part of Proust's disapproval of Balzac is also directed at the latter's inability to separate his life and his art. Balzac actually wrote to his sister that if he didn't make his mark by *La Comédie humaine*, he would succeed by his marriage with Mme Hanska. The force of his personal needs and ambitions invaded his literary discourse: the dramatic arrangement of events in some of his letters is indistinguishable from that in his fiction; he inserts real-life individuals into his novels alongside fictional characters; and he inserts himself into his fiction, providing the reader with naïve views of history and art, and shamelessly (and implausibly, for the purposes of fiction) making references to his other novels. Part of the problem, admits Proust, is that a writer like Balzac spends as much time with his fictional characters as with real-life ones.

In the final years of his life, Proust moved to a different and firmer view of the author in his work that brought him much closer to Balzac. The Proustian voice, speaking about the novel from outside, in letters and articles, or from inside, begins to sound very much like a single voice. Intra-fictional identifications of the Narrator with the author Marcel Proust coincide with a parallel set of equivalencies in non-fictional texts. I would agree with the judgement of Gérard Genette that Proust's initial success in writing in the first person was accomplished via a certain distancing of the author from himself, a 'mise en perspective' that freed him up from the early conundrum of the meaning of saying 'I':

Proust first had to overcome a certain adherence to himself, he had to detach himself so as to win the right to have his hero say «I», that hero who is not completely himself and not completely someone else.[62]

But what I see in the not-so-subtle interplay of authorial cross-references at the heart of Proust's writings is a kind of enthusiastic and wilful readherence to the biographical self, that is at the same time an affirmation of personal identity. To me, this is a deliberate shift (backward, in a sense) towards a Balzacian practice of the inextricability of life and art. I would argue, as well, that part of Proust's desire to reconnect himself publicly to the author who had written *Les Plaisirs et les jours* and articles in *Le Figaro*, and who had prefaced and translated works by Ruskin, stemmed from a realization that the work he was completing as his life ended was a reintegration not only of all aspects of his self, but of all aspects of his writing. It was a living patchwork, a living dialogue of the forms and voices adopted earlier in his career, all of which found their place and their justification in the 'sort of novel' that his work eventually became. By co-opting into fiction the pastiche, the critical article, the society column and the letter, the first-person voice of *A la recherche* joyously asserts its own dilation, a dilation that can easily take it beyond the formal borders of the traditional novel. This same sense of authorial play crosses over easily into Proust's late non-fiction. It is at some point in 1918–19,[63] when he reviews his pastiches for republication, that Proust adds an extravagant episode to his 1908 Goncourt pastiche. In it, the eccentric Marcel Proust makes an appearance, becomes involved in a fist fight, then a duel, with Zola, and later is reported to have committed suicide following investment losses.

As critical readers, we must, of course, indicate our alarm at the degree to which the Proustian text infringes upon the proprieties and plausibility of fiction. Genette has done so in connection with the Goncourt pastiche, which he presents as the most troublesome example of a series of impossibilities (others relate to temporal and spatial questions) contained within *A la recherche*. It may be plausible at the level of fiction in general, he argues, to have Proust's characters become personalities who are reviewed in the *Journal des Goncourt*. But he finds that, at the level of *A la recherche* as a work of fiction, the Goncourt sequence is impossible from the reader's vantage point, for it is fiction once removed, truly 'pure fiction'. Richard Sayce has taken Genette nicely to task for his failure to suspend disbelief,[64] but the conclusion of Genette's remarks remains suggestive:

this strange episode ... represents, within the work, a kind of door opening on to something other than the work, something that the work cannot know without destroying itself, a door which is there but which cannot be opened or closed.[65]

Indeed, it seems to me that the entire set of structural and technical anomalies we have noted in Proust's fiction deliberately point beyond the work at hand to a work conceived of as even more broadly open than has been admitted to date. And this is not such a paradox, for Proust's aesthetic imperative of self-contemplation places emphasis on the relationship between reflections that happen outside the work of art, and the work of art itself.

The acceptance, indeed the flaunting, of 'improper' views of fictional status and voice, is one of the striking characteristics of the mature Proustian novel. The mood has changed between 1908 and 1922. Instead of doubts, Proust's text exudes a complex mood of play, irony and confrontation. Discussions of form retain elements of tension, and are always demonstrations, but some of these nodes of formal anxiety – the bogus Goncourt text and the article in *Le Figaro* are two of them – have become pranks at the junctures of the story. Pranks with a purpose, of course, for as they make fun of the notion of purity in literature, they also have instructional value. What the *Figaro* article and Goncourt pastiche do, as they intervene in the textual flow, is to foreground in a dramatic way not only the ambiguity of the novel's own form, and the mixed nature of its texture, but the stubborn insistence of Marcel Proust that 'form is myself', that 'form is what I have written'. The self perceives itself, as one critic has said, as 'a multiplicity of constantly changing forces, energies and vectors that "meet", as it were, to form a "given" individual in time and space'.[66] But the Proustian self desires a more permanent assemblage, and one of the stubborn, ongoing instincts in Proust's text is to claim for itself all of its authorship. In the same sense as one can speak of the flowing together of the arts in Proust, that is, painting, music and literature,[67] one is conscious of a very deliberate attempt to have all literary forms coincide and fit within the same envelope.

Proust's utter nonchalance concerning the loss of fictional verisimilitude has its tonic side. Anxiety is done. The author of *A la recherche du temps perdu* has become the anomalous man-in-his-works, the man of his works, that an equally contradictory Balzac had become before him.

Conclusion

It is thus Bakhtin's conception of the novel as a carnivalesque, parodic meeting-place of all genres which seems to elucidate best the Proustian project. Perhaps because dialogism is essentially an oral concept, it applies particularly well to Proust's written discourse, itself so connected to orality. Dialogues of structure and genre exist alongside the dialogues of words. Meaning is located in the dialogic process of interaction between various types of texts, voices and languages. As David Lodge and Lennard Davis have each suggested in a slightly different context, as soon as a variety of literary forms or genres is allowed into a textual space – highly reader-conscious discourses like journalism or letters, expressly ironic forms like parodies or pastiches, third-person narration alongside first-person – a resistance is established to the domination of any single form.[1]

Does the advent of this newly purposeful author at the end of *A la recherche* mean that peace has been made with the question of the nerves and their anxieties? In his discussions of artistic individuality, Proust connects the idea of intermittence and recurrence to the individual's nervous makeup. But what thematic recurrence lays bare is a purified version of the composer's or the painter's nervous physiognomy, the essence of their individuality which, in the case of normal human exchange, remains incommunicable:

I sensed that ... whatever gave me the sort of joy which I had found from time to time and at certain moments in my life, I could no more express it than the peculiar *nervous* quality of intoxication. Now this inexpressible quality is precisely what we experience and is, as it were, the generalization of what is none the less most distinctive *in the nerves and in the soul*, as if it were that inexpressible quality exteriorized that one senses in Elstir's colours, in Vinteuil's harmonies, as the colours of the spectrum make external and visible the intimate composition of stars that we will never see.

[je sentais que ... ce qui me donnait cette sorte de joie que je retrouvais de temps en temps à certains moments de ma vie, je ne pouvais pas plus l'exprimer que la qualité particulière, *nerveuse*, d'une ivresse. Or ce genre d'inexprimable c'est justement cela que nous retrouvons, et comme la généralisation de ce qu'il y a pourtant de plus particulier *dans les nerfs et dans l'âme*, comme si cela projetait au-dehors celui qu'ils ressentirent, dans les couleurs d'un Elstir, dans les harmonies d'un Vinteuil, comme les couleurs du spectre extériorisent la composition intime des astres que nous ne verrons jamais.] (III, 1169; the emphasis is mine.)

Thus the semi-conscious pulsations of the nerves are satisfied – and a structuring figure acknowledged – at one level. At another, anxiety remains, visible in the obvious efforts to organize a closure that will be the perfect closure of form.

Proust has interiorized Théodule Ribot's lesson on the intermittence of intuitive willpower, and intermittence becomes the essential figure explaining his Narrator's spiritual life and his own compositional practice as a novelist. Not only does Proust replace the notion of narrative exposition by the intermittent repetition of important situations and episodes, the intermittent, repeated resumption of writing appears, at a certain level, to constitute Proust's method of structuring his text. Iteration might be viewed as a sign of neurotic obsession, but this particular narrative not only accommodates what may be obsessional in these recurrences, it also calms the anxiety by recognizing that recursiveness is the essence of the author's effort towards style. The repeated investigations of a feeling or sensation are not a source of frustration, but a vehicle for transporting the Proustian individual beyond the anxiety that language initially provokes. In a letter to Antoine Bibesco, Proust describes the final serenity which writing affords:

But I hide my deep, clarified impression, the one I truly possess, beneath a unified style and beside fifteen others where one day, I hope and believe, penetrating eyes will discover it. And all that remains of exhilarating hours is a sentence, sometimes only an epithet, and they are calm.

[Mais mon impression approfondie, éclaircie, possédée, je la cache à côté de quinze autres sous un style uni où j'ai foi qu'un jour des yeux pénétrants la découvriront. Et d'heures exaltées il ne reste qu'une phrase, parfois qu'une épithète, et calmes.] (*Corr.*, XI, 235)

In superimposing episodes and condensing impressions via recurrence and reiteration, Proust arrives at a linguistic peace. A dizzying set of impressions can be made to coalesce, through repeated metaphor, into a single word. Repetition isolates essence, and it is the contemplation of this essential part-self, distilled into language, that is the final relaxant for Proustian anxieties.

Notes

INTRODUCTION

1 Frédéric Fladenmuller uses this term. See note 8 below.
2 Quoted by Mark Micale, *Approaching Hysteria*, p. 116.
3 Paris: Masson, 1904. Translated as *The Psychic Treatment of Nervous Disorders (The Psychoneuroses and their Moral Treatment)*. Chapter 24 discusses intermittent heart-beat in nervous individuals.
4 See *Marcel Proust: écrits de jeunesse, 1887–1895*, pp. 101–9.
5 'New hysteria studies' is the title of Mark Micale's introduction to his useful, wide-ranging study *Approaching Hysteria*. The interest in hysteria-based narrative may be seen in studies such as Emily Apter's *Feminizing the Fetish*, Janet Beizer's *Ventriloquized Bodies* and Jann Matlock's *Scenes of Seduction*.
6 Georges Rivane, *Influence de l'asthme sur l'œuvre de Marcel Proust* (Paris: La Nouvelle Edition, 1945). See also René Etiemble, 'Le Style de Marcel Proust est-il celui d'un asthmatique?' in *Cinq états des 'Jeunes filles en fleurs', avec les placards et manuscrits de Marcel Proust* (Alexandria: Editions du Scarabée, 1947), and François-Bernard Michel, *Le Souffle coupé* (Paris: Gallimard, 1984), especially chapter 4, 'Marcel Proust: son asthme et sa recherche mortelle du sens'.
7 Paris: Lefèbvre, 1950.
8 See, for example, Jean Milly, 'Le Style de la maladie chez Proust', *BMP*, 43 (1993), 58–71; Frédéric Fladenmuller, 'Le Nerveux Narrateur dans *A la recherche du temps perdu*' and Marie Miguet, 'Idéologie du *Traité d'hygiène* d'Adrien Proust'.
9 Henry, *Marcel Proust: théories pour une esthétique*.
10 In one letter he complains that he has no overall conception of the work (*Corr.*, II, 124).
11 The asthma study (*L'Hygiène des asthmatiques*) was by his colleague Dr Eugène Brissaud, while the work on neurasthenia was co-authored with Dr Gilbert Ballet (*L'Hygiène du neurasthénique*).
12 Antoine Compagnon has emphasized this point; see *Proust entre deux siècles*, p. 134.

13 See Jean-Louis Baudry, *Proust, Freud et l'autre*, pp. 31–2.
14 Luc Fraisse uses the term 'réinvestissement', and gives wonderful examples of the process in *L'Œuvre cathédrale*, pp. 210–11.
15 As has the publication of much manuscript material in the journal *Bulletin d'informations proustiennes*.
16 See Luc Fraisse, *Le Processus de la création chez Marcel Proust: Le fragment expérimental*.
17 Annick Bouillaguet has demonstrated that Proust lifted Elstir's detailed description of the church at Balbec (II, 485–7; II, 196–8) verbatim from Emile Mâle's work *L'Art religieux au XIIIe siècle en France*. See her article 'Intertextes proustiens', 83, and her book *Marcel Proust: le jeu intertextuel*, especially chapter 4, 'La Citation devenue plagiat'.

1 PROUST BETWEEN NEURASTHENIA AND HYSTERIA

1 Micale, *Approaching Hysteria*, p. 3. His comments on hysteria in literature are of particular interest (chapter 3, 'Hysteria as Metaphor').
2 See chapter 4 of Jann Matlock's book, *Scenes of Seduction*, and p. 338 nn. 14 and 15.
3 In her study *Feminizing the Fetish*.
4 Flaubert's entry for hysteria in the *Dictionnaire des idées reçues* reads, 'Hysteria. Confuse it with nymphomania.'
5 This definition is Debora Silverman's in *Art Nouveau in Fin-de-Siècle France*, p. 80.
6 Paris: Dentu, 1881.
7 Under the pseudonym Charles Epheyre, Richet published a novel dealing with hysteria, hallucination and hypnotism called *Possession* (Paris: Ollendorff, 1887); in an 1880 article in *La Revue des Deux Mondes*, he defers to Flaubert's portrait of the hysteric as being the most accurate. See Beizer, *Ventriloquized Bodies*, pp. 61, 138.
8 Goncourt wonders if the disapproval is the result of rivalry: 'Does he resent that since I entered literature I have worked on nervous maladies? Would he prefer that he alone in the world have that monopoly?' *Journal des Goncourt*, 4 vols. (Paris: Fasquelle/Flammarion, 1956), III, 885 (1888).
9 *Œuvres complètes*, II, 83.
10 *Idées et sensations* (Paris: Librairie Internationale, 1866), p. 228.
11 *Ibid.*, p. 126.
12 Outside fiction, Proust seems to still hold to the Goncourt view. In a letter of 1918 to Lionel Hauser, he suggests that deviance and ill-health (Musset's drunkenness, Flaubert's epilepsy, Rimbaud's perversions) are necessary components of a writer's genius: 'physical malady is (in these degenerate times) almost a condition of intellectual strength that approaches genius' ['la maladie physique est (dans nos jours dégénérés)

presque une condition de la force intellectuelle un peu géniale'] (*Corr.*, XVII, 215).

13 *The Anxiety of Influence.*

14 *Félicité* was the early title of *Un Cœur simple.*

15 Some of the parallels drawn here are suggested by Mireille Naturel in her article 'Le Rôle de Flaubert ', 78–9.

16 Quoted by Naturel, 'Le Rôle de Flaubert', 79.

17 Gustave Flaubert, *Correspondance* (Paris: Pléiade, 1973), I, 229. For a discussion of Flaubert's nervous malady, see Bruneau, *Les Débuts littéraires de Gustave Flaubert*, pp. 359–83 and 578–84; Sartre, *L'Idiot*, III, 1771–920; and Beizer, *Ventriloquized Bodies*, pp. 93–8.

18 Gustave Flaubert, *Correspondance*, I, 214.

19 *Ibid.*, p. 229.

20 Sainte-Beuve, whose *Portraits contemporains* Proust was reading in 1908, mentions that Senancour had developed a strange nervous malady after drinking a white wine from Saint-Maurice (see *Textes retrouvés*, ed. Philip Kolb, p. 51, n. 2).

21 Letter quoted by Sartre, *L'Idiot*, III, 34–5.

22 '[Flaubert] will have great difficulty making [of words] the living instruments of his own movement outside himself and he will never succeed completely because he was *passivized* by his mother's attentions and because that movement and his project – his permanent possibilities for action – were, from the beginning, *passed over in silence.*' Sartre, *L'Idiot*, I, 151.

23 Quoted by Sartre, *L'Idiot*, I, 36.

24 Michel Raimond, *La Crise du roman* (Paris: José Corti, 1966), pp. 269–70.

25 Quoted by Naomi Schor, *Breaking the Chain*, p. 26. See also Gérard Genette's essay 'Silences de Flaubert' in *Figures I.*

26 Quoted by Sartre, *L'Idiot*, III, 1472.

27 *Ibid.*, I, 619.

28 *Breaking the Chain*, p. 13.

29 Letter to Louise Colet, 16 January 1852 (*Correspondance*, II, 31).

30 *L'Idiot*, III, 1618.

31 *The Golden Notebook* (London: Michael Joseph, 1972), p. 14.

32 *Correspondance*, II, 483.

33 *Ibid.*, p. 335.

34 *Ibid.*, pp. 483–4.

35 Quoted by Philip Kolb, ed., *Textes retrouvés*, p. 52, n. 13.

36 Nerval is felt to be especially close on this score. In the article on Flaubert's style, Proust says, 'This phenomenon of [involuntary] memory served as a transition for Nerval, that great genius almost all of whose works could take as their title that which I gave first of all to one of my own: *The Intermittences of the Heart*' (*ASB*, 273) ['Ce phénomène de mémoire [involontaire] a servi de transition à Nerval, à ce grand génie dont presque toutes les œuvres pourraient avoir pour titre celui que

j'avais donné d'abord à une des miennes: *Les Intermittences du cœur*']
(*CSB*, 599).

37 See the article 'Sentiments filiaux d'un parricide' (*CSB*, 150–9).

38 *Le Journal pour Rire*, no. 28 (9 April 1852).

39 Baudelaire, *Mon Cœur mis à nu*, in *Œuvres complètes*, I, 703.

40 *Œuvres complètes*, II, 83.

41 See *Le Carnet de 1908*, p. 65; and *ASB*, 26; *CSB*, 234–5.

42 In addition to the Goncourt parodies in *Pastiches et mélanges* and *Le Temps retrouvé*, Proust composed a pastiche in an album he offered to the wife of Georges de Lauris. A portion of it is quoted in *Corr.*, XI, 161, n. 5.

43 See Richard Sayce's thoughtful article on the relationship between Proust's style and that of the Goncourt *Journal*, 'The Goncourt Pastiche in *Le Temps retrouvé*', Jean Milly's chapter 'Le Pastiche Goncourt dans *Le Temps retrouvé*' (in *Proust dans le texte et l'avant-texte*), his chapter on the Goncourts in *Les Pastiches de Proust*, and the Pléiade notes on the Goncourt pastiche (IV, 287–95).

44 In fact, the younger Goncourt admitted he had contracted syphilis in 1850, twenty years before his death. See André Billy, *Vie des frères Goncourt* (Editions de l'Imprimerie Nationale de Monaco, 1956), II, 89. Similar symptoms caused considerable confusion, in the second half of the century, between various nervous ailments and syphilis. See Alfred Fournier, *Les Affections parasyphilitiques* (Paris: Rueff, 1894), pp. 110–22. On 23 January 1862, Baudelaire suffered a first debilitating attack which he thought to be hysterical in origin.

45 Billy, *Vie des frères Goncourt*, II, 88.

46 *Nouveaux Essais de psychologie contemporaine* (Paris: Alphonse Lemerre, 1885), p. 173.

47 Edmond and Jules de Goncourt, *Charles Demailly* (Paris: Charpentier-Fasquelle, 1913), pp. 279–80.

48 Odette de Crécy is described as 'surrounded by Dresden pieces' (II, 221–2; I, 605). Laure Hayman, on whom the character of Odette was at least partially based, had the same tastes (*Corr.*, I, 189).

49 Milly, *Les Pastiches de Proust*, p. 161.

50 And not in February 1892, as stated in some biographies.

51 *Journal des Goncourt*, 9 vols. (Paris: Charpentier, 1887–96), IX, 91–2.

52 Tics such as the use of the conditional of conjecture ('serait'), the delayed apposition of certain nouns ('bouton'), and the colloquial 'et c'est …'. These are mentioned by Sayce, 'The Goncourt Pastiche', pp. 105–7.

53 *Ibid.*, pp. 110–14.

54 Proust saw the play either in 1891 – if Philip Kolb's dating of this letter is correct – or during its first run in 1888 (cf. *CSB*, 643, n. 1). Given the impact the production had on Proust, it may be significant that he saw it with Bizet, a young man for whom he felt a strong (though apparently unrequited) sexual attraction.

55 Letter of 19 February 1918 to Jacques Porel (*Corr.*, XVII, 120). See Annick Bouillaguet, 'Le Pastiche des Goncourt dans *Le Temps retrouvé*', 82–91. There are other brief comments on Réjane in *CSB*, 600–1.

56 *Germinie Lacerteux* (Paris: Livre de Poche, 1990), p. 145. Subsequent page references are to this edition.

57 Pierre Sabatier, '*Germinie Lacerteux*' *des Goncourt* (Paris: SFELT, 1948), p. 138.

58 *Journal des Goncourt* (Paris: Fasquelle/Flammarion, 1956), IV, 583, 2 June 1894.

59 Letter from Schwob to Gide, quoted by Eric Deschodt in *Gide: le 'contemporain capital'* (Paris: Perrin, 1991), pp. 36–7.

60 See the Pléiade editors' comments, I, 167, n. 1.

61 In the view of one of Proust's doctors, Paul Sollier, the symptoms of hysteria were the result of the same deficiency as neurasthenia, nervous exhaustion (*L'Hystérie et son traitement*, p. 10).

62 New York: Wood, 1880. Beard's first article on neurasthenia appeared earlier, in 1869 ('Neurasthenia, or Nervous Exhaustion', *Boston Medical and Surgical Journal*, 80 (1869), 245–59). See F. G. Gosling, *Before Freud: Neurasthenia and the American Medical Community 1870–1910* (Urbana: University of Illinois Press, 1987), especially chapter 1.

63 New York: G. P. Putnam's Sons, 1881.

64 New York: E. B. Treat, 1884. It was translated as *La Neurasthénie sexuelle, hygiène, causes, symptômes et traitement* (Paris: Société d'éditions scientifiques, 1895).

65 Edward Shorter, *From Paralysis to Fatigue*, pp. 220 ff.; also, p. 221, n. 87.

66 Paris: A. Maloine.

67 Elaine Showalter describes this treatment in *The Female Malady*, pp. 138–9. Sollier's sensitive handling of female hysteric patients is investigated by Martha Noel Evans in *Fits and Starts*, pp. 66–7.

68 See Shorter, *From Paralysis to Fatigue*, pp. 223–4; cf. Showalter, *The Female Malady*, p. 135, and Adrien Proust, *L'Hygiène du neurasthénique*, p. 11.

69 Micale, *Approaching Hysteria*, pp. 163–5.

70 Silverman, *Art Nouveau*, p. 82, n. 35.

71 Max Nordau, *Degeneration*, 1895 (rpt. New York: Howard Fertig, 1968), pp. 115–16. Quoted by Silverman, *Art Nouveau*, p. 82.

72 Fouillée, 'Dégénérescence: le passé et le présent de notre race', *Revue des Deux Mondes*, 131 (1895), 793–824.

73 Sander Gilman, *Difference and Pathology*, p. 278, n. 52.

74 *Les Morticoles* (Paris: Editions Fasquelle, 1956), p. 344.

75 Micale, *Approaching Hysteria*, p. 197.

76 Paul Dubois, *The Psychic Treatment of Nervous Disorders*, p. 18.

77 *Marius* (Paris: Editions de Fallois, 1988), p. 26.

78 See Gosling, *Before Freud*, p. 13.

79 Micale, *Approaching Hysteria*, p. 292. Neurasthenia has been equated with chronic fatigue syndrome by proponents of the view that both con-

ditions are 'culturally sanctioned forms of illness behaviour'. See Abbey and Garfinkel, 'Neurasthenia and Chronic Fatigue Syndrome', 1638.

80 Dr Proust's study of neurasthenia appeared during a decade that witnessed a deluge of books on nervous disorders. On hysteria, there were the two major studies, Pierre Janet's *L'Etat mental des hystériques* (Paris: Alcan, 1894) and Paul Sollier's *Genèse et nature de l'hystérie* (Paris: Alcan, 1897), the latter followed by Sollier's *L'Hystérie et son traitement* (Paris: Alcan, 1901). In 1893 Emile Laurent published a *Guide pratique pour le traitement des névrosés* (Paris: Société d'Editions Scientifiques) and in 1895 *La Neurasthénie et son traitement* (Paris: Maloine). Alcan published *La Famille névropathique* by Charles Féré in 1894, and several authors examined the relationship between nervousness and genius: Edouard Toulouse, *L'Enquête médico-psychologique sur les rapports de la supériorité intellectuelle avec la névropathie* (Paris: Société d'Editions Scientifiques, 1896); Emile Laurent, *La Poésie décadente devant la science psychiatrique* (Paris: Maloine 1897). To this list one may add the works cited in the article by Frédéric Fladenmuller ('Le Nerveux Narrateur dans *A la recherche du temps perdu*') and those referred to by Jo Yoshida in 'Proust et la maladie nerveuse'.

81 See Jean Milly, 'Le Style de la maladie chez Proust', *BMP*, 43 (1993), 58–71; Jo Yoshida, 'Proust et la maladie nerveuse' and 'La Maladie nerveuse chez Proust: genèse du portrait du docteur Boulbon'; Dominique Mabin, *Le Sommeil de Marcel Proust* (Paris: Presses Universitaires de France, 1992); Frédéric Fladenmuller, 'Le Vocabulaire nerveux dans l'œuvre de Marcel Proust', *BIP*, 15 (1984), 53–64, and 'Le Nerveux Narrateur dans *A la recherche du temps perdu*'; and several articles by Marie Miguet: 'La Neurasthénie entre science et fiction'; '*La Recherche*, tombeau d'Adrien Proust?', *BIP*, 22 (1991), 99–109; and 'Idéologie du *Traité d'hygiène* d'Adrien Proust'.

82 The quotation marks are Proust's. He is alluding to the title of Théodule Ribot's work, *Les Maladies de la volonté*.

83 See a letter to Marie Nordlinger, *Corr.*, II, 377.

84 This line may be an echo of Adrien Proust (*L'Hygiène du neurasthénique*, p. 76): 'Often obsessed by some fixed idea or some hypochondriac preoccupation, *[neurasthenics] live, so to speak, in a state of perpetual absent-mindedness*' ['Souvent obsédés par quelque idée fixe, quelque préoccupation hypocondriaque, *[les neurasthéniques] vivent pour ainsi dire en état de distraction perpétuelle*']. The emphasis is mine.

85 Henry, *Marcel Proust: théories pour une esthétique*, p. 81. Séailles' major publications were *Essai sur le génie de l'art* (Paris: Baillière, 1883) and *Léonard de Vinci* (Paris: Perrin, 1892).

86 *Le Monde comme volonté et comme représentation* (Paris: Alcan, 1888), translated by Burdeau. The true first translation of this work into French dates from 1886, though it was published in Leipzig.

87 *Théories pour une esthétique*, pp. 46–55 and 70–1.
88 Czoniczer, *Quelques antécédents de A la recherche du temps perdu*, pp. 11–14.
89 *La Philosophie de Schopenhauer*, p. 150.
90 Shorter, *From Paralysis to Fatigue*, p. 393, n. 48. The full title of the Camus-Pagniez work is *Isolement et psychothérapie: traitement de l'hystérie et de la neurasthénie, pratique de la rééducation morale et physique* (Paris: Alcan, 1904).
91 *L'Etat mental des hystériques* (Paris: Alcan, 1894), translated as *The Mental State of Hystericals*. Dr Proust appears to borrow directly from Janet in discussing willpower deficit in neurasthenics: 'Aboulia, in other words, the collapse of the will, is one of the most common characteristics of *the mental state of neurasthenics*' (*L'Hygiène du neurasthénique*, p. 75).
92 *Mental State of Hystericals*, p. 409.
93 *Ibid.*, p. 104.
94 This article is included in *La Psychologie des sentiments* (Paris: Alcan, 1896), pp. 140–70. Ribot returns to the question of affective memory in *Problèmes de psychologie affective*. Another researcher-colleague of Ribot who wrote from a very Proustian position on affective memory was Frédéric Paulhan (*La Fonction de la mémoire et le souvenir affectif* (Paris: Alcan, 1904)). See Elisabeth Czoniczer's excerpts from his texts (*Quelques antécédents*, pp. 104–9). He also wrote a study of the will (*La Volonté* (Paris: Octave Doin, 1903)).
95 *L'Hérédité, étude psychologique sur ses phénomènes, ses lois, ses causes, ses conséquences* [title of the first edition] (Paris: Ladrange, 1873); *Les Maladies de la mémoire* (Paris: Alcan, 1881).
96 Ribot, *Problèmes de psychologie affective*, p. 36.
97 *Ibid.*, p. 1.
98 The allusions to Chateaubriand and Nerval (*Problèmes de psychologie affective*, pp. 169–70, 365–6) recall, of course, the Narrator's connection to the same two writers as aesthetic mentors.
99 Ribot, *Problèmes de psychologie affective*, p. 161.
100 *Les Maladies*, pp. 102–3.
101 *Ibid.*
102 *Ibid.*, p. 105.
103 *De l'action des aimants sur quelques troubles nerveux et spécialement sur les anesthésies* (1879).
104 Quoted by Marie Miguet, 'Idéologie du *Traité d'hygiène* d'Adrien Proust', pp. 222–3.
105 *American Nervousness*, p. 52.
106 Freud, who diagnosed himself as neurasthenic, believed that sexual neurasthenia was caused by the replacement of 'adequate' sexual relations by inadequate behaviour (masturbation or nocturnal emissions). See *Collected Papers* (London: Hogarth Press, 1949), I, 76, 98, 146.

107 *L'Hygiène du neurasthénique*, pp. 14–19. These pages provide an interesting discussion that is very likely a source for Marcel Proust's own theory of the heredity of transformation.

108 *L'Hygiène du neurasthénique*, p. 18. Elsewhere in his study Dr Proust condemns over-long schooling and, especially in residential schools, the lack of physical exercise and excessive onanism. Marcel Proust mentions an argument with his father during which the latter begged him to stop masturbating for at least four days. Marcel was seventeen at the time (*Correspondance avec Daniel Halévy*, p. 43).

109 See Marie Miguet's article, 'Le "Père Norpois" et le roman familial'.

2 AN ANXIETY OF LANGUAGE

1 *Proust*, pp. 56–7.
2 See the remarks of Yves Sandre (*CSB*, 690), and Frédéric Fladenmuller, 'Le Nerveux Narrateur', p. 36.
3 Note to *Sésame et les lys*, p. 70.
4 Lois Jaeck, *Marcel Proust and the Text as Macrometaphor*, p. 16.
5 Note to *Sésame et les lys*, p. 70.
6 Albert Flament, *Le Bal du Pré Catelan*, p. 41.
7 Fernand Gregh, *Mon Amitié avec Marcel Proust*, pp. 8–9.
8 Elisabeth de Clermont-Tonnerre, *Robert de Montesquiou et Marcel Proust*, p. 34.
9 *Ibid.*, p. 136.
10 *Correspondance générale*, I, 181.
11 *Mon Amitié avec Marcel Proust*, p. 49.
12 Fernand Gregh believed that Proust borrowed the three-adjective habit from Anatole France (*Mon Amitié*, p. 19).
13 Corr., p. 121.
14 *Robert de Montesquiou et Marcel Proust*, p. 10.
15 *Le Visiteur du soir* (Geneva: La Palatine, 1949), pp. 10–11.
16 See George Painter, *Marcel Proust: A Biography*, II, 160–3, for a discussion of the beginning of their friendship.
17 *Hommage à Marcel Proust*, pp. 77–8.
18 Edmond de Goncourt had labelled not Racine, but Phèdre 'the great legendary hysteric' (*La Faustin* (Paris: Charpentier, 1882), p. 112).
19 Lacan quoted by Catherine Millot, *Nobodaddy: l'hystérie dans le siècle* (Paris: Point hors ligne, 1988), p. 156.
20 *Ibid.*, p. 106.
21 G. W. F. Hegel, *Phenomenology of Spirit*, trans. A. V. Miller (Oxford: Clarendon Press, 1977), p. 66. Quoted by Malcolm Bowie, *Freud, Proust and Lacan*, p. 146.
22 *Le Livre à venir* (Paris: Gallimard, 1959), pp. 27–8.
23 Once more, a Charles, and, like Charles Swann, Charlus, Charles

Morel, Charles Demailly, overly devoted to the social, rather than the permanent values of art.

24 Hanotaux had met the monocled Leconte de Lisle when the latter was a librarian at the Senate and had been entertained by stories of Sainte-Beuve's time as a library employee. See my article 'Norpois, père ou mentor', *Revue d'Histoire Littéraire de la France*, 1 (January–February 1993), 123–4.

25 The editors of *Contre Sainte-Beuve* quote part of this passage as the one which disturbed Proust (*CSB*, 224, n. 2).

26 I borrow this analysis, which I have compressed considerably, from Bourdieu's *Distinction: A Social Critique of the Judgement of Taste*, a translation of *La Distinction: Critique sociale du jugement*. See especially Bourdieu's discussion of the 'aesthetic disposition' and the postscript 'Toward a "Vulgar" Critique of "Pure" Critiques' (pp. 28–50 and 485–500). Bourdieu does not apply his ideas explicitly to Proust, although he refers to him not infrequently.

27 Bourdieu, *Distinction*, p. 47.

28 In the same issue of *La Revue Blanche* in which Proust's article appeared (15 July 1896), Lucien Muhlfeld depicts Proust's literary tastes as those of a salon habitué. Mallarmé's own response (*La Revue Blanche*, 1 September 1896) suggests that certain contemporaries are incapable of reading, 'except the newspaper'. See the full discussion of the quarrel in Bertrand Marchal, *La Religion de Mallarmé* (Paris: José Corti, 1988), pp. 467–79.

29 Stéphane Mallarmé, *Œuvres complètes* (Paris: Pléiade, 1945), p. 368.

30 'Discourse in the Novel', in *The Dialogic Imagination*, pp. 259–422.

31 *Distinction*, p. 485.

32 *Etudes sur le temps humain*, I, 386.

33 Proust also chides Paul Morand for attempting to cover over a lack of profound sentiment in some of his poetry with dramatic voice intonation (*Corr.*, XVIII, 423).

34 There are a number of references to the bodily language of Sainte-Beuve in sketches (see IV, 810–11, 858).

35 *Marcel Proust romancier*, I, 341–2.

36 See Georges de Lauris, *A un ami* (Paris: Amiot-Dumont, 1958), p. 16.

37 I refer especially to the passages on the Narrator's admiration for Bergotte (I, 110–14; I, 92–6), then his meeting with and impressions of the writer (II, 138–58; I, 536–52), and a number of sketches related to these texts (I, 781–90; 1027–34).

38 Marie Miguet discusses aspects of Adrien Proust's voice and style in 'Le "Père Norpois" et le roman familial'.

39 The kernel of this text seems to appear first in a sketch describing a symphony that is variously attributed to César Franck or Vinteuil (III, 1145–6), and in another manuscript note about Franck: 'For Franck / It

is not a motif that was recurring, it is the beginning of a neuralgia, difficult to localize, vague and ganglionic' ['Pour Franck / Ce n'est pas un motif qui revenait, c'est une névralgie qui commence, difficile à localiser, vague et ganglionnaire']. See Compagnon, *Proust entre deux siècles*, p. 46, n. 6.

3 TRANSITIVE WRITING

1 Montreal: Presses de l'Université de Montréal, 1967, 2 volumes.
2 *Proust, Freud et l'autre*, p. 13.
3 *The Dialectics of Isolation*, p. 96.
4 'Proust and the Art of Incompletion', in *Marcel Proust's Remembrance of Things Past*, ed. Harold Bloom, p. 176.
5 The preference for Flaubert's letters was a commonplace at the turn of the century and is mentioned in the criticism of Jules Lemaître, Albert Thibaudet and Sainte-Beuve (see *Recherche*, II, 780, n. 3).
6 Gabriel de la Rochefoucauld reported that Proust had actually met a lady at a dinner who asked him if he had heard of *Salammbô* and knew its author. She then apparently misheard Proust's whispered response to be 'Paul Bert' (see *Hommage à Marcel Proust*, p. 64).
7 For example, Alain Buisine in *Proust et ses lettres*, p. 33.
8 *Le Bal du Pré Catelan*, p. 67.
9 'Un Scandale littéraire', *Le Journal* (3 March 1893).
10 Gilles Deleuze and Félix Guattari argue that Kafka's letters and fiction had a similar function, and they include his correspondence, short stories and novels within a single 'writing machine', partly because, as they say, none of the material was meant for publication (*Kafka: pour une littérature mineure*).
11 See *Autour de soixante lettres de Marcel Proust* (Paris: Gallimard, 1929), pp. 15, 26 and 27.
12 Marcel Proust, *Choix de lettres* (Paris: Plon, 1965), p. 17.
13 *Proust*, pp. 56–7.
14 *Lettres à Reynaldo Hahn*, ed. Philip Kolb (Paris: Gallimard, 1956), pp. 127 and 172.
15 'Topographies of obstacles and lists of conditions are elevated to great heights by Proust, as functions of the letter, to the point that the correspondent no longer understands whether the author wishes him to visit, has ever wished it, is dismissing him in order to attract him, or the opposite.' Deleuze and Guattari, *Kafka: pour une littérature mineure*, p. 61. Quoted by Buisine, *Proust et ses lettres*, p. 29.
16 The poem is 'Aux amis inconnus', quoted in a letter to Jacques Copeau (*Corr.*, XII, 156).
17 Quoted from *Madame Bovary* by Naomi Schor, *Breaking the Chain*, p. 25.
18 It is Norpois who labels the Narrator a hysterical flatterer (III, 311; II, 568).

19 *Lettres à Milena* (Paris: Gallimard, 1978), p. 85. See Buisine, *Proust et ses lettres*, p. 86.

20 In her preface to the first publication of Proust's letters to herself, *Lettres à la comtesse de Noailles*, *Correspondance générale*, II, 9.

21 Robert Vigneron has documented the special blend of acrimony and flattery in their relationship ('Marcel Proust et Robert de Montesquiou: Autour de *Professionnelles Beautés*', in *Etudes sur Stendhal et sur Proust*, pp. 352–86).

22 See, for example, a beautiful letter of condolences sent to the son of the deceased marquise de Brantes (*Corr.*, XIII, 145).

23 Comments that Montesquiou wrote in the margins of some of Proust's letters show his true feelings: 'impertinent', 'pee-pee', 'insolent and stupid', 'light-minded', 'insolent and untrue'. See *Corr.*, II, 167–70 as an example.

24 *Les Pas effacés: mémoires* (Paris: Emile-Paul Frères, 1923), III, 289.

25 *Journal 1889–1939*, p. 1067.

26 See *Correspondance générale*, II, 26–7.

27 Alain Roger notes this borrowing in *Proust: Les Plaisirs et les noms* (Paris: Denoël, 1985), p. 37.

28 Cf. *Corr.*, XI, 188, including Philip Kolb's notes.

29 See *Recherche*, III, 663, n. 1, and *Corr.*, XIII, 368.

30 Most of these transpositions are noted by Philip Kolb as he discusses individual letters in the Plon *Correspondance*.

31 See Painter, *Marcel Proust: A Biography*, II, 212.

32 'L'Ecrit et le lu: statut de l'épistolaire dans *A la recherche du temps perdu*', 24.

33 As Baudry points out, this theme is also at the heart of Proust's *Figaro* article 'Sentiments filiaux d'un parricide', and Proust proposes it to Reynaldo Hahn (again in a letter) as the central idea of a literary work he is planning (*Proust, Freud et l'autre*, pp. 31–2).

34 *Proust et ses lettres*, p. 127.

35 *Correspondance générale*, II, 9. She also observes, as other of Proust's contemporaries do not, that Proust's flattery sprang from a serious, sober part of his personality: 'You expressed the gravity of your heart in these tender witticisms' (*Hommage à Marcel Proust*, p. 11).

36 *Mon Amitié avec Marcel Proust*, p. 47.

37 See Yves Sandre's article, 'Proust chroniqueur'.

38 In a letter to Lucien Daudet (*Autour de soixante lettres de Marcel Proust*, p. 220). Proust used the term 'article' as a catch-all; see the letters to Georges de Lauris and Mme Strauss referred to in the notes to *Pastiches et mélanges* (*CSB*, 681, n. 1).

39 Françoise Giroud, editor of *L'Express*, interviewed by Maria-Antonietta Macciocchi in 'L'Ecriture du journalisme', p. 30.

40 Jean Milly, *Les Pastiches de Proust*, p. 225.

41 The description of the salon of the comtesse Aimery de la Roche-

foucauld (*CSB*, 436–9) was not published during Proust's lifetime; it probably dates from 1901 or earlier. Proust's article on the comtesse de Guerne (*CSB*, 503–6) is more a high-society music review than the presentation of a salon.

42 A number of examples are put forward by Jean-Yves Tadié (*Proust*, pp. 131–3). It is an exaggeration to suggest, as does Genette (*Figures I*, p. 58), that almost all these chronicles are to be found intact in *A la recherche*.

43 See *Recherche*, IV, 148, n. 1.

44 'Le Dormeur éveillé: genèse d'un roman de la mémoire'. See also the following sketches in the Pléiade *Recherche*: I.1, I.2, I.3 and I.8 (I, 633–6); XII.1, XII.2, XII.3 and XII.4 (IV, 671–6).

45 Parts of this text migrate in and out of published material of this period. See the description of the 'abominable act of reading the newspaper' in 'Sentiments filiaux d'un parricide' (*CSB*, 150–9).

46 Letter of November 1908, *Corr.*, VIII, 289–90. Elsewhere Proust compares *Colette Baudoche* unfavourably with 'Sylvie' of Nerval (see *Le Carnet de 1908*, p. 67 and n. 408) and speaks of Barrès's pretentious style.

47 The prime model for Norpois, Gabriel Hanotaux, appears to have shared Norpois' taste in clichés and his wrongheaded sense of international realities: 'I have heard Hanotaux, with my own ears, declare that the alliance with Russia would be the bridge leading to an alliance with Germany, announce for tomorrow the inevitable conflict between France and England, decree that William II was the only sovereign having a clear and distinct view of the "chessboard", and that Franz-Joseph, "the Nestor of monarchs", was the firmest supporter of peace in Europe.' Léon Daudet, *Souvenirs des milieux littéraires, politiques, artistiques et médicaux* (Paris: Nouvelle Librairie Nationale, 1920), p. 366.

48 Proust's nomenclature circles undecidedly here. The critic attempts to identify 'the moral physiognomy of the artist', 'the spiritual life of a writer', 'the peculiar physiognomy of Ruskin'. These three references are from the foreword to *La Bible d'Amiens*, pp. 9, 11 and 14. He incorporated large parts of this text into the notes for 'Journées de pèlerinage' (*CSB*, 75–6).

49 Claude Pichois uses the term 'critique d'identification' to describe Baudelaire's critical stance (*Œuvres complètes*, II, 1071).

50 *The Anxiety of Influence*, p. 141.

51 Letter to Théophile Thoré cited by Claude Pichois in Baudelaire, *Œuvres complètes*, II, 1070–1.

52 Philip Kolb was one of the first to discuss this illumination in 'Proust et Ruskin: nouvelles perspectives'.

53 See Paul de Man's famous deconstruction of Proust's argument in *Allegories of Reading*, pp. 57–78.

54 It is the title of an article devoted to Serge Doubrovsky in *Lettres Romanes*.

55 Stern, *Swann's Way*, p. 89.

56 See *Corr.*, XI, 161, n. 5.

57 Proust knew Reboux (pseudonym of Paul Amilet, 1877–1963) and had written to him in connection with his collection of verse *Les Iris noirs*. See *Corr.*, II, 231–2.

58 See Anthony Pugh, *The Birth of 'A la recherche du temps perdu'*, pp. 21–2.

59 For example, the letter to Lauris, *Corr.*, VIII, 59, and a later one to Ramon Fernandez, *Corr.*, XVIII, 380.

60 Bloom, *The Anxiety of Influence*, p. 26.

61 Letter to Henri de Régnier, *BMP*, 40 (1990), 15.

62 Both texts are quoted by Milly in *Les Pastiches de Proust*, pp. 46–7; the first now appears in a Pléiade sketch (I, 836). Citing what appears to be the same second text, Françoise Leriche's reading is, 'others speak of the beautiful language of France', i.e. Anatole France ('Du Nouveau sur le Cahier 14', 7).

63 Cf. his comment, 'Our minds are never satisfied unless they can provide a clear analysis of what they had first produced unconsciously, or a living recreation of what they first patiently analysed' (*ASB*, 269) ['Notre esprit n'est jamais satisfait s'il n'a pu donner une claire analyse de ce qu'il avait d'abord inconsciemment produit, ou une recréation vivante de ce qu'il avait d'abord patiemment analysé'] (*CSB*, 595), and similar thoughts in a letter to Ramon Fernandez about the intent of his pastiches (*Corr.*, XVIII, 380).

64 Milly dates the writing between 17 November 1917 and 9 October 1918 (*Proust dans le texte et l'avant-texte*, p. 186), though others have opted for 1915–16 (see Annick Bouillaguet, *Proust et les Goncourt*, pp. 7–8, 12).

4 FORM: FROM ANXIETY TO PLAY

1 *The Dialogic Imagination*, p. 279.

2 From Michael Holquist's introduction to *The Dialogic Imagination*, p. xxxi.

3 *Mensonge romantique et vérité romanesque*, p. 307.

4 This is Frank Kermode's phrase in *The Sense of an Ending*, p. 133.

5 R. Pascal has summarized some of these views in 'Narrative Fictions and Reality'.

6 See Jacques Derrida, *L'Ecriture et la différence*, pp. 360–1, and cf. a remark by Alistair Duckworth: 'From a Derridean point of view all closure is ideological, not because there is in [a work of literature] 'literally' too much to say ... but because literary language, lacking a 'centre' in text or author, without 'end' or 'origin', excludes totalization

and permits only the 'freeplay' of infinite substitution'; '*Little Dorritt* and the Question of Closure', 130. Quoted by Armine Mortimer, *La Clôture narrative*, p. 220.

7   *The Open Work* (Cambridge, Mass.: Harvard University Press, 1989), chapter 1, 'The Poetics of the Open Work'.

8   Quoted by Jean Levaillant, 'Inachèvement, invention, écriture, d'après les manuscrits de Paul Valéry', p. 102.

9   Quoted by Luc Fraisse, *Le Fragment expérimental*, pp. 293–4, and, in a slightly different context, by Jean-Yves Tadié, the Pléiade editor (I, p. ci).

10 Proust does in fact seem to find length important. A propos of *A la recherche*, he says, 'I will not go so far as to say, along with Maeterlinck who was speaking, I think, of *King Lear*, that I believe that, all other qualities being equal, the longer a work is, the more merit it has. What is amazing is that Lemaître wrote me the same thing when my pastiches (the least good ones) appeared in *Le Figaro*' ['Je n'irai jusqu'à dire avec Maeterlinck parlant je crois du *Roi Lear* qu'à qualités égales, plus un ouvrage est long, plus il a de mérites. Chose singulière, à propos de mes Pastiches quand ils parurent (les moins bons) dans le *Figaro*, Lemaître m'écrivit la même chose'] (*Corr.*, XIX, 342).

11 See Philippe Hamon, 'Clausules', 499.

12 Ending as incompletion, one of Marianna Torgovnick's models of closure (*Closure in the Novel*), is deeply Proustian. I refer extensively, in what follows, to Armine Mortimer's study, *La Clôture narrative*.

13 *La Clôture narrative*, p. 24.

14 Roland Barthes, *S/Z* (Paris: Editions du Seuil, 1970), p. 194, quoted by Mortimer, *La Clôture narrative*, p. 28.

15 *Mensonge romantique et vérité romanesque*, chapter 12, 'La Conclusion', pp. 289–312.

16 See Kermode, 'Sensing Endings'.

17 Quoted from *Cahier* 55 by Jean Milly, *Proust dans le texte et l'avant-texte*, pp. 201–2. See also his article '*Albertine disparue*: la vie posthume d'un texte littéraire', 259.

18 One may compare the shortened version of *Albertine disparue* published by Nathalie Mauriac and Etienne Wolff (Paris: Grasset, 1987) with the new Pléiade text of *Albertine disparue*, edited by Anne Chevalier (IV, 3–272), and Jean Milly's 'édition intégrale' (Paris: Librairie Honoré Champion, 1992). Milly's introduction to this latter volume is the most complete and dispassionate discussion of the controversy, but Nathalie Mauriac Dyer has published a series of interesting articles on the question, for example, 'Les Mirages du double. *Albertine disparue* selon la Pléiade'.

19 See Milly's introduction to his Champion edition, pp. 34–5.

20 *Albertine disparue*, Nathalie Mauriac edition, p. 17.

21 See *Recherche*, IV, 625, n. 2, the photo of the last page of the manuscript
   (IV, 1319), and 'Note sur le texte' (IV, 1177).
22 *Monsieur Proust* (Paris: Robert Laffont, 1973), pp. 402–3.
23 See *Matinée chez la princesse de Guermantes*, p. 113, and *Recherche, Esquisse*
   XXIV (IV, 799).
24 Torgovnick, *Closure in the Novel*, p. 18.
25 Letter to Louis Bouilhet, 4 September 1850, *Correspondance*, I, 679.
26 See the fine article of Pierre-Marc de Biasi, 'Flaubert et la poétique du
   non-finito', pp. 45–73, especially p. 56.
27 Cahiers 55 and 59–62, for example. The point is made by Bernard
   Brun in his introduction to *Le Temps retrouvé* (Paris: Garnier-
   Flammarion, 1986), pp. 51–3.
28 *Le Fragment expérimental*, p. 328.
29 *Figures III*, pp. 148–9.
30 Claudine Quémar, 'Autour de trois "Avant-textes" de l'"ouverture" de
   la *Recherche*: nouvelles approches des problèmes du *Contre Sainte-Beuve*',
   BIP, 3 (1976), 7–29.
31 Almuth Grésillon, Jean-Louis Lebrave and Catherine Viollet, *Proust à la
   lettre*, p. 84.
32 Martin Walser, 'Ecrire', in *La Naissance du texte*, ed. Hay, p. 153.
33 'Proust et la superposition descriptive'.
34 *Proust entre deux siècles*, p. 135.
35 The list of critical works that have examined quotation and inter-
   textuality in Proust is enormous. Jacques Nathan's *Citations, références et
   allusions de Marcel Proust* (Paris: Nizet, 1969) is a helpful guide. Since 1991
   the *Bulletin d'informations proustiennes* (*BIP*) has a regular sub-section of
   articles on intertextualities. Françoise Leriche offers some brief but
   penetrating theoretical considerations in 'La Citation au fondement du
   Côté de Guermantes?' I have found the research of Luc Fraisse very
   pertinent (*Le Fragment expérimental*, 'Du Bon Usage des citations',
   pp. 336–42), as well as that of Antoine Compagnon (*Proust entre deux
   siècles*, for example, chapter 3, 'Racine est plus immoral'). See also
   Annick Bouillaguet, *Marcel Proust: Le jeu intertextuel*, and Genette's
   Palimpsestes.
36 Cited by Fraisse, *Le Fragment expérimental*, pp. 339–40.
37 This point is made by Gerhard Kaiser, *Proust, Musil, Joyce*, pp. 68–73.
38 Proust appears to have had a belief, however hedged and reluctant, in
   previous lives. In one letter he writes, 'Personally, the constant study of
   internal phenomena, with my ear attuned to inexplicable reminiscences, would lead me to believe that our current life is, in fact, not our
   first life, and that our mind has not fully erased the memories of the
   preceding ones' ['Personnellement, l'étude constante des phénomènes
   intérieurs, l'oreille prêtée à d'inexplicables réminiscences, me porterait
   à croire qu'en effet notre vie actuelle n'est pas la première et que

l'éponge de l'oubli n'a pas complètement effacé les souvenirs des précédentes'] (*Corr.*, XVII, 214).

39 I have taken the English translation of these lines from *Against Sainte-Beuve*, p. 306.

40 The Pléiade editors credit Anatole France with the other three (I, 93, n. 1).

41 In his article 'Les Phrases de Bergotte', Jean Milly studies Bergotte as a literary and stylistic model of the Narrator-as-writer.

42 From 'The Poet', Ralph Waldo Emerson, *Selected Essays* (New York: Penguin, 1982), p. 276. The French translation appeared in 1894 (see *JS*, 104, n. 2).

43 Fraisse, *l'Œuvre cathédrale*, p. 116.

44 'L'Autocitation chez Proust'.

45 'Impressions de route en automobile', published 19 November 1907 in *Le Figaro*.

46 See *Le Carnet de 1908*, p. 52, and the editorial notes to *Le Temps retrouvé*, IV, 1149.

47 This is one of the self-quotations noted by Luzius Keller.

48 Gilles Deleuze, *Proust et les signes* (Paris: Presses Universitaires de France, 1963), p. 176.

49 There are a variety of references, in *Le Côté de Guermantes* and *La Prisonnière*, to this transformation of the Martinville prose poem into an article (III, 400; II, 643 – III, 459; II, 691–2 – V, 5; III, 523 – V, 128 ; III, 626).

50 *Marcel Proust romancier*, I, 276.

51 Michihiko Susuki wrote about the naming of the Narrator as early as 1959 in 'Le «Je» proustien', *BMP*, 9 (1959), 69–82.

52 Leo Spitzer, *Stilstudien* (Munich: M. Hueber, 1961), II, 447–72; Brian Rogers, *Proust's Narrative Techniques*, p. 120; Louis Martin-Chauffier, 'Proust et le double «je» de quatre personnes'; Marcel Muller, *Les Voix narratives dans la Recherche du temps perdu*. See also Gérard Genette, *Figures III*, pp. 225–67, and Grésillon *et al.*, 'Quand tous mes autres moi seront morts', in *Proust à la lettre*, pp. 109–39.

53 I borrow this provocation from Grésillon *et al.*, *Proust à la lettre*, p. 116.

54 By 'dilated I' Benveniste means, however, 'we'; see *Problèmes de linguistique générale*, p. 235.

55 *Marcel Proust romancier*, I, 296.

56 This note was printed at the bottom of the page in the first edition of *Le Temps retrouvé*. Clarac and Ferré removed it in publishing the 1954 Pléiade edition, but the editors of the second Pléiade edition reinserted it into the text. It has been omitted completely from the Scott Montcrieff, Terence Kilmartin translation updated by D. J. Enright (VI, 442).

57 A compilation of these notes is available in *Matinée chez la princesse de Guermantes*, pp. 287–472. See also Florence Callu, '"Capital, capital-

issime", un mode de composition chez Marcel Proust?', in *Leçons d'écriture: ce que disent les manuscrits*, ed. Grésillon and Werner, pp. 79–90, and Eugène Nicol, 'L'Auteur dans ses brouillons'.

58 Callu, 'Capital, capitalissime', p. 84
59 Cited by Antoine Compagnon, *Proust entre deux siècles*, p. 75.
60 Fragment of *Cahier* 57 quoted by Jean Milly in his Garnier-Flammarion edition of *La Prisonnière*, pp. 50–1.
61 Muller, *Les Voix narratives*, pp. 162–3, and *Corr.*, XIX, 35.
62 *Figures III*, p. 256.
63 See Milly, *Les Pastiches de Proust*, pp. 21–2, 153, 164.
64 'The Goncourt Pastiche in *Le Temps retrouvé*', pp. 118–21.
65 *Figures III*, p. 61.
66 Patrick O'Donnell, *Echo Chambers: Figuring Voice in Modern Narrative* (Iowa City: University of Iowa Press, 1992), p. 117, n. 1.
67 Emile Bedriomo, *Proust, Wagner et la coïncidence des arts*.

CONCLUSION

1 See Lodge, *After Bakhtin*, p. 22.

Bibliography

PROUST'S WORKS AND CORRESPONDENCE

A la recherche du temps perdu, 4 vols. Paris: Bibliothèque de la Pléiade, 1987–9.

Albertine disparue, ed. Jean Milly. Paris: Librairie Honoré Champion, 1992.

Albertine disparue, ed. Nathalie Mauriac and Etienne Wolff. Paris: Grasset, 1987.

La Bible d'Amiens. Paris: Mercure de France, 1904.

Le Carnet de 1908, ed. Philip Kolb. Paris: Gallimard, 1976.

Contre Sainte-Beuve. Paris: Bibliothèque de la Pléiade, 1971.

Correspondance, ed. Philip Kolb, 21 vols. Paris: Plon, 1970–93.

Correspondance avec Daniel Halévy, ed. Anne Borrel and Jean-Pierre Halévy. Paris: Editions de Fallois, 1992.

Correspondance générale, 6 vols. Paris: Plon, 1930–36.

Ecrits de jeunesse 1887–1895, ed. Anne Borrel. Illiers-Combray: Institut Marcel Proust International, Société des Amis de Marcel Proust et des Amis de Combray, 1991.

Jean Santeuil. Paris: Bibliothèque de la Pléiade, 1971.

Matinée chez la princesse de Guermantes, ed. Henri Bonnet and Bernard Brun. Paris: Gallimard, 1982.

Sésame et les lys. Paris: Mercure de France, 1906.

Textes retrouvés, ed. Philip Kolb and Larkin Price. Urbana: University of Illinois Press, 1968.

BOOKS AND ARTICLES

Abbey, Susan, and Paul Garfinkel. 'Neurasthenia and Chronic Fatigue Syndrome: The Role of Culture in Making a Diagnosis', *American Journal of Psychiatry*, 148, 12 (December 1991), 1638–46.

Apter, Emily. *Feminizing the Fetish: Psychoanalysis and Narrative Obsession in Turn-of-the-Century France*. Ithaca: Cornell University Press, 1991.

Aragon, Debray-Genette, *et al. Essais de critique génétique*. Paris: Flammarion, 1979.

Bakhtin, M. M. *The Dialogic Imagination*, trans. Caryl Emerson and Michael Holmquist. Austin: University of Texas Press, 1981.

Bardèche, Maurice. *Marcel Proust romancier*, 2 vols. Paris: Les Sept Couleurs, 1971.

Barthes, Roland. 'Une Idée de recherche', in *Recherche de Proust*, ed. G. Genette and Tzvetan Todorov. Paris: Editions du Seuil, 1980, pp. 34–9.

Baudelaire, Charles. *Œuvres complètes*, I. Paris: Bibliothèque de la Pléiade, 1975.

Œuvres complètes, II. Paris: Bibliothèque de la Pléiade, 1976.

Baudry, Jean-Louis. *Proust, Freud et l'autre*. Paris: Editions de Minuit, 1984.

Beard, George. *American Nervousness, its Causes and Consequences*. New York: G. P. Putnam's Sons, 1881.

Sexual Neurasthenia (Nervous Exhaustion, its Hygiene, Causes, Symptoms and Treatment). New York: E. B. Treat, 1884.

Bedriomo, Emile. *Proust, Wagner et la coïncidence des arts*. Tübingen: Gunter Narr; Paris: Editions Jean-Michel Place, 1984.

Beizer, Janet. *Ventriloquized Bodies: Narratives of Hysteria in Nineteenth-Century France*. Ithaca: Cornell University Press, 1993.

Benveniste, Emile. *Problèmes de linguistique générale*, 2 vols. Paris: Gallimard, 1966.

Biasi, Pierre-Marc de. 'Flaubert et la poétique du non-finito', in *Le Manuscrit inachevé: écriture, création, communication*, pp. 45–73.

Bloom, Harold. *The Anxiety of Influence*. New York: Oxford University Press, 1973.

Bonnet, Henri. '*Le Temps retrouvé* dans les Cahiers', *Etudes proustiennes*, I, Cahiers Marcel Proust 6. Paris: Gallimard, 1973, pp. 111–62.

Bouillaguet, Annick. 'Intertextes proustiens', *BMP*, 41 (1991), 83–90.

Marcel Proust: Le jeu intertextuel, Paris: Editions du Titre, 1990.

'Le Pastiche des Goncourt dans *Le Temps retrouvé*: aspects stylistiques et thématiques de l'insertion', *BMP*, 43 (1993), 82–91.

Proust et les Goncourt: Le pastiche du 'Journal' dans 'Le Temps retrouvé'. Paris: Archives des Lettres Modernes, 1996.

'Proust et les Goncourt: la phrase cachée d'une réécriture', *BMP*, 45 (1995), 132–52.

Bourdieu, Pierre. *Distinction: A Social Critique of the Judgement of Taste*, trans. Richard Nice. Cambridge, Mass.: Harvard University Press, 1984. Translation of *La Distinction: Critique sociale du jugement*. Paris: Editions de Minuit, 1979.

Bowie, Malcolm. *Freud, Proust and Lacan: Theory as Fiction*. Cambridge University Press, 1987.

Brachet, Jean-Louis. *Traité de l'hystérie*. Paris: Baillière, 1847.

Briquet, Pierre. *Traité clinique et thérapeutique de l'hystérie*. Paris: Baillière, 1859.

Brissaud, Eugène. *L'Hygiène des asthmatiques*. Paris: Masson, 1896. Introduction by Adrien Proust.

Brun, Bernard. 'Le Carnet de 1908 de Marcel Proust: les jeux de l'intertextualité', *BIP*, 25 (1994), 27–37.

'Le Dormeur éveillé: genèse d'un roman de la mémoire', in *Etudes proustiennes*, IV. Paris: Gallimard, 1982, pp. 241–316.

'Histoires d'un texte: les cahiers de la *Recherche*', *BIP*, 16 (1985), 11–18.

'Roman critique, roman philosophique ou roman', *BMP*, 39 (1989), 37–44.

Bruneau, Jean. *Les Débuts littéraires de Gustave Flaubert*. Paris: Armand Colin, 1962.

Buisine, Alain. *Proust et ses lettres*. Lille: Presses Universitaires de Lille, 1983.

Callu, Florence. '"Capital, capitalissime", un mode de composition chez Marcel Proust?', in *Leçons d'écriture*, pp. 79–90.

Clermont-Tonnerre, Elisabeth de. *Robert de Montesquiou et Marcel Proust*. Paris: Flammarion, 1925.

Cocteau, Jean. 'La Voix de Marcel Proust', in *Hommage à Marcel Proust*, pp. 77–9.

Colloque 'Marcel Proust et la médecine', La Gazette du CHU, 4, 8 (November 1992).

Compagnon, Antoine. *Proust entre deux siècles*. Paris: Editions du Seuil, 1989.

Czoniczer, Elisabeth. *Quelques antécédents de 'A la recherche du temps perdu'*. Geneva: Droz, 1957.

Deleuze, Gilles, and Felix Guattari. *Kafka: pour une littérature mineure*. Paris: Editions de Minuit, 1975.

De Man, Paul. *Allegories of Reading*. New Haven: Yale University Press, 1979.

Derrida, Jacques. *L'Ecriture et la différence*. Paris: Editions du Seuil, 1967.

Dezon-Jones, Elyane. 'L'Ecrit et le lu: statut de l'épistolaire dans *A la recherche du temps perdu*', *BIP*, 17 (1986), 21–6.

Dubois, Paul. *The Psychic Treatment of Nervous Disorders (The Psychoneuroses and their Moral Treatment)*. New York: Funk and Wagnalls, 1909, 6th edn. Translation of *Les Psychonévroses et leur traitement moral*. Paris: Masson, 1904.

Duckworth, Alastair. '*Little Dorrit* and the Question of Closure', *Nineteenth-Century Fiction*, 33, 1 (1978), 110–30.

Evans, Martha Noel. *Fits and Starts: A Genealogy of Hysteria in Modern France*. Ithaca: Cornell University Press, 1991.

Fernandez, Ramon. *Proust*. Paris: Nouvelle Revue Critique, 1943.

Fladenmuller, Frédéric. 'Le Nerveux Narrateur dans *A la recherche du temps perdu*', *BIP*, 17 (1986), 35–42.

Flament, Albert. *Le Bal du Pré Catelan*. Paris: Fayard, 1946.

Fraisse, Luc. *L'Œuvre cathédrale: Proust et l'architecture médiévale*. Paris: José Corti, 1990.

Le Processus de la création chez Marcel Proust: le fragment expérimental. Paris: José Corti, 1988.

Freud, Sigmund. *Collected Papers*, 1. London: Hogarth Press, 1949.

Genette, Gérard. *Figures I*. Paris: Editions du Seuil, 1966.

Figures II. Paris: Editions du Seuil, 1969.

Figures III. Paris: Editions du Seuil, 1972.

Palimpsestes. Paris: Editions du Seuil, 1982.

Gide, André. *Journal 1889–1939*. Paris: Bibliothèque de la Pléiade, 1951.

Gilman, Sander. *Difference and Pathology: Stereotypes of Sexuality, Race and Madness*. Ithaca: Cornell University Press, 1985.

Girard, René. *Mensonge romantique et vérité romanesque*. Paris: Grasset, 1961.

Goujon, Henry. 'Neurasthénie', *Le Figaro*, 23 September 1904.

Gregh, Fernand. *Mon Amitié avec Marcel Proust*. Paris: Grasset, 1958.

Grésillon, Almuth, Jean-Louis Lebrave, Catherine Viollet. *Proust à la lettre: les intermittences de l'écriture*. Tusson: Du Lérot, 1990.

Haig, Stirling. *Flaubert and the Gift of Speech*. Cambridge University Press, 1986.

Hamon, Philippe. 'Clausules', *Poétique*, 6 (1975), 495–526.

Henry, Anne. *Marcel Proust: théories pour une esthétique*. Paris: Klincksieck, 1981.

Proust romancier: le tombeau égyptien. Paris: Flammarion, 1983.

Hommage à Marcel Proust. Paris: Gallimard, 1927.

Jaeck, Lois Marie. *Marcel Proust and the Text as Macrometaphor*. University of Toronto Press, 1990.

Janet, Pierre. *The Mental State of Hystericals*. Washington, DC: University Publications of America, 1977. (Reprint of the first English-language edition of G.P. Putnam's Sons, 1901.) Translation of *L'Etat mental des hystériques*. Paris: Alcan, 1894.

Jullien, Dominique. *Proust et ses modèles*. Paris: José Corti, 1989.

Kaiser, Gerhard. *Proust, Musil, Joyce: Zum Verhältnis von Literatur und Gesellschaft am Paradigma des Zitats*. Frankfurt: Athenäum, 1972.

Keller, Luzius. 'L'Autocitation chez Proust', *Modern Language Notes*, 95 (May 1990), 1033–48.

Kermode, Frank. 'Sensing Endings', *Nineteenth-Century Fiction*, 33, 1 (June 1978), 144–58.

The Sense of an Ending: Studies in the Theory of Fiction. Oxford University Press, 1967.

Kolb, Philip. 'Proust et Ruskin: nouvelles perspectives', *Cahiers de l'Association internationale des études françaises*, 12 (1960), 259–73.

Leçons d'écriture: ce que disent les manuscrits. Hommage à Louis Hay, ed. Almuth Grésillon, Michael Werner. Paris: Minard, 1985.

Leriche, Françoise. 'La Citation au fondement du *Côté de Guermantes*? hypothèses pour un séminaire', *BIP*, 22 (1991), 31–6.

'Du Nouveau sur le Cahier 14', *BIP*, 21 (1990), 7–21.

Levaillant, Jean. 'Inachèvement, invention, écriture d'après les manuscrits de Paul Valéry', in *Le Manuscrit inachevé: écriture, création, communication*, pp. 101–25.

Lodge, David. *After Bakhtin: Essays on Fiction and Criticism*. New York: Routledge, 1990.

Macciocchi, Maria-Antonietta. 'L'Ecriture du journalisme', *Tel Quel* (Fall 1979), pp. 26–36.

Le Manuscrit inachevé: écriture, création, communication, ed. Louis Hay. Paris: Editions du CNRS, 1986.

Marcel Proust's Remembrance of Things Past, ed. Harold Bloom. New York: Chelsea House, 1987.

Martin-Chauffier, Louis. 'Proust et le double «je» de quatre personnes', in *Les Critiques de notre temps*, ed. Jacques Bersani. Paris: Garnier, 1971, pp. 54–66.

Matlock, Jann. *Scenes of Seduction: Prostitution, Hysteria and Reading Difference in Nineteenth-Century France*. New York: Columbia University Press, 1994.

Mauriac Dyer, Nathalie. 'Les Mirages du double. *Albertine disparue* selon la Pléiade', *BMP*, 40 (1990), 117–53.

Mein, Margaret. *A Foretaste of Proust: A Study of Proust and his Precursors*. Westmead: Saxon House, 1974.

Micale, Mark. *Approaching Hysteria: Disease and its Interpretations*. Princeton University Press, 1995.

Miguet, Marie. 'Critique/autocritique/autofiction', *Lettres Romanes*, 63, 3 (August 1989), 195–208.

'Idéologie du *Traité d'hygiène* d'Adrien Proust', in *Colloque 'Marcel Proust et la médecine'*, *La Gazette du CHU*, 4, 8 (November 1992), 219–25.

'La Neurasthénie entre science et fiction', *BMP*, 40 (1990), 28–42.

'Le "Père Norpois" et le roman familial', *Revue d'Histoire Littéraire de la France*, 2 (March–April 1990), 191–207.

Miller, J. Hillis. 'The Problematic of Ending in Narrative', *Nineteenth-Century Fiction*, 33, 1 (1978), 3–7.

Milly, Jean. '*Albertine disparue*: la vie posthume d'un texte littéraire', *Revue d'Histoire Littéraire de la France*, 2 (March–April 1992), 254–69.

Les Pastiches de Proust. Paris: Armand Colin, 1971.

'Les Phrases de Bergotte', *Etudes proustiennes*, 1, Cahiers Marcel Proust 6. Paris: Gallimard, 1973, pp. 35–67.

Proust dans le texte et l'avant-texte. Paris: Flammarion, 1985.

Morand, Paul. *Le Visiteur du soir*. Geneva: La Palatine, 1949.

Mortimer, Armine Kotin. *La Clôture narrative*. Paris: José Corti, 1985.

Muller, Marcel. *Les Voix narratives dans la 'Recherche du temps perdu'*. Geneva: Droz, 1965.

La Naissance du texte, ed. Louis Hay. Paris: José Corti, 1989.

Naturel, Mireille. 'La Citation de salon, ou une parodie de critique littéraire', *BIP*, 22 (1991), 71–82.

'Le Rôle de Flaubert dans la genèse du texte proustien', *BMP*, 43 (1993), 72–81.

Nicole, Eugène. 'L'Auteur dans ses brouillons: *marginalia* des Cahiers de Proust', *BMP*, 39 (1989), 60–7.

Pagès, Alain. 'Correspondance et genèse', in *Leçons d'écriture*, pp. 207–14.

Painter, George. *Marcel Proust: A Biography*, 2 vols. London: Chatto and Windus, 1966.

Pascal, R. 'Narrative Fictions and Reality: A Comment on Frank Kermode's *The Sense of an Ending*', *Novel*, 11, 1 (1977), 40–50.

Porter, Agnes. 'Proust's Final Montesquiou Pastiche', in *Marcel Proust: A Critical Panorama*, ed. Larkin Price. Urbana: University of Illinois Press, 1973, pp. 124–46.

Poulet, Georges. *Etudes sur le temps humain*, 1. Paris: Plon, 1952.

Proust, Adrien, and Gilbert Ballet. *De l'action des aimants sur quelques troubles nerveux et spécialement sur les anesthésies*. Paris: Masson, 1879.

L'Hygiène du neurasthénique. Paris: Masson, 1897.

Pugh, Anthony R. *The Birth of 'A la recherche du temps perdu'*. Lexington: French Forum Publishers, 1987.

Ribot, Théodule. *La Philosophie de Schopenhauer*. Paris: G. Baillière, 1874.

Les Maladies de la volonté. Paris: Alcan, 1883.

Problèmes de psychologie affective. Paris: Alcan, 1910.

Robitaille, Martin. 'Etudes sur la correspondance de Marcel Proust: une synthèse', *BMP*, 46 (1996), 109–26.

Rogers, Brian. *Proust's Narrative Techniques*. Geneva: Droz, 1965.

Rousset, Jean. *Forme et signification*. Paris: José Corti, 1964.

Sandre, Yves. 'Proust chroniqueur', *Revue d'Histoire Littéraire de la France*, 71, 5–6 (September–December 1971), 771–90.

Sartre, Jean-Paul. *L'Idiot de la famille: Gustave Flaubert de 1821 à 1857*, 3 vols. Paris: Gallimard, 1971.

Sayce, R. A. 'The Goncourt Pastiche in *Le Temps retrouvé*', in *Marcel Proust: A Critical Panorama*, ed. Larkin Price. Urbana: University of Illinois Press, 1973, pp. 102–23.

Schor, Naomi. *Breaking the Chain: Women, Theory and French Realist Fiction*. New York: Columbia University Press, 1985.

Shorter, Edward. *From Paralysis to Fatigue: A History of Psychosomatic Illness in the Modern Era*. New York and Toronto: The Free Press and Maxwell Macmillan Canada, 1992.

Showalter, Elaine. *The Female Malady: Women, Madness and English Culture, 1830–1980*. New York: Pantheon, 1985.

Silverman, Debora. *Art Nouveau in Fin-de-Siècle France: Politics, Psychology and Style*. Berkeley: University of California Press, 1989.

Simon, Anne. 'Proust et la superposition descriptive', *BIP*, 25 (1994), 151–66.

Sollier, Paul. *L'Hystérie et son traitement*. Paris: Alcan, 1901.

Stern, Sheila. *Swann's Way*. Cambridge University Press, 1989.

Tadié, Jean-Yves. *Proust*. Paris: Pierre Belfond, 1983.

'Proust et l'inachèvement', in *Le Manuscrit inachevé: écriture, création, communication*, pp. 75–85.

Terdiman, Richard. *The Dialectics of Isolation*. New Haven: Yale University Press, 1976.

Torgovnick, Marianna. *Closure in the Novel*. Princeton University Press, 1981.

Van Buuren, Maarten. 'Hystérie et littérature: la fissure par laquelle l'Esprit du Mal pénètre dans l'âme', *Poétique*, 25 (November 1994), 387–409.

Vigneron, Robert. *Etudes sur Stendhal et sur Proust*. Paris: Nizet, 1978.

Weber, Eugen. *France Fin de Siècle*. Cambridge, Mass.: Belknap Press, 1986.

Yoshida, Jo. 'Proust et la maladie nerveuse', in *Marcel Proust 1: A la recherche du temps perdu, des personnages aux structures*. Paris: Minard/Lettres Modernes, 1992, pp. 101–24.

'La Maladie nerveuse chez Proust: genèse du portrait du docteur Boulbon', *BMP*, 42 (1992), 43–62.

Index